THE DARK SIDE OF ECLIPSES

Do the Heavens Still Issue Warnings of Things to Come?

The sun shall be turned into darkness and the moon into blood, before the great and terrible day of the Lord come. --Joel 2:31 KJV

Marcha "Whobeda" Fox

B.S. Physics, Dipl. IAA

KALLIOPE RISING PRESS
NAPLES, NEW YORK

I sought for the greatness and genius of America in her commodius harbors and her ample rivers, and it was not there...in her fertile fields and boundless forests, and it was not there...in her rich mines and her vast world commerce, and it was not there...in her democratic congress and her matchless constitution, and it was not there. Not until I went into the churches of America and heard her pulpits aflame with righteousness did I understand the secret of her genius and power. America is great because she is good, and if American ever ceases to be good, she will cease to be great.

--Alexis de Tocqueville

No part of this book may be reproduced or transmitted in any form or by any means, electronic or mechanical, including photocopying or recording, or by any information storage and retrieval system without written permission from the author and publisher with the exception of brief excerpts used in the context of reviews. Requests and inquiries may be made via email to:

marcha@kallioperisingpress.com.

The opinions offered in this book are the author's based on her knowledge of astrology, ancient prophecies, religion, research, and observation during several decades of residence on this planet. Their intent is to inform and perhaps to warn. As with all speculation, time will tell.

Copyright © 2024 by Marcha Fox

All Rights Reserved

First Printing: February 2024

ISBN 978-1-7334186-7-6

Library of Congress Control Number: 2024906937

Horoscopes and Eclipse paths generated with Sirius 3.0 Astrological Software from Cosmic Patterns

Cover and interior design by the author.

Cover photo credit Pete Linforth, The Digital Artist, Pixabay

Back cover: New Madrid Seismic Zone By Sara Boore and Susan Mayfield - USGS, Public Domain, https://commons.wikimedia.org/w/index.php?curid=68822765

Back cover composite with 2017 and 2024 eclipse paths created by the author

Other illustrations as attributed within.

* * *

KALLIOPE RISING PRESS
NAPLES, NEW YORK 14512

DEDICATION

I dedicate this work to my fellow truth seekers.

To those who question everything rather than trust what someone says, no matter how famous or important they may be.

To those who see through the curtain of lies cloaking our planet and discern their source.

To those who believe a battle wages between good and evil for the hearts and souls of men facilitated by those whose wickedness exceeds their worst imaginings.

To those who recognize that astrology has endured for millennia because it was given to mankind as a gift to know and understand these things.

Astrology Books by Marcha Fox

ValkyrieAstrology.com

Whobeda's Guide to Basic Astrology (ebook and paperback)

Lilith: Dark Maid of the Sith (ebook)

Asteroid Goddesses: A Primer (ebook)

The Definitive Guide to Astrological Reports (ebook)

With Ena Stanley

Examining the Chart's Structure (ebook)

Award Winning Mystery/Suspense by Marcha Fox and Pete Risingsun

Dead-Horse-Canyon.com

The Curse of Dead Horse Canyon: Cheyenne Spirits

Return to Dead Horse Canyon: Grandfather Spirits

Revenge of Dead Horse Canyon: Sweet Medicine Spirits (Coming soon)

Science Fiction by Marcha Fox

StarTrailsSaga.com

Available as ebooks, paperbacks, and audiobooks narrated by T. W. Ashworth

Beyond the Hidden Sky

A Dark of Endless Days

A Psilent Place Below

Refractions of Frozen Time

The Terra Debacle: Prisoners at Area 51

Family History

The Family History Fun Factor: How to Gather and Preserve Family Folklore

TABLE OF CONTENTS

Introduction 1
1. Types of Eclipses 4
2. Mundane Astrology 101 8
3. The United States "Birth Chart" 13
4. There's More than Planets Out There 17
5. Partial Solar Eclipse 25 December 2000 27
6. September 1, 2016 Solar Eclipse 34
7. February 26, 2017 Annular Solar Eclipse 46
8. August 21, 2017 Total Solar Eclipse 65
9. December 26, 2019 Solar Eclipse 84
10. Anthony Fauci and the December 26, 2019 Eclipse 94
11. June 21, 2020 Solar Eclipse 99
12. July 5, 2020 Lunar Eclipse 109
13. December 14, 2020 Solar Eclipse 119
14. June 10, 2021 Annular Solar Eclipse 130
15. December 4, 2021 Solar Eclipse 140
16. April 30, 2022 Solar Eclipse 151
17. October 25, 2022 Solar Eclipse 160
18. April 20, 2023 Solar Eclipse 170
19. October 14, 2023 Annular Solar Eclipse 181
20. February 14, 2024 Mars-Pluto Conjunction 197
21. February 28, 2024 Double Cazimi 205
22. March 25, 2024 Lunar Eclipse 212
23. Sibly Progressed New Moon 217
24. April 8, 2024 Total Solar Eclipse 221
25. Mars-Saturn Exact Conjunction April 10, 2024 233
26. U.S. Sibly Chiron Return April 20, 2024 239
27. A Step Back in Time 247
28. The Comet is Back! 257
29. Eclipse Paths that Cross 262
30. Enough is Enough 272
Appendix A 275
Appendix B 281
Appendix C 290
Appendix D 292
About the Author 295

INTRODUCTION

Witnessing the total eclipse on August 21, 2017 gave me a bad feeling. My impression? That God was fed up with the United States and withdrawing his light. I understood at a visceral level how terrifying it was for those who believed the Sun represented God and were not aware of the details of celestial mechanics that caused the Moon to obscure the Sun.

Today, conversely, we understand the mechanics, but not the meaning. Astrology and seeing "signs in the heavens and the earth beneath" are now considered little more than superstition. Am I the only one who sees the irony of the period known as *The Enlightenment* that debunked ancient knowledge with 17th - 19th Century science?

Or was the intent more devious? Were the powers that be, that persist to this day, depriving the common man from esoteric wisdom the elite would use to their own advantage? Has mankind in general become more or less intelligent since then?

For those that believe the Universe in general and our solar system in particular "evolved" by chance, consider the astronomical odds of our single Moon being EXACTLY the correct size and distance to occult the Sun.

Unbelievers who point to science should pay closer attention to recent discoveries and theories in quantum physics, which already include additional dimensions in which astrology could easily operate at frequencies we have yet to detect.

My training to earn a bachelor's degree in physics at Utah State University definitely denigrated astrology. Being a person who demands proof, I investigated it myself. Much to my surprise, I discovered that it worked!

Upon retiring from a career at NASA that spanned twenty-one years, I studied it formally at the International Academy of Astrology, graduated, and became a professional astrologer, much to the horror of my college professors.

But that's who I am.

I'm skeptical of many things, but open-minded enough (thanks to my Sagittarius Mercury) to investigate, then adjust my stance accordingly.

This book is my attempt to share some of what I've discovered, specifically regarding critical astrological messages contained in eclipses regarding the days ahead.

Messages we've been brainwashed to ignore.

If you're an astrologer you're likely to learn something new. If you're not, I've done my best to explain where the interpretations come from based on the symbolism of the planets, signs, and houses.

Also included is a group of minor planets and asteroids categorized as the "Trans-Neptunians" as well as a few others. These are identified with their symbolism in the following pages as well as in a Cheat Sheet for your convenience.

I don't go into the astrological meaning of the planets in great detail. If you're familiar with astrology your eyes would glaze over. No doubt you want to jump right into the "good stuff," not be told something you already know.

If your only familiarity with this ancient craft is Mercury retrograde (if that), this isn't the place to learn the basics. At one time I was in that very place and had a difficult time finding a book that constituted Astrology 101.

So I wrote one.

"Whobeda's Guide to Basic Astrology" is available on Amazon in both print and ebook formats.

As someone who grew up asking "Why?" frequently enough to frustrate my parents and annoy my instructors, I felt it essential to include details from which I draw my conclusions for three reasons: 1) So readers learn some astrology via assimilation; 2) For me to remember how I came up with it; 3) So fellow astrologers can set me straight if I'm out in deep space or wish to share their own insights.

If your only source of information is mainstream media, you think everything on this planet is just hunky-dory, and are blissfully unaware of the state of the world, please skip to the Appendices. It includes information that summarizes some key points that explain the world situation and context of these eclipses.

That said, I have done all I could to make this understandable, because this really is critical information.

Brace yourself. The road ahead gets rather rough.

1. Types of Eclipses

Thousands of years ago various cultures learned how to predict eclipses. Some speculate that the Antikythera device, which dates back to the ancient Greeks, was invented by Pythagoras and used to predict eclipses among other things.

Why would anyone bother to invest so much time, calculations, and innovation to know when they'd occur?

Maybe because they knew they contained esoteric wisdom that was important, particularly for those to whom the eclipses were visible.

If you're already familiar with what causes eclipses, you might want to skip ahead to the next section and start getting into the "good stuff."

For those who aren't, there are two categories of eclipses, Solar and Lunar.

Solar Eclipses

Solar eclipses occur when the Moon blocks the Sun and Lunar eclipses are when the Earth's shadow covers the Moon.

There are three types of solar eclipse: Partial, Annular, and Total. Which one occurs depends on the position of the

Moon. For a partial, the Moon is not lined up perfectly with the Sun which results in seeing a "bite" out of the Sun, but not total obstruction. (See C in Figure 1.)

An annular eclipse results when the Moon is farther away from Earth, which makes it appear smaller and thus not big enough to cover the Sun. Also known as a "ring of fire" eclipse, a thin band of sun remains visible (See B in Figure 1.)

A total eclipse is when the Moon is closer to Earth and thus of sufficient size to cover the entire solar disk. These are the most spectacular as the moment of totality reveals the Sun's corona, which is normally not visible due to the glare of the Sun. (See A in Figure 1.)

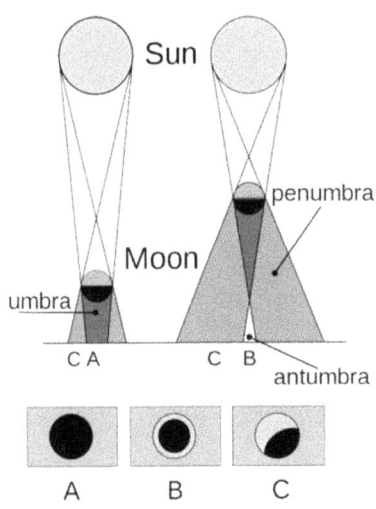

1. 1. *Types of Solar Eclipses. (Licensed under Creative Commons Attribution 2.5 Generic License)*

There are usually two sets of eclipses each year, though occasionally another one slips in. The reason there's not an eclipse every month is because the line-up simply isn't right. I could go into the details of that, but all I'm going to say is that it depends on whether the lunation occurs in close enough proximity to the lunar nodes, which is where the Moon's orbit crosses the ecliptic, or apparent path of the Sun.

Even when one occurs, its visibility could be anywhere on the planet. Thus, it's rare to be able to see one, much less more in your lifetime.

Most people celebrate the chance to see one, but there would be far less rejoicing if their meaning were evident.

Which is why I'm writing this book.

Safety Issues

If you're planning to view an eclipse, be sure to do so safely. The only time you can look directly at it is when it's at totality, not while the Moon creeps across the face of the Sun.

For that you need special glasses or a piece of dark welder's glass. You can even get binoculars that have protective coating. The website GreatAmericanEclipse.com has all the products you need as well as maps and other paraphernalia. Check them out.

If you're going to travel, plan ahead. Hundreds of thousands of people travel to see eclipses when they're within driving distance.

If you haven't already made your reservation to see the April 8 eclipse, it's probably already too late. Traffic is worse than coming out of stadium following a professional football game. Plan your route and where you'll stay accordingly to avoid disappointment and frustration.

LUNAR ECLIPSES

There are three types of lunar eclipses: penumbral, when the Moon crosses only the Earth's penumbra; partial, when the Moon crosses partially into the Earth's umbra; and total, when the Moon crosses entirely into the Earth's umbra, giving it a reddish color.

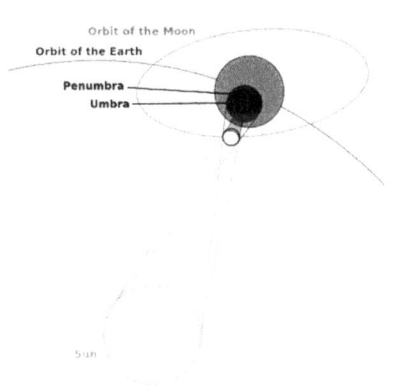

2. *Solar Eclipse Diagram. (Licensed under Creative Commons Attribution 2.5 Generic License.)*

When you read about "Blood Moons" that's what they're referring to. For example, references in The Holy Bible to the end times and the "Moon turning to blood" isn't literal, but refers to a lunar eclipse.

Remember that we were given the heavenly bodies for a reason, one of which was "for times and for seasons." Another, of course is for "signs in the heavens and in the Earth beneath" with respect to the End Times.

Somewhere along the line, those "signs in the heavens" were ignored and dismissed as superstition.

Why?

What were they trying to hide?

2. Mundane Astrology 101

Who hasn't consulted a Sun Sign horoscope, hoping to learn what was happening in their life? Has it ever worked?

Probably not.

Mass horoscopes may occasionally have personal meaning, but the odds are against it. Sadly, this is why so many think astrology is stuff and nonsense.

If a duly trained and experienced astrologer examines your natal chart generated for the date, time, and place of your birth, however, it's another story. That's when the Universe's plan for your life emerges with startling details through the signs, houses, as well as the luminary and planetary sign placements, especially when advanced methods are employed.

But guess what?

Astrology is not limited to individuals (natal horoscope astrology). There are numerous subsets within the broad category known as Mundane Astrology. These include weather cycles (astrometeorology); corporations and the stock market (financial astrology); as well as governments and their leaders (geo-political astrology).

This book shares my results upon examining several eclipses and a few other relevant charts through the lens of

Geo-Political astrology. The following tables give you the bare-bone basics, though I include keywords or other reminders along the way.

What I describe herein is based on charts cast for Washington, D.C. unless indicated otherwise.

If you're not an astrologer you may be unaware that there is more than one zodiac. The charts in this book are based on the Tropical Zodiac, which derives from the relationship between the Sun and Earth. The equinoxes and solstices mark the beginning of the four Cardinal signs, *i.e.* Aries, Cancer, Libra and Capricorn.

On the other hand, the Sidereal Zodiac is tied to the constellations. These two systems differ by approximately 23 degrees. For example, if a planet is in Leo per the Tropical zodiac, it's likely to be seen in the constellation Cancer.

It's my experience that the Tropical zodiac relates to events on Earth while the Sidereal is tied to spiritual and eternal subjects. If you're looking for "signs in the heavens" related to religious prophecy, then what is visible in the sky (and captured by the Sidereal zodiac) applies.

Vedic astrology uses the sidereal zodiac. Vedic astrologer, Juliana Swanson, who was one of my instructors at IAA, offers predictions that are very similar to mine since both of us concentrate on the planets rather than their sign placement.

For heavenly matters, where they are in the sky, however, is going to determine their deepest interpretation.

Mundane Astrology Cheat Sheets

HOUSE	INCLUDES
1st/Ascendant	National identity/myth; the populace; how the U.S. is seen by others.
2nd	Finances, treasury, resources in general. Standard of living and general prosperity.
3rd	Roads, mail, telephone, communications, infrastructure, primary education (K-12), blogs, states, local areas, and municipalities versus the entire country, bordering countries such as Mexico and Canada.
4th	Land (values, speculation, usage), history and historical self-perception, family policies, opposition party, endings and new beginnings.
5th	Senate, House of Lords, children, entertainment industry, sports, recreation, stock speculation, gambling, how citizens perceive their country and their place in it.
6th	Working class, farmers, army, labor unions, healthcare industry.
7th	Treaties, alliances, our relationship with other countries, open enemies.
8th	Foreign debts, mortality, banking, insurance, military treaties, reserves, lobbying, sedition, natural disasters, wars.
9th	Ambassadors, higher education/academia, courts, religious institutions, mass media, other countries and cultures.
10th (Midheaven)	Head of state/government (president, prime minister, king, dictator, governor, mayor), party in power, national/civic reputation, ruling party.
11th	Legislative bodies (congress, parliament, assemblies), other clubs and associations, stock exchange, lobbyists.
12th	Charities, non-profit foundations, hospitals, prisons, secret police, spies, hidden enemies, subversion, sedition, treason.

LUMINARY OR PLANET	GLYPH	RULERSHIP
Sun	☉	Head of state/government
Moon	☽	The people, women, children, waterways, water tables, national mood.
Mercury	☿	Intelligentsia, writers, trade (retail).
Venus	♀	Artists, cultural attaches, gems, prosperity, profits, standard of living.
Mars	♂	Military, fires, disputes, conflicts, war.
Jupiter	♃	Bankers, merchants (wholesale), judges, clergy.
Saturn	♄	The elderly, conservatives, bureaucrats, authority figures, boundaries, structure in general.
Uranus	♅	Aeronautics, eccentrics, political agitators (mostly the left, but not always), explosions, science, electrical grid, humanitarian efforts, rebellion, disturbances, sudden change.
Neptune	♆	Socialism, idealism, pollution, oil, overseas trade, pharmaceuticals, deception, illusions, delusions, propaganda, subversion.
Pluto	♇	Secret societies, revolutionaries, political extremists, power grabs, subversion, organized crime, colonialism, underground mineral resources

Specific resources may have other rulers, *i.e.* Mars for iron and coal, Venus for copper and gemstones, Sun for gold, Moon for silver, water, etc.

MINOR PLANET OR ASTEROID	GLYPH	RULERSHIP
Eris (Goddess of Discord)	♀	Minority groups, factions, immigrants.
Chiron (The Wounded Healer)	⚷	Injury, casualties, scars, wounds that never heal, compassion for those with similar wounds.
Cupido	⚴	Merge, bring together, unite, integrate like-minded individuals, e.g., culture, society, arts.
Hades	⚴	Brings destruction characteristic to its resident sign; unattractive side of life; lower self, base, unprincipled, and evil; ruins, waste, deprivation, decay, antiquity, ancient secrets.
Zeus	⚴	Directed energy; desire to project the self; leadership; guns, fire, explosions, weaponry.
Kronos	⚴	Polar opposite to Hades. Mastery, excellence, in-tune with laws of nature; what it touches is raised to higher levels.
Apollon	⚴	Peace, commerce, honors, fame, cross-cultural exchange, multitudes/many. What he touches grows, multiplies and reaches many. Exploration and discovery.
Admetos	⚴	Compression, density, circular motion, penetration, concentration. Distills an issue to its essence.
Vulcanus	⚴	Great power and potential. Magnifies what it touches.
Poseidon	⚴	Clarity, politics, education, philosophy. In lowest form can indicate propaganda.

3. The United States "Birth Chart"

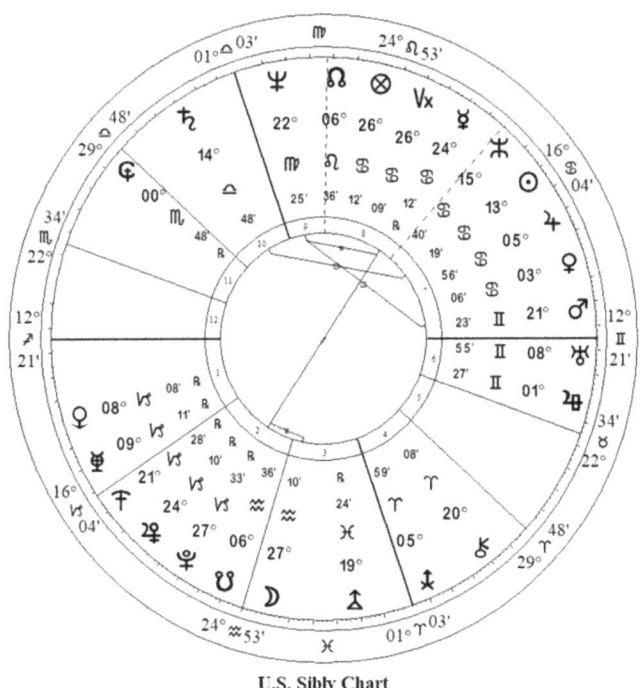

U.S. Sibly Chart
NATAL CHART

July 4, 1776
5:10 PM
Philadelphia, PA
39N57'08" 75W09'51"
Time Zone: 0 hours West
Local Mean Time

Tropical Placidus
True Node

Mean Moon's Node 7 ♌ 36
Birth Time Accuracy XX
G.M.T. 22:10:39

Marsha Fox
B.S. Physics, Dipl. IAA whobeda@valkyrieastrology.com ValkyrieAstrology.com "Timing is Everything"

This is the U.S. "Birth" Sibly chart cast for July 4, 1776. Some use alternative charts, (such as the Kelleher version, which has the same date but a birth time of 6:30 pm), but Sibly is most common.

The basic premise of the Sibly chart is that the U.S. was "born" when colonists rebelled against the Crown. Others consider its birth when the United Stated legally became a country and signed a treaty with England.

However, this is the horoscope I typically use and have found it represents the transit-triggered events in this country with reasonable accuracy.

Where did it come from, you ask?

Astrologer Ebenezer Sibly (1751–1799), an English physician and occult writer, rectified a birth chart for the United States set for July 4th, 1776 at 5:10 PM in Philadelphia, Pennsylvania. ("Rectifying" a chart entails comparing it to the transits for several important events to determine the ascendant, from which the structure for the entire horoscope is derived.)

I will be comparing eclipse charts to the Sibly Chart in a similar manner. When the eclipse chart activates houses that reflect events occurring in a close timeframe, it further validates its accuracy. Note that eclipses are powerful enough that sometimes their effects occur before the actual eclipse as well as after. However, as explained later, there are no "sudden" or "unexpected" events that didn't evolve over time.

Bear in mind that "time" is something humans invented and doesn't apply to such things as astrology. The cosmos is essentially "timeless," which is what makes providing prognostications so difficult. Like so many things in that category, 20:20 hindsight is most accurate. It's always there, just not a simple matter to pin-point before the fact.

Along those lines, awhile back I posted a three-part series of astroblogs about the USA's Pluto Return on my website (https://valkyrieastrology.com). For those of you unfamiliar with returns in general, much less this one, a "return" occurs when a planet completes an orbit that delivers it back to its natal position, beginning a new cycle.

In geo-political astrology Pluto represents secret societies; underground mineral resources in general (e.g. oil, coal, gold, etc.); revolutionaries; political extremists; and exploiting other's resources (such as in colonialism).

Pluto takes approximately 250 years to complete a trip around the sun. As the natural ruler of death, rebirth, destruction, power, and transformation, it's not much of a surprise that this is often how long a democracy lasts before it collapses, at which time it's usually replaced with a dictatorship.

U.S. parallels to the demise of the Holy Roman Empire are considerable, but beyond the scope of this book.

There were three Pluto returns due to retrograde motion. These occurred on February 20, 2022, July 11, 2022, and December 28, 2022.

Note the cycle completed approximately six weeks after the U.S. mid-term 2022 election.

During that same timeframe Neptune had a demi-return (opposed its natal position) on March 1, 2022. Neptune represents socialism, idealism, pollution, oil, and pharmaceuticals. This super-charged such matters and drew attention to them as never before.

These cycles often light the fuse on situations that explode (figuratively or otherwise) with the energy provided by an eclipse.

It's important to note, however, that per Vedic astrology, the Pluto returns will occur in 2024. Considering everything else occurring at that time, it makes a lot of sense.

I suggest you read the blog Vedic Astrologer, Juliana Swanson posted on the subject here:

https://astralharmony.substack.com/p/the-first-ever-united-states-pluto/

Juliana states: *"Based on my extensive research of previous Pluto Return cycles that occurred throughout history in various empires, I discovered that Pluto Return is not an apocalypse. It is, however, a turning point whose long-range effects may extend for many years before and after the window of exactitude (the period of exact conjunctions of transiting Pluto with natal Pluto)....*

The Pluto Return will be within an effective orb of influence until early 2025. It will be strongest throughout all of 2024, during which time Pluto will make three separate exact conjunctions to its natal position. These exact conjunctions will occur on February 22, July 16, and December 30, 2024."

4. There's More than Planets Out There

There are various chart delineations elsewhere (including some of my blogs) of the United States Sibly chart's planets and houses, so I'm not going to repeat that. That horoscope coupled with transits since the USA's founding is a book in itself.

Rather, I'm going to focus more on the minor planets, Eris, Chiron, and the eight Trans-Neptunians: Cupido, Hades, Zeus, Kronos, Apollon, Admetos, Vulcanus and Poseidon. Astrologer Bill Meridian, who specializes in eclipses, uses them and that's good enough for me.

As with the asteroids, for which I have a great fondness, these lesser known cosmic entities lend another layer of detail beyond the planets alone.

The Trans-Neptunian definitions that follow are mostly based on Meridian's descriptions in his book, *The Predictive Power of Eclipse Paths,* coupled with my own commentary. These are slightly more detailed that the "Cheat Sheet" previously included.

[NOTE:--If you're new to astrology you may not be aware that trines and sextiles are not always friendly. When malefics like Mars, Saturn, Uranus, and Pluto are involved, it indicates a strong energy exchange, which is seldom beneficial. Personally, I don't trust any of them. Oppositions demand balance, and squares tend to represent a crisis or challenge. Quincunxes are unstable, hard to predict much like Uranus, and demand an adjustment, change of course, or in some cases an unresolvable Catch-22.]

Meet the Star Players

Eris (Discord): Eris is a minor planet in the far reaches of the solar system. Named for the Goddess of Discord, she represents immigrants, minorities, and other factions such as LGBT+ and the Woke crowd. Such groups feel marginalized and have no problem making plenty of noise to demand that from which they believe they've been deprived.

Eris resides in the Sibly 1st house, which includes the populace. Remember that the people who originally founded the United States were in this category, though with time those who have been here for generations have merged to form the population as a whole.

Nonetheless, as other groups immigrated over the centuries, they often began their place in society within those ranks. Citizenship in the United States required disavowing one's previous affiliations and does not recognize dual-citizenship.

If you come to America, become an American. Unity is essential to a strong country and its lack explains much of why the U.S. is in the situation it's in today.

The quincunx from Eris to Uranus in the 6th shows that protests, riots, demonstrations, and general rebellion are vehicles employed to demand changes that fit their agenda.

The Founding Fathers's rebellion against the British Crown, which started the American Revolution, epitomizes this aspect.

In other words, Eris can be a trouble-maker, but often has justification. I'm sure that Blacks, Irish, Italian, Hispanic, Middle Easterners, and East Asians would agree as they've sought equality in "the land of the Free."

But don't get me going about how indigenous people who occupied this land for millennia were treated--and still are, for that matter--by the U.S. government. (If you're unaware, I suggest you read my *Dead Horse Canyon* books.)

Cupido (The Facilitator): Cupido in his most basic sense represents the urge to merge, the gathering together of people into a like-minded group. He's in the 2nd House of finances, treasury, and resources in general. It's interesting that he opposes Mercury in the 8th house of foreign debts, banking, and reserves. This brings to mind the National Reserve. Oppositions require balance, trouble initiated when it's lost.

Hades (The Destroyer): Hades symbolizes anything that is base, unprincipled and downright evil. It represents ruins, carnage, decay, and deprivation. He has no respect for the laws of nature, which causes damage and pain. Hades is in the 11th house, which includes legislative bodies such as the House of Representatives, as well as various clubs and associations.

I'm inclined to add lobbyists, too, as the ones who run this country more that we realize. They brought the U.S. into corporatism, *i.e.*, collusion between corporations and government to the detriment of citizens. When the Supreme Court declared corporations "citizens" and legalized lobbying, it set the U.S. up for delivering the country into the hands of the rich and elite.

In addition, Hades rules ancient secrets, which brings me to secret societies. He's appropriately placed at 00:48 Scorpio, a sign where he is surely capable of demonstrating his full power. He does not aspect any natal planets.

Remember that many of the Founding Fathers were members of the Masonic Order. While their initial intent may have been noble enough, it's my opinion that it has deteriorated since.

Zeus (Thunder): Surely everyone is familiar with Zeus. His energy represents projecting the self, including those in leadership positions and directed energy (think thunderbolts). He's in the 4th house, which includes land, history, family policies, and the opposition party (ruling party is the 10th).

In generalized astrology, this is also the house of endings and new beginnings. At the bottom of the horoscope, the 4th house cusp represents where the Sun is at midnight, which marks the ending of one day and beginning of the next.

Zeus's placement at 05:59 Aries squares Jupiter in Cancer in the 7th. Jupiter represents bankers, wholesale merchants, judges and the clergy while the 7th is generally treaties and alliances, though open enemies reside there, too.

It doesn't require a lot of imagination to consider the defense of our land and family policies squared off with bankers, wholesalers, and judges as they relate to treaties and alliances. The Boston Tea Party comes to mind as do the financiers of war.

How much do bankers and big business policies benefit the typical family?

Kronos (Mastery): Kronos is virtually the opposite of Hades. He rules all that is excellent and that which is in tune with the laws of nature. He's in the 2nd house quincunx Mars in the 7th, indicating the need for adjustments with finances and resources when it comes to treaties and alliances.

A quincunx is an unstable aspect that requires vigilance. Without diligent management it can go awry.

Being exploited by the Crown before U.S. independence comes to mind, though this has continued to be an issue since America is rich in resources. Trade agreements are in this category.

I place foreign aid and restitution to our enemies (who typically attacked us!) as related to this quincunx as well. This aspect is unstable and unpredictable, causing constant adjustments and sometimes a Catch-22 situation where neither side can win.

Think about some of the deals various politicians have cut with foreign countries using our resources, such as uranium, oil, etc., for their personal financial gain. This should be a no-brainer if you've paid any attention whatsoever to numerous scandals the past few years.

Apollon (Publicist): Per astrologer, Bill Meridian, Apollon represents "peace, commerce, honors, fame, and cross-cultural exchange." Apollon relates to multitudes, growth, and that which affects many. He's in the 6th house, which includes the working class, farmers, army, labor unions, and healthcare.

His placement at 01:27 Gemini quincunxes Hades/11th, suggesting the inclination for some of these entities to be influenced in an evil way by certain groups.

Remember that "peace" and "freedom" are not synonymous as well as the questionable money-driven behavior of the healthcare industry during the COVID-19 pandemic.

Flawed protocols caused numerous unnecessary deaths for which hospitals collected $48,000 per patient who allegedly died from infection by the coronavirus. However, many have reported that anyone who died of any cause was reported to have died of COVID to collect these funds.

The non-partisan watch-dog organization, Judicial Watch, prepared a thirty-five page report, *"The Judicial Watch COVID Project: A Special Investigative Report,"* released in July 2023. It exposed the COVID "plandemic" for what it was from the "lab leak" lie to psyops to scare the public while suppressing and censoring those who promoted safe and effective medications to say nothing of hiding the ill-effects caused by the toxic vaccines. You can learn more about their good work at *https://www.judicialwatch.org*.

I can think of numerous examples of groups that have a detrimental effect on the public. Do you trust Monsanto? The Pentagon? Especially the DOD's "black" budget? Labor Unions? Powerful entities rarely resist the temptation to dupe the public for financial gain.

Admetos (Distiller): This represents such things as compression, density, circular motion, concentration and penetration. Meridian refers to him as a "drill." Admetos is in the 1st house of national identity and the populace at 09:11 Capricorn and conjunct Eris.

Like the Goddess of Discord, he's quincunx Uranus at 08:55 Gemini in the 6th house. Examples of what Uranus represents include technological discoveries, innovation, political agitators, rebellion, explosions, and the power grid.

You can see how these influences promoted development of electronics. Not necessarily a bad thing, but can be used that way by unscrupulous people/organizations.

Admetos and Eris work well together to attain what those represented by Eris want to obtain.

Vulcanus (Transformer): He symbolizes great power and potential. He magnifies what he encounters, whether for good or evil. I see his influence as a combination of Jupiter and Pluto. I nicknamed him the "Transformer" after the electrical components in a power grid.

He's in the 3rd house at 19:24 Pisces where he relates to roads, mail, communications, infrastructure, early education (K-12) and disseminators of information. There are no aspects between him and natal planets. The 3rd house in natal astrology relates to thoughts, ideas, siblings, and neighbors. Mundane matters relate strongly to neighborhoods, local culture, and leadership. Communities influence your life more directly than the Feds. I think neighboring countries, such as Canada and Mexico, fit, too.

Poseidon (Clarity): This lord of the deep represents clarity and ideally, enlightenment, similar to his fellow ruler, Neptune, though the latter is more likely to cause confusion, delusions, and illusions as well.

In a negative sense, Poseidon relates to politics, education, and philosophy. Idealism fits, too. Big surprise there, right? He's placed in the 7th house of alliances and treaties at 15:40 Cancer. He squares Saturn at 14:48 Libra in the 10th house, which includes the president, heads of state, and the national reputation. The square shows there will be challenges and sketchy areas related to fairness in these deals with other countries.

Trans-Neptunian Aspects in the U.S. Sibly Chart

Apollon in the 6th quincunx Hades in the 11th is the only major aspect between these minor planets in the Sibly chart. All others noted in the previous section were between them and planets.

When you look as this unstable aspect as irreconcilable differences between the Peacemaker and the Destroyer, their energies are likewise antithetical, adding to its volatility. Apollon in the 6th distributes information to unify the working class, farmers, labor unions, and the healthcare industry, hoping for a peaceful convocation.

Hades, on the other hand, has nothing positive to convey to Congress, groups (which we can assume include government agencies and lobbyists), or various other disreputable associations.

His placement in this house lends an inherently destructive influence that has evolved over the past two-hundred forty-seven years. "The squeaky wheel gets the oil" versus "the silent majority" comes to mind, if you'll pardon the clichés.

People who are satisfied, complacent, or patient don't protest. Anger is a natural motivator of those who do.

While an opposition seeks balance, a quincunx is not inclined toward mutually acceptable compromise. Rather it waits until one or the other has an advantage to prevail, perhaps through a favorable aspect from a lunation.

For example, a hypothetical New Moon in Cancer in their common degree would trine Hades, infusing him with emotional energy that's likely to express as rage, while a semisextile to Apollon brings friction and annoyance, giving Hades the advantage.

Their sign placements are likewise incompatible. Apollon is in logical, objective, data-driven Gemini while Hades is in passionate and potentially devious Scorpio. Each will function well in its respective sign, but never the twain shall meet.

What are Anaretic Degrees?

For future reference, the first degree or so of a sign is referred to as anaretic, where a planet, minor planet, asteroid, or comet is immersed in a new cosmic environment. It grabs its attention, its expression shocked by the sudden change and need to acclimate, like visiting an unfamiliar city or country for the first time.

Situational awareness at the cosmic level, if you will.

How does it feel? How will it influence his function? Is it comfortable? Stressful? Stubborn? Receptive? Will it exacerbate or squelch the cosmic entity's characteristics?

By the time it reaches the sign's last degree or two, which is also considered anaretic, he's saturated with energy absorbed during his transit. If a retrograde cycle within that sign prolonged his stay, it will be even stronger. It's like being in the town where you lived long enough for everything to be familiar. He knows his environment, his purpose there, and how to express himself in the most effective manner.

Note that Apollon (01:27 Gemini) and Hades (00:48 Scorpio) in the Sibly chart are both anaretic, the former slightly less so. Zero degrees of Cardinal Signs (Aries, Cancer, Libra, Capricorn) are considered "world points."

Placement in those degrees is critically important since it indicates something that affects the entire world.

5. Partial Solar Eclipse 25 December 2000

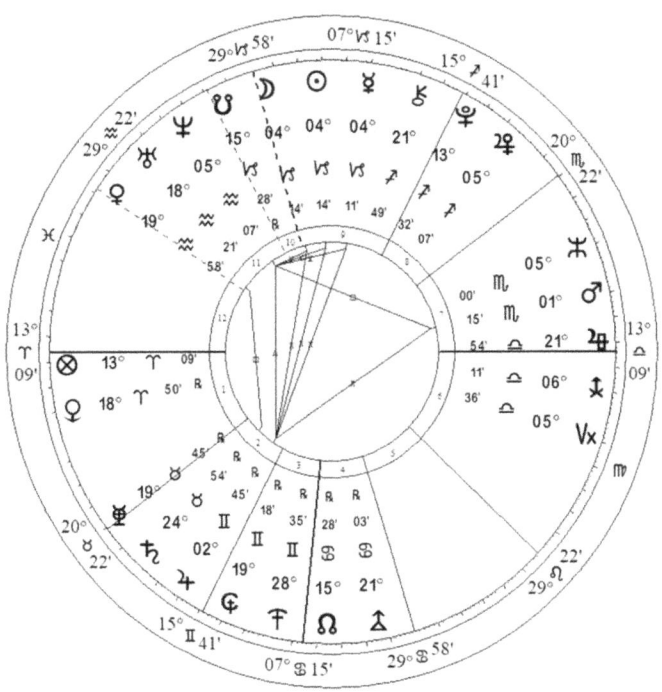

Solar Eclipse Dec 25 2000
Partial Solar Eclipse (astrological) Saros Cycle 122 = 57

December 25, 2000
12:21:37 PM
Washington, D.C
38N53'42" 77W02'12"
Time Zone: 5 hours West
Standard Time

Tropical Placidus
True Node

Mean Moon's Node	16 ♋ 01
Birth Time Accuracy	AA
G.M.T	17:21:37

Marsha Fox
B.S. Physics, Dipl. IAA whobeda@valkyrieastrology.com ValkyrieAstrology.com "Timing is Everything"

This eclipse's path of visibility in the U.S. was limited to Idaho, arriving from high into Canada and across the Arctic and North Atlantic. As I write this book, it's over twenty years later. However, it's worth study in the historical context of a new millennium and the country's evolution.

Eclipse guru and master astrologer, Bernadette Brady, states in her book *"Predictive Astrology: The Eagle and the Lark,"* that this eclipse is "concerned with unusual groups and the individuals involved. People will be drawn to these groups with concerns such as healing, the arts, or the love of humanity. Individuals will feel that they will gain much from their involvement."

As the world entered into the first official year of the 21st Century, that may have been the case as they got past the Y2K debacle. For those of you who don't recall, that was the panic that every computer on the planet would crash as the date rolled from the 1900s into the new millennium.

The eclipse takes place in the 9th house which relates to the courts, other countries/cultures, academia, religious institutions, and the mass media. The triangular aspect pattern is a "course adjustment loop." Generally it shows a conflict (square) that requires adjustment (quincunx) before harmony can be restored (trine).

Mars/7th/Scorpio (dignity) sqr Neptune/11th/Aquarius

This aspect is one component of the course adjustment loop. It suggests problems with countries overseas that could be related to the oil and pharmaceutical industries.

Mars/7th/Scorpio qnx Jupiter/2nd/Gemini

This is another leg of the course adjustment loop. It implies the need for vigilance and possible adjustments on the part of merchants and bankers relative to U.S. finances and resources. Sounds like trade issues, which need to be resolved.

If oil is the resource in question, its price affects the entire economy. In other words, to get anything from Point A to Point B requires transportation, which involves oil. This aspect suggests increasing the U.S. supply of oil to compensate for issues with other oil-producing countries, perhaps high prices.

Jupiter/2nd/Gemini tri Neptune/11th/Aquarius

This is the final portion of the course adjustment loop and should indicate where harmony is gained to resolve the conflict. If oil is the issue, this shows the increase in production will benefit various groups (including the stock market, retailers, and of course oil companies.)

Jupiter/2nd/Gemini qnx Sun/Moon/Mercury/9th/Capricorn

Jupiter makes five major aspects, four of them quincunxes. Besides the one to Mars noted above, three connect with the eclipse itself as well as Mercury, suggesting this relates to retail trade.

Sun/Moon/Mercury/9th/Capricorn ssxtl Neptune/11th/Aquarius

The semisextile indicates friction or an annoyance. The eclipse in the house that involves the courts as well as Mercury, which represents the retail industry, is causing friction that somehow relates to the oil industry. Transportation, perhaps?

Venus/11th/Aquarius sqr Saturn/2nd/Taurus

This suggests that profits and prosperity, perhaps on a national level, were being restricted due to a resource shortage.

Pluto/8th/Sagittarius tri Ascendant/1st/Aries

Pluto relates to secret societies and underground resources of which oil is one, even though its actual significator is Neptune. This suggests aggressive action financed by bankers to effect a transformation and enhance the national identity, which would undoubtedly relate to the economy.

North Node/4th/Cancer opp South Node/10th/Capricorn

The lunar nodes operate like gateways where something is left behind (South Node) as something new is attained (North Node). With the 4th house representing the opposition party, this suggests the switch to a different ruling party.

* * *

December 2000 Eclipse with Sibly Chart

The eclipse falls in the Sibly 1st house, suggesting its effects will directly affect the people.

The Course Adjustment Loop from the eclipse chart repeats in the biwheel through connections to the Sibly chart in a rather interesting manner.

Eclipse Ascendant/4th/Aries sqr Sun/7th/Cancer

The square leg of the loop entails the eclipse bringing a new beginning that creates a challenge for the Sun, which represents the president.

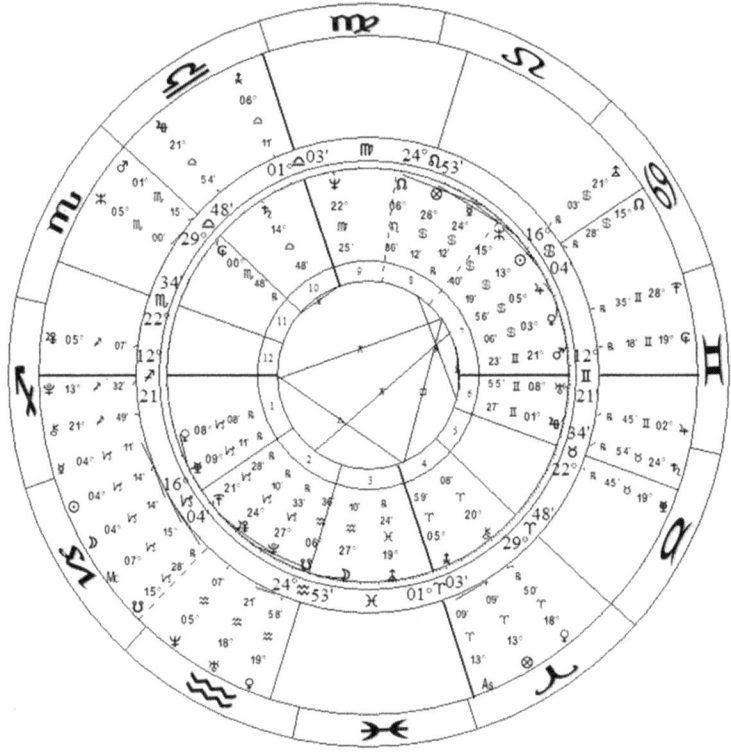

Eclipse Pluto/1st/Sagittarius qnx Sibly Sun/7th/Cancer

A change of direction related to a power play by the president that involves oil will transform the National Identity.

Pluto/1st/Sagittarius cnj Sibly Asc trine Eclipse Ascendant/4th/Aries

These changes of direction effect a positive new beginning.

Eclipse Mercury/1st/Sagittarius, rules 7th and 9th

Mercury's rulership of houses that include allies and other countries suggests public awareness of foreign relations, their impact, and court action via media reporting.

The cosmic climate involving the Trans-Neptunians is relatively quiet.

Eclipse Cupido/12th/Sagittarius tri Sibly Zeus/4th/Aries

This implies there will be fireworks to come from various groups that are currently hidden because of this change of leadership.

Eclipse Zeus/10th Triangle of Potential with Sibly South Node/2nd - North Node/8th

Specific action by government leadership will increase foreign debt, banking, and reserves. Resources in general will be reduced, including the treasury.

Eclipse North Node cnj Sibly Poseidon/7th

Dealing with other countries will increase, but need to be monitored for questionable political entanglements.

Eclipse Vulcanus/8th/Cancer opp Sibly Kronus/2nd/Capricorn sqr Eclipse Apollon/10th/Libra (Cardinal T-square)

Oppositions demand balance, in this case to avoid financial chaos and dependence on foreign nations for our fuel supply versus impact to our own resources. This suggests doing so peacefully will be difficult and up to the government to oversee.

Eclipse Venus/2nd/Aquarius sextile Eris/4th/Aries

Hints at protests regarding foreign oil and faction issues to come, perhaps related to land use and the environment.

* * *

This eclipse set the tone for the new millennium and hints at future issues and their related conflicts.

The Bush and Obama administrations would be target-rich environments, but would easily triple the size of this book if I were to review every eclipse that occurred during that time. While it would be very revealing and show the cosmic tracks that got us to where we are today, let's leave that for another time and skip forward to see where we were sixteen years later.

* * *

Truth does not mind being questioned. A lie does not like being challenged.

6. September 1, 2016 Solar Eclipse

Bernadette Brady states this eclipse carries "realism, a "coming down to earth. The individual will become aware of an old situation, and see it for what it is rather than what he or she thought. This can be a constructive time for tackling the truth."

Take a moment to consider that statement through the lens of 20:20 hindsight.

This was approximately two months before the 2016 election. Thus, this represents the hottest period of the Trump vs. Hillary Clinton campaign trail when both parties would be doing everything in their power to convince the people to embrace their respective platforms.

Visually, the eclipse contains a reverberating T-square, illustrating the discord and division in these two camps. This was the most controversial presidential race since the Bush - Gore debacle in 2000.

Pondering Brady's description, I can't help but wonder whether "seeing a situation for what it is" was a factor in Trump's landslide victory?

That said, there was clear conflict at this time, illustrated by the eclipse's presence in the house that represents the populace, many of whom felt as if they were being "eclipsed," their will trampled beneath policies that victimized the working class.

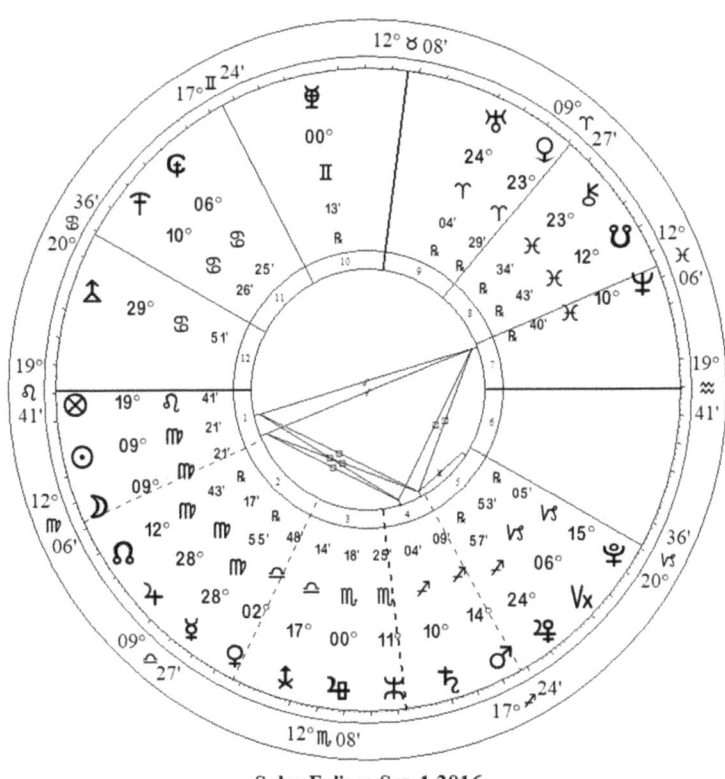

Solar Eclipse Sep 1 2016

Mutable T-Square: Eclipse/1st/Virgo opp Neptune/7th/Pisces; sqr Saturn/4th/Sagittarius; Mars/4th/Sagittarius sqr Neptune/7th/Pisces

The populace was polarizing into different camps, based on foreign interests and possibly oil. One side was practical, the other idealistic. A new beginning was in effect with vast philosophical differences between the two opponents. The populace recognized the need for directed structural change.

Admetos anaretic/10th/Gemini

Admetos illustrates that issues were concentrated, seen in a factual and objective manner in the public eye.

Admetos/10th/Gemini qnx Apollon/3rd/Scorpio

The acerbic nature of the campaign drove people out to vote in droves, some of which hadn't done so for years.

Jupiter and Mercury conjunct/2nd/Virgo; both retrograde

Resources were an important issue being reconsidered as well as various ethical issues. Numerous scandals involving Hillary and Bill were no secret, but their contingents had no problem looking the other way.

Trump was obnoxious and controversial, but brutally honest. He rallied the masses behind his "Drain the Swamp" and "Make America Great Again" promise. Republicans and Democrats alike were saturated in corruption.

Hades/11th/Cancer opp Vertex/5th/Capricorn

The country was on the cusp of major change, one way or the other. Many voters wondered what happened to the America they grew up in while others wanted it changed, according to the direction Obama had taken it--a path Hillary would continue to pursue.

Cupido/5th/Sagittarius trine Uranus/9th/Aries

Multitudes were ready for major change. Their country was becoming unrecognizable.

Eris/9th/Aries cnj Uranus/9th/Aries

Minorities, immigrants, and other factions were pushing for change, too, but didn't favor "America First" that Trump promised. The courts and media would be their allies in expressing their desires.

Trump's promise to "drain the swamp" likewise threatened thousands of comfy bureaucrats and congress critters with whom much of the populace was fed up. His reference to his opponent as "Crooked Hillary" was inflammatory to both sides, albeit for different reasons.

During this time Conservatives were the ones who felt marginalized after Obama's two terms of sweeping changes. The 9th house includes the media, which was definitely vying for the status quo and did all in their power to maintain it.

Bear in mind as well that the 9th is inherently philosophical. It's where people's ideologies lie, the chasm between them widening at an alarming rate. These differences would receive a cosmic blast driving that division even deeper in less than a year when another eclipse occurs.

To the surprise of many (particularly liberals), the people's voice was heard, loud and clear. The Swamp critters were horrified. Both Democrats and Republicans entrenched in the system for personal gain sensed the hounds sniffing at their respective heels.

The path of visibility of this eclipse crossed the Indian Ocean, South Africa, then diminished in the South Atlantic. Thus, the effects of this eclipse were apparent, but not as dramatic as those to come.

September 2016 Eclipse with Sibly Chart

While the eclipse chart itself is relatively crisp, when it interacts with the Sibly chart numerous issues emerge. The eclipse falls in the 9th, which includes ambassadors, academia, courts, religious institutions, and the mainstream media. In basic astrology, it's where belief systems and expectations reside.

Eclipse/9th/Virgo tri Sibly Admetos/1st/Capricorn (partile i.e. same degree of respective signs.)

Issues of concern to the populace were compressed.

Jupiter RX/9thVirgo cnj Mercury RX/9th/Virgo tri Pluto/2nd/Capricorn

Massive rethinking thru legislation and the judicial system would be required to bring about transformational change.

Trump's proposal to make America energy-independent plays into this aspect as a fresh approach from previous administrations.

E-Mars/1st/Sagittarius cnj Sibly Ascendant sxtl Saturn/10th/Libra

The people made their voices heard demanding action for structural change in leadership.

The Dark Side of Eclipses

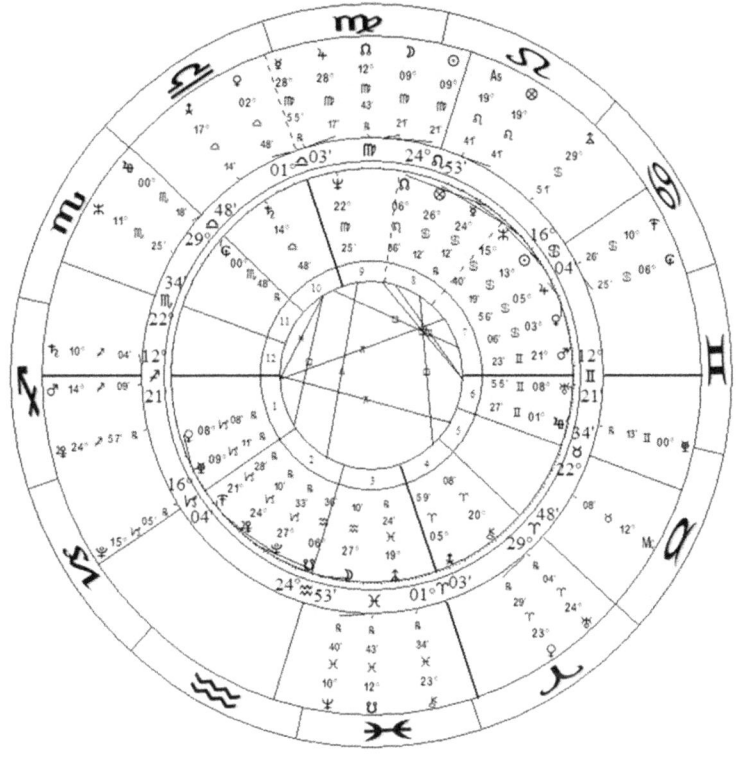

E-Pluto/1st/Sagittarius sqr Saturn/10th/Libra

This aspect shows how down and dirty the campaign would be, exposing corruption with promises to "drain the swamp," a statement so Plutonian it illustrates the prevailing cosmic energy.

Capricorn rules government and corporations while Pluto functions much like a roto-rooter that clears your clogged sewer lines.

E-Eris/4th/Aries cnj E-Uranus/4th/Aries sqr Sibly Mercury RX/8th/Cancer

Eris and Uranus, two proponents for change by whatever means necessary, are well-placed in the house of new beginnings. Remember it was conservatives who felt marginalized at this time.

Their square to Sibly Mercury in the house that includes foreign debt, banking, insurance, and mortality, indicate strong disapproval of the status quo.

Health insurance costs for the working class skyrocketed with Obamacare. While it benefitted some deserving individuals, it definitely didn't please the majority of taxpayers as insurance premiums and the healthcare industry spiraled out of control, eroding their paychecks. To those footing the bill, this ploy to redistribute wealth was hugely unpopular.

The national debt was of great concern. Even worse, it put us at the mercy of China, our avowed enemy.

E-Midheaven/5th/Taurus qnx Sibly Ascendant

This Midheaven placement suggests that which is in the public view and draws attention to the country's status as a whole. The people will make their wishes clear by effecting a change that impacts the country's reputation. This was illustrated by Trump's landslide victory.

Other countries were not pleased, either, since they stood to lose much, along with career politicians and bureaucrats.

As America grew weaker under Obama, it was looked on favorably by other countries, jealous U.S. prosperity.

The "Land of the free and home of the brave" had deteriorated significantly at the hands of those who benefited personally from foreign entanglements.

This did not set well with the American people who considered themselves patriots.

Since Obama's two terms were over, clearly a new person was heading for the White House, one way or the other. Hillary Clinton was seen by most as Obama Part 2.

Eclipse/9th/Virgo sqr S-Uranus/6th/Gemini

The eclipse squaring Uranus in the house of the working class and healthcare indicates yet another key issue that needed to be changed. Some questioned the legality of the government requiring citizens to carry insurance.

Am I the only one who noticed, perhaps due to my over three-quarters of a century on this planet, that as soon as the government gets involved prices escalate at an obscene rate?

The cost of healthcare for routine doctor visits back in the 1950s wasn't prohibitive. It got worse when insurance came on the scene, when premiums far exceeded what the average person or family would be paying for medical care.

Virgo, where the eclipse occurred, is the sign that rules health. Uranus, the planet that rules sudden change and rebellion, is in Gemini, an Air Sign that thrives on logic and sound data.

Look at how tuition rates have risen since the advent of student loans. These days colleges and universities, components of the 9th house, often have more employees than students. To afford an education the average student relies on loans. When they can't afford to pay them, guess who gets stuck?

Remember Fanny Mae and the housing crash? The government encourages people who can't afford a house to buy one, pumping up profits for builders, real estate brokers, and banks. When foreclosures swamp the market years later and banks start to fail, who bails them out?

Then there's the pharmaceutical industry. Why are prescription drugs more expensive in the U.S. that other countries? It's obvious that the "healthcare" industry wants to keep you sick. That way they keep reaping profits from your misery as doctors write multiple scripts, many to treat side-effects of the other drugs. Natural cures and physicians who promote them are frequently blacklisted or censored.

How much of the diabetes epidemic is due to a flawed "food pyramid" promoted by the USDA that was anything but healthy? What about GMOs? All the toxic chemicals in everything from packaged food to toothpaste? Chemicals that are banned in countries that care about maintaining a healthy populace.

C'mon, people. Wake up. The U.S. government is not your friend. Pluto started doing a number on its pervasive corruption in 2022. Subsequent eclipses are finishing the job, but you can see it goes back decades.

There's a vicious circle that comprises government going into debt to pump money into an industry that profits, then when the loses hit, they get bailed out at taxpayer expense. Going off the gold standard and our fiat currency, which gets printed as needed, causes inflation, which further contributes to rising costs.

What's wrong with this picture?

So, moving right along, what additional insights might the Trans-Neptunians tell us?

E-Hades cnj Sibly Jupiter/7th/Cancer

This aspect implies foreign relations will be decimated. Trump's promise to put America first put other countries on notice they were going to lose benefits. The U.S. would no longer subsidize them, especially those who hated us, anyway.

Of course they preferred Clinton to win. Everyone wanted a piece of American pie. The sad truth was that the citizens of those countries never saw a penny's worth of the aid we sent while crooked leaders and dictators got filthy rich.

There are four Trans-Neptunians in anaretic degrees which carry a huge punch, especially since this quartet also forms a quincunx, indicating an adjustment or change of course.

E-Admetos cnj Sibly Apollon/6th/Gemini

This one indicates a concentration of issues relative to the wellbeing of the working class, which includes the cost of healthcare as well as other issues.

E-Apollon cnj Sibly Hades/11th/Scorpio

The destruction of certain groups exploiting the country for personal gain is suggested. This includes numerous members of Congress and corrupt agencies such as the FDA to say nothing of other "alphabet agencies."

E-Hades/7th/Cancer qnx Sibly South Node/2nd/Aquarius semisextile S-North Node/8th/Leo

A change of direction is indicated that will affect our resources as well as borrowing money from our avowed enemies. It will be a bumpy ride as a new administration breaks down various foreign financial relations with a strong dose of nationalism.

The election two months later showed these issues to be paramount and apparent to the majority of voters when Trump won by a landslide. Considering the fact the Universe was pointing out these issues, it shouldn't have been a surprise.

Unlike previous candidates, Trump listed his campaign promises on the White House website and showed his progress in achieving them. It's intuitively obvious the media not only did not tout his accomplishments, but made him out to be a dangerous and crazed potential dictator.

Never did he receive a single word of praise for his passion to restore the country to the one he grew up in.

A former Democrat, he switched to Republican to run for the office of Chief Executive. His heart is that of a patriot, one who has seen his country lose ground throughout his lifetime and deviate farther and farther from what the Founding Fathers envisioned.

People who draw their opinions from the mainstream media, however, are very susceptible to being duped regarding what is really happening. Social media can be even worse since its infested with bots and an artificial intelligence presence programmed to promote an agenda that fits Big Tech desires--not that of the majority of responsible people. In fact, they actively censor those who try to spread the truth.

I'm amazed how many astrologers expected Clinton to win. A careful assessment of these eclipse charts populated with the Trans-Neptunians should have made it obvious.

Or did they not like what they saw, given many astrologers lean toward the left?

Major upsets to the status quo are shown everywhere. I don't know where their predictions hailed from, but apparently they gave little if any heed to what this eclipse clearly stated.

Astrologers are only human. They see what they want to see when they examine a chart. Being objective is a considerable challenge. I hate it when I have to give clients bad or disappointing news. For this reason I do an abysmal job reading my own chart.

Objectivity is essential, but not always easy to maintain.

I get that.

7. February 26, 2017 Annular Solar Eclipse

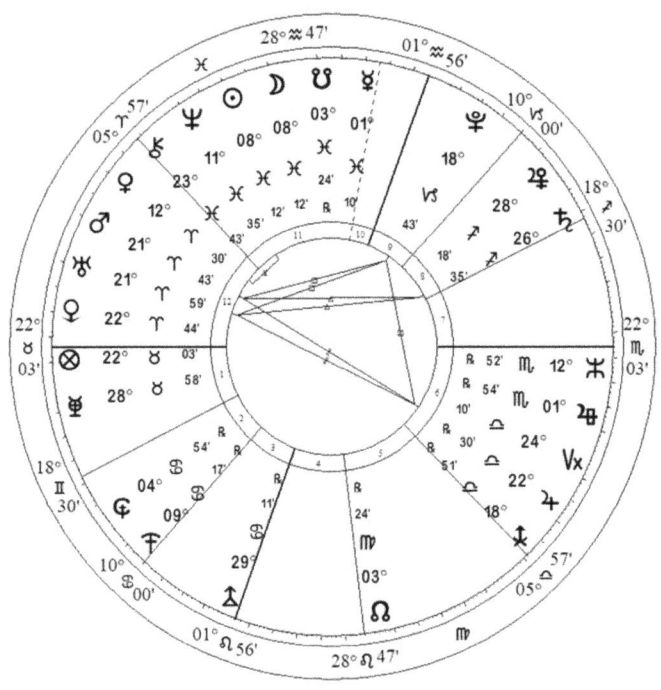

Solar Eclipse Feb 26 2017
Annular Solar Eclipse (astrological) Saros Cycle 140 # 29

February 26, 2017 Tropical Placidus
9:58:18 AM True Node
Washington, D.C.
38N53'42" 77W02'12" Mean Moon's Node 3 ♍ 14
Time Zone: 5 hours West Birth Time Accuracy AA
Standard Time G.M.T. 14:58:18

Marcha Fox
B.S. Physics, Dipl. IAA whobeda@valkyrieastrology.com ValkyrieAstrology.com "Timing is Everything"

The path of this eclipse stretched from South Africa, across the Atlantic, over the southern tip of South America, and into the South Pacific. Remember an eclipse does not have to be visible in the United States to have an impact, as previously shown.

When visible, however, the impact increases dramatically, which will be apparent for the next one that occurs six months later.

Brady describes this eclipse family as one that "brings with it the element of the pleasant surprise. Sudden happiness, a joyful event, the lucky break, the lucky win."

So let's see how that played out.

This eclipse occurred in the 11th house, which includes legislative bodies (e.g., The House of Representatives), assemblies, and other clubs and associations. This suggests heavy influence in this area. Another way to look at it is that legislation enacted by the previous administration would be negated (eclipsed).

(Note that a chart's house structure changes with location. Thus, for other countries the focus is likely to be different.)

Mars cnj Uranus cnj Eris/12th/Aries (partile) opp Jupiter/6th/Libra sqr Pluto/9th/Capricorn (T-square)

The 12th, 6th and 8th houses are considered unfortunate as the domains of hidden enemies, health, and death, respectively. The Mars-Uranus-Eris triple conjunction shows an aggressive rebellion brewing a little over a month following Trump's inauguration.

Eris shows where much of the protesting will hail from. This ominous trio is part of a Cardinal T-square with Pluto influencing the media, courts, and academia while Jupiter provokes labor unions and the healthcare industry. Trouble was clearly afoot.

Indeed, trouble already began as early as Trump's inauguration with a Women's March. To pull such an event together so quickly following the election indicates that Trump's win was not a total surprise to some (perhaps astute astrological consultants to the left who didn't go public).

It also illustrates that some matters shown in an eclipse can occur before the Sun and Moon align in their cosmic dance. Another possibility was being triggered by routine lunations (New and Full moons). They likewise have an influence, albeit not as intense.

Pluto represents corruption, the top item on Trump's agenda expressed in his promise to "drain the swamp." This god of the underworld contributed seething, unstoppable power to resisting his efforts. The reign enjoyed by labor unions as well as healthcare in cahoots with insurance companies under Obama was likewise threatened.

Saturn/8th/Sagittarius trine Mars-Uranus-Eris/12th/Aries (~5 deg orb)

The trine from Saturn to this ominous 12th trio is a bit wider than I prefer, but nonetheless viable. It suggests conservative values will be applied to foreign debt, banking, insurance, and reserves in a transformational manner, which will be one of many protest targets.

Admetos/1st/Taurus sextile Vulcanus/3rd/Cancer (anaretic) qnx Cupido/8th/Sagittarius

The people have spoken and aren't backing down, their combined power unprecedented. These three Trans-Neptunians form a yod with Cupido at the eye. The issues are clear and voters have banded together to demand change.

What specific issues might be pursued may become apparent when integrated with the Sibly Chart.

According to Brady, this eclipse is one that "brings a pleasant surprise, sudden happiness, a joyful event, the lucky break, the lucky win. The events which will be occurring can be believed and can positively change the person's life."

Trump voters were definitely pleased. The people had spoken, mostly the "silent majority" of some seventy million voters who were unhappy with Obama. Liberals, members of "the swamp," the mainstream media, and various others with a lot to lose, not so much.

Eris rising conjunct the Part of Fortune does not bode well for moving forward. The opposition will not go down without a fight.

February 2017 Eclipse with Sibly Chart

This biwheel is a hot mess if I've ever seen one. Brace yourself for a detailed look at what was happening roughly six weeks after Trump's inauguration.

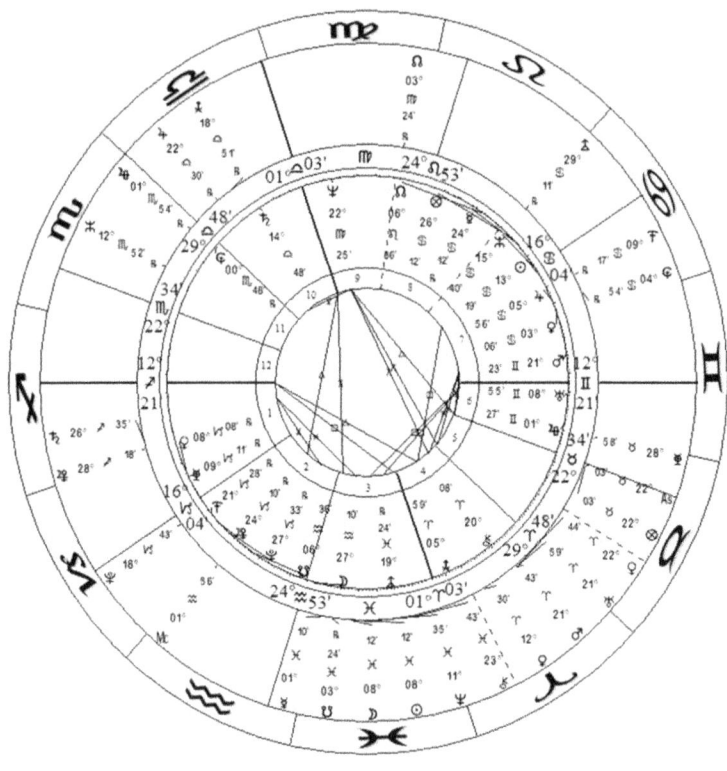

Let's think about the eclipse itself for a moment. The Sun represents the president or head of state. It's eclipsed in the 3rd house of communications. In other words, the media will "eclipse" Trump's intent and actions to suit their own purposes. This house includes infrastructure, which Trump was trying to transform by making the country energy independent with secure borders.

Eclipse/3rd/Pisces sxtl S-Eris/1st/Capricorn

Unfavorable media coverage will provide an advantage to protestors, which include minorities, immigrants, and women's rights groups.

As a side note, however, many journalists state that they lost more rights during the Obama administration than any other. While he promised his administration would be "transparent" it was indeed the most secretive in history and besieged with doubletalk. His birth records, college records, even his voting record as a senator, were locked up tighter than Fort Knox. Anyone daring to venture into forbidden territory was quickly debunked or silenced.

Knowing legislation limiting information would impinge on the First Amendment of the Bill of Rights, he took an alternate approach. He limited journalists' access to government sources in such a way that left them hamstrung as far as getting to the facts in any government issue.

Reporters were only allowed to contact the agency's assigned "Public Affairs" contact and were forbidden from talking to anyone within the organization itself, thus controlling the narrative.

This was a subtle but effective form of censorship and restriction to free speech that violated the First Amendment which states: *Congress shall make no law respecting an establishment of religion, or prohibiting the free exercise thereof; or abridging the freedom of speech, or* of the press; or the right of the people peaceably to assemble, and to petition the Government for a redress of grievances.

However, as the president, he could control government policy. More information and details straight from a journalist's blog can be found here:

https://www.usnews.com/opinion/articles/2017-01-27/president-obamas-dangerous-precedent-on-press-freedoms

Memes and other questionable material implicate H.R.4310 - National Defense Authorization Act for Fiscal Year 2013, a bill Obama signed in 2012, as making it legal for the press to lie to the American people. According to snopes.com, this was not true. Being skeptical of anything they say since they've been known to lie before (taking advantage of this bill, too, no doubt), I decided to read it myself.

Or I might add, *try*.

My eyes glazed over trying to slog through this lengthy bill, most of which relates to military funding and policies, but I did find a few sections that did just that. Legislative language is not always easy for someone without legal training to fully understand, particularly any implications that are purposely cloaked in legalese.

From what I understand, the Smith-Mundt Act of 1948 that followed World War II made it illegal to impose propaganda on the American people. The big caveat, however, was that doing so in other countries to preserve or possibly improve America's image was acceptable. Here is what it states in H.R. 4310, Section 1078:

*(Sec. 1078) Revises provisions of the United States Information and Educational Exchange Act of 1948 authorizing the Secretary of State and the Broadcasting Board of Governors to provide for the preparation and **dissemination of information intended for foreign audiences abroad about the United States,** including about its people and policies, through press, publications, radio, motion pictures, the Internet, and other information media, including social media, and through information centers and instructors.*

*Authorizes the Secretary and the Board to **make available in the United States** motion pictures, films, video, audio, and other materials disseminated abroad pursuant to such Act, the United States International Broadcasting Act of 1994, the Radio Broadcasting to Cuba Act, or the Television Broadcasting to Cuba Act. Amends the Foreign Relations Authorization Act of Fiscal Years 1986 and 1987 **to remove statutory limitations on the ability of the Board and the State Department to provide information about their activities to the media, the public, or Congress.** [Emphasis added.]*

"Statutory limitations" could easily relate to the Smith-Mundt Act that prohibited propaganda much less overt lying.

If you're so inclined to search the bill yourself, have at it. You can find it on the government website:

https://www.congress.gov/bill/112th-congress/house-bill/4310

If the media was granted permission to lie, this gave them license to get as creative as they wanted with news stories. The more sensational, the better has always been the case to draw readers or an audience, but now there were no limits or restrictions to assure accurate reporting.

It used to be that papers like The National Enquirer were obviously comprised of fiction. They actually paid quite well for these stories, but anyone with the intelligence of a turnip knew the majority were fake.

Now the mainstream media, that far too many people continue to trust, is in that same category.

Welcome to the world of fake news! Ironically, much of what was labeled "Fake" or outright censored since COVID was actually true. Apparently labeling it as false was also legitimate under HR-4310.

Have you ever heard of "crisis actors?" I suggest you look it up. Then check how the same faces keep appearing as victims at diverse tragedies, such as school shootings. Have you noticed that often the same pictures are used to illustrate different events that occurred in different part of the world? Unbelievable, but yes, it happens.

This has destroyed all faith I ever had in the accuracy of media stories. It's somewhat sad that when actors are used in commercials, such as those for pharmaceuticals, they state if it's an actor. I suppose that falls under "truth in advertising." However, it doesn't apply to news stories.

What's wrong with this picture?

Did you read George Orwell's *1984* or Aldous Huxley's *Brave New World* in high school? If not, you might want to read it now, before it's banned.

[NOTE:--If you've made it this far you're apparently not horribly offended by my commentary. Yes, I have an entire millinery of tin foil hats and I'm proud of every single one. Stay tuned. It gets better.]

Okay, enough commentary. Moving right along....

Eclipse/3rd/Pisces sqr S-Uranus/6th/Gemini

Abrupt changes are coming for the working class, military, and healthcare industry, but these will meet considerable resistance.

As a wealthy businessman, Trump was presented as the epitome of everything wrong with Republicans. Trump, in reality, was apolitical. His platform was his own for what he believed was best for the country and American people.

He reduced regulations for corporations and drilled for oil in places that fueled opposition to his objective to become energy-independent.

Being of the belief that greedy corporations exploit regulations already, I didn't agree with much of this. I'm not a fan of pollution and I definitely opposed fracking. Nonetheless, he created jobs, drove down the cost of gasoline, and the economy improved.

E-Mars cnj E-Uranus/4th/Aries qncx Sibly Neptune/9th/Virgo

Well, look at what we have here. Neptune, planet that rules deception, is in the 9th house that includes the mainstream media. Consider this in the context of my earlier rant to see how even the Universe knew they'd do everything they could to undermine Trump's accomplishments.

Well, well, well.

As I've often said about astrology, you can't make this stuff up.

The media consistently presented videos of Trump ranting like a crazed demagogue without including the context. The fact he was really fighting for the country was spun in such a way to demonize his intent. They even fooled some of the people who voted for him with their smear campaign.

He resorted to "mean tweets" to communicate directly with the public because anything he said or did was either ignored or distorted.

E-Mars cnj Uranus cnj Eris/4th/Aries

This trio's placement is a clear indicator that there's going to be a plethora of discord and protests. Remember that the 4th represents the opposition party as well as endings and new beginnings.

E-Mars cnj Uranus cnj Eris/45th/Aries sxtl S-Mars/7th/Gemini (partile)

This connection points to Mars in the house that contains foreign relations which implies protests over his crackdown on illegal immigration.

Eclipse/Aries/4th trine Sibly Mars/7th/Gemini

The eclipse's trine to Sibly Mars indicates U.S. partnerships overseas are threatened and hints that treaties will be cancelled or renegotiated as Trump looks out for U.S. interests.

Trump's call for energy independence was definitely unpopular, particularly to those proposing a "Green" agenda.

The eclipse Midheaven falling in the Sibly 2nd shows resources would be something that got a lot of public attention.

Eris not only represents minorities and other factions, but also fits this country's first occupants, Indigenous Americans, who were (and still are) opposed to the oil pipeline crossing their land. The eclipse's connection to Sibly Eris points out that protestors will have a target-rich environment.

Mars-Uranus-Eris/Aries/4th qncx Neptune/9th/Virgo

This trio of trouble makers aspecting Neptune shows the media's shift from support of the past administration to overt opposition to the current one, no matter what it takes in distorting the truth. It also reflects issues related to foreign oil as the USA began producing again.

E-Mercury/3rd/Pisces qncx Sibly Midheaven/10th/Libra

This further shows the shift in media support, implying the only support for the proposed changes was from bloggers and individuals in communities across the nation who elected Trump in the first place.

There were seventy million of them, whether or not you were among them.

E-Ascendant and Part of Fortune/5th/Taurus tri Sibly Neptune/9th/Virgo

Once again this suggests involvement of the media, perhaps in a deceptive way, as well as input from those in the entertainment and sports industries who opposed Trump's policies.

E-Midheaven/2nd/Aquarius tri Sibly Midheaven/10th/Libra

This indicates the country's status and/or reputation will involve finances and resources in general, confirming the energy independence issue.

E-Saturn/1st/Sagittarius semisxtl Sibly Pluto/2nd Capricorn

Saturn in the Sibly 1st house, which indicates the populace, shows those who support restructuring. The aspect it forms to Pluto in the house of resources, specifically those underground, fits well. A semisextile is a minor aspect that usually indicates friction or an annoyance. In other words, not everyone would agree and there would be a lot of resistance.

Becoming energy independent was obvious to Trump, but not so much to the public. Instead, they were busy protesting fracking, which admittedly is not environmentally friendly or safe. Most of the populace, myself included, was unaware that the increased drilling for oil and the unpopular practice of fracking were about making American energy independent.

Did the end justify the means?

E-Saturn sxtl Sibly Moon/3rd/Aquarius

The national mood is focused on these infrastructure issues with their pros and cons.

E-Neptune/3rd/Aquarius sqr Sibly Ascendant/1st/Sagittarius

Neptune, the natural significator for oil, squaring the Sibly ascendant shows this agenda is not going to be popular with much of the populace. Neptune's involvement further suggests that information forthcoming may not be accurate at best and deceptive at worst.

E-Jupiter/10th/Libra ssxtl Sibly Neptune/9th/Virgo

There will be major friction against the President with regard to foreign oil.

We were led to believe by the press that it was about greed. However, the economic boom that followed benefited most everyone. When gas prices go down, the price of just about everything transported via truck or train holds steady or decreases, simple economics most do not understand.

Seriously, people, how do you think consumer goods get to the store?

E-Venus/4th/Aries tri Ascendant

Venus is the natural significator of love and money and rules the 6th house of the working class and 10th house of national status. This suggests financial and job advantages, most of which were ignored by the media in favor of the far more interesting and news-worthy protests.

E-Venus/4th/Aries sqr Sibly Sun/7th/Cancer

Energy independence will have a detrimental affect on foreign relations as part of Trump's "America First" agenda and no more popular overseas than it was with the press.

So that's what constitutes the "hot mess" referred to as far as the planets and chart angles are concerned.

As if that's not enough, believe or not, there's more when we examine how Eris, Chiron, and the Trans-Neptunians contributed to the fray.

Trans-Neptunian Influences

E-Cupido/1st/Sagittarius

Many will have a vested interest in current events related to the country.

E-Cupido/1st/Sagittarius ssxtl Sibly Pluto/2nd/Capricorn activates natal Sibly Pluto ssxt Sibly Moon

There will be considerable friction and emotional involvement regarding various policies, which is a major factor in dividing the nation. When people's sentiments are involved, they're not easily resolved with data. In case you haven't figure it out already, emotions are not generally affected by logic, no matter how sound it may be.

Not that logic or sound data were in abundance.

E-Chiron/4th/Pisces sxtl Sibly Cupido/2nd/Capricorn

Numerous individuals are concerned for the environment and the consequences of rapid and dramatic change and its affects on national resources.

E-Mars/Uranus/Eris/Aries sqr Sibly Kronos/2nd/Capricorn

The concept of vying for energy independence to help the U.S. economically was sound, but it would not be simple to achieve with so much opposition.

E-Kronos/7th tri Eclipse/3rd/Pisces

The involvement of Kronos indicates this was a masterful approach for strengthening the country's infrastructure, in spite of any opposition from those who couldn't grasp the big picture.

E-Hades/7th/Gemini cnj Sibly Jupiter-Venus midpoint

There will be damage to foreign relations as the U.S. withdrew international agreements to protect its own interests.

E-Kronos/7th/Gemini opp Sibly Admetos/1st/Sagittarius

This further captures the essence of the domestic versus foreign oil issue and the people being split on the pros and cons. It reflects the impact of "Make America Great Again" versus our relationship with other countries.

This contributed to it becoming a hot political debate that pitted "Green Agenda" proponents versus what was touted as greedy corporate interests. Blinded by the media to what the advantages could be economically to the populace as a whole, opposition to all the drilling and fracking had plenty of support except from those in the oil industry benefiting from the sudden boom.

Eclipse Apollon cnj Sibly Hades/11th/Scorpio

This is the house of legislative bodies, assemblies, other clubs and associations, including the stock exchange and lobbyists. Apollon represents peace for the many while Hades is destruction, often due to ignoring the laws of nature.

Oil is controversial with its significator (Neptune) cloaking various facts about it as well. Green energy sounds all well and good, but comes at a price that is typically ignored or lost in idealistic, Neptunian fog.

This is driven home when you see an electric vehicle (EV) towing a gas-driven generator or barely survive an unexpected winter freeze that induces demands on the power grid such that rolling blackouts are the only solution because wind turbines are frozen up.

If the power grid can't handle a hot summer day or exceptionally cold winter spell without going into rolling blackouts, then how can it deal with millions of electric cars plugged in every night? Are those ugly wind turbines really the answer, or cause environmental issues of their own?

The real issue here is what other solutions might be out there, but covered up by the corporate greed everyone opposes, liberal and conservative alike.

In case you're unfamiliar with Nikola Tesla, I suggest you look him up. He discovered a means to give everyone FREE electricity, but was suppressed, silenced, and bankrupted by forces that wanted to profit by selling electricity. All of his files were confiscated, assumedly by the FBI, upon his death.

What was in those files? If they still exist, where are they?

Tesla's methods employed drawing energy from the Earth itself. It was clean and free, other than the infrastructure involved to get it established. Modern day experiments have demonstrated his premise was accurate.

Think about everyone benefitting from the "Green Agenda." Are their motives really for the good of the planet or solely their bank account?

E-Poseidon/11th/Scorpio tri Sibly Sun/7th/Cancer

Did Trump see something far more clearly that we have yet to understand? Was he a loud-mouthed, obnoxious billionaire or visionary trying to save the country from what it had become?

E-Apollon/11th/Scorpio qnx Sibly Apollon/6th/Gemini

Were these two bringers of peace trying to point to a new direction that would satisfy all the people, not just greedy corporate interests? Would economic prosperity lead the way to new breakthroughs that would ultimately benefit us all, making oil dependence fade away in a more natural and economically feasible way?

Corporatism, the collusion between corporations and government, hurts everyone except those profiting from it. The majority of liberals and conservatives as well can typically agree on that, while their elected officials are equally guilty in the political arena.

Harry Truman said, "Show me a man that gets rich by being a politician, and I'll show you a crook." If I were to list those who have gotten rich in politics over the past few decades it would be longer than this book.

Trump, on the other hand, went into politics with enough money of his own to not be subject to such temptations. Rather than increase his assets while president, they declined. That alone should show he was apolitical and had the interests of the country in mind versus his own wealth, which he earned himself.

However, what he believed to be for the country's benefit clashed violently with the millions who didn't vote for him and a few of them who did.

It doesn't take a rocket scientist to see where this was headed.

In case you're unaware, Trump is a Gemini, so his thought process is based on data, though at times it may be lacking or inaccurate. Tweeting inaccurate data made him a target for being booted off that social media platform.

This was the preamble to the eclipse on August 21 when the path of visibility divided the country like never before, though admittedly Trump's actions were definitely a factor.

8. August 21, 2017 Total Solar Eclipse

3 Path of visibility of August 21, 2017 Total Eclipse (Map generated by Sirius v. 3.0)

This eclipse occurred in Leo. If you know anything about Leos, you know they love attention and this one got plenty. It even got a name, "The Great American Eclipse" because its path crossed the United States from coast to coast as shown in the map. Whether or not it was "great" is rather questionable considering its impact.

The effects of an eclipse are stronger along the path of visibility. Bill Meridian, a master astrologer who does extensive study of eclipses as noted earlier, states that *when an eclipse path crosses a country it suggests/prognosticates division.*

In the map above you can see its path extended northwest from South Carolina across the tip of Georgia and North Carolina, through Tennessee, Kentucky, Illinois, Missouri, Kansas, Nebraska, Wyoming, Idaho, and Oregon. Visually, it's clear that it literally "divided" the country. Millions flocked to view it, but a rare few like myself were even vaguely aware of its astrological implications.

I witnessed this eclipse from Swan Valley, a tiny resort town in Western Idaho near the Wyoming border. By choosing a remote area we avoided much of the traffic involved versus those who viewed the event from cities.

If you're planning on viewing the upcoming eclipse in April, bear that in mind. I knew people who did otherwise and were stuck in traffic jams on Interstate highways for hours and hours.

Maps of the path of visibility are readily available so if you have to travel to one, choose one that's a bit off the beaten path. Even then, get reservations early. Most have no clue how popular viewing an eclipse is or how many converge on the path of visibility when it's only a comfortable drive a few hours away.

While it was a remarkable experience and a pleasant road trip with my eldest daughter and her husband, the feeling I received while viewing it was far from positive. My impression was that of God withdrawing his light, that he would no longer look favorably upon our nation.

I sensed we were in trouble.

Indeed, the stage was set by the preceding eclipse in February.

Eclipse guru, Bernadette Brady states that the effects of this one will *"bring unexpected events that involve friends or groups which will stress personal relationships."*

She goes on to say that information is distorted and possibly false, so individuals should not make any hasty decisions. Tiredness or health problems were also attached to it. She bases her remarks on the planetary aspects of the first eclipse in any given series, the energy of which carries through the entire family.

Clearly, the controversy during this time brought numerous divisions between friends and family members as each held tightly to their reasons for their chosen party or issue.

Without further ado, let's look at the eclipse chart and how the Trans-Neptunian Planets affected its energy, which as we've already seen, yields additional information.

August 21, 2017 Total Solar Eclipse Chart

What jumps out first and foremost if you're paying any attention to these charts is the partile trine between the Leo eclipse and Uranus. An eclipse in the 9th suggests the president will be "eclipsed" and not find legislative or media support for his ambitions in this area.

In this case, it will be facilitated by 9th house matters such as the mass media and other cultures, within and without the United States. It also implies that Trump will "eclipse" other countries/cultures as his focus turns toward his "Make America Great Again" agenda.

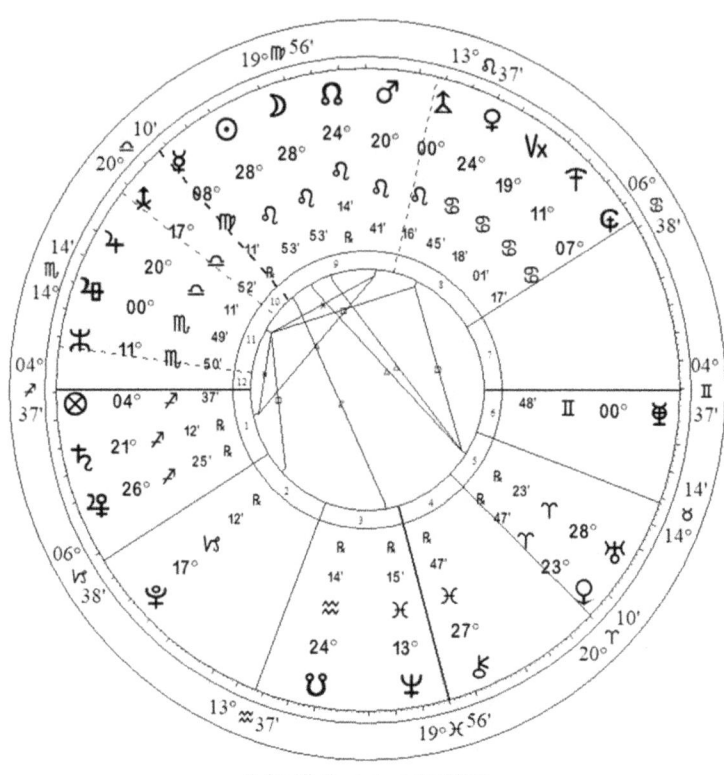

Solar Eclipse Aug 21 2017
Total Solar Eclipse (astrological) Saros Cycle 145 #22

August 21, 2017
2:30:06 PM
Washington, D.C.
38N53'42" 77W02'12"
Time Zone: 5 hours West
Daylight Saving Time

Tropical Placidus
True Node

Mean Moon's Node   23 ♌ 54
Birth Time Accuracy   AA
G.M.T.   18:30:06

Marcha Fox
B.S. Physics, Dipl. IAA whobeda@valkyrieastrology.com ValkyrieAstrology.com "Timing is Everything"

This eclipse occurred around the time that Trump was making sweeping changes to U.S. policy. He was determined to make America "First" as opposed to being continually exploited and stepped on by other countries. He tightened up the border with Mexico and questioned treaties and alliances that took unfair advantage of the U.S.

If you don't know what a "Nationalist" is, look it up. You'll see Trump's photo beside it. (Just kidding, but the reference is accurate.)

Saturn/1st/Sagittarius sxtl Jupiter/11th/Libra tri Mars/9th/Leo

This closed loop aspect pattern represents an easy energy flow, but not necessarily a positive one. Saturn and Mars are labeled malefics with good reason. When they're trined with both in Fire signs, it suggests moving forward like a controversial government program, with or without consent or approval. Jupiter connected to both Saturn and Mars inflates the effects.

The most fundamental delineation is someone in a position of power wields their influence to bring about changes they see as necessary in a big way.

Venus/8th/Cancer ssxtl N. Node/9th/Leo/ qnx S. Node/3rd/Aquarius

The Lunar Nodes show legislative change is coming as the result of a new philosophy relative to America's relationship with her neighbors. This will cause friction, even if it's a good thing economically.

Eris/5th/Aries sqr Venus/8th/Cancer

This is where Eris and her protestors come into play, though Venus in the house of transformational change is pushing back for the sake of prosperity.

Eris/5th/Aries tri North Node/9th/Leo and Eris/5th/Aries sxtl South Node/3rd (Triangle of Potential)

Eris/5th/Aries cnj Uranus/5th/Aries

Change is coming that will affect immigrants and Eris has a lot of influence in the outcome.

In mundane astrology the 5th relates to children, sports and recreation; the entertainment industry; playing the stock market; its cousin, gambling; and oddly enough, the Senate. This implies upsets in those areas that involve the courts, legislation, other cultures, and the media.

This manifested in Trump's objection to the DACA (Deferred Action for Childhood Arrivals) program that Obama instituted via Executive Order in 2012. Its purpose was to protect illegal immigrants from deportation who came to the country as children before 2007 when they were between the ages of 15-31. It issued these individuals work permits, but did not provide any other benefits. Approximately 900,000 individuals have been involved in the program at one time or another.

Trump attempted to cancel the program, but this action was denied by the Supreme Court. However, a district court judge declared DACA illegal because of the way it was created with an Executive Order versus Congressional approval. Nonetheless, it remained in effect.

Protests against cancelling this program were massive. Since it was directed at children of illegal immigrants who came to this country at a young age and considered the U.S. their home, abruptly making them subject to deportation was viewed in a very negative manner and considered inhumane.

Mercury Rx/9th/Virgo opp Neptune RX/3rd/Pisces

Mercury is exalted in Virgo where he functions more efficiently than anywhere else as he draws from that sign's propensity for detail and precision. Being retrograde suggests that reworking, rethinking, or resolving previous legislation will occur.

Neptune is dignified in his home base of Pisces, so his vibes are not being inhibited by an unfriendly zodiacal environment, either. He tends to be idealistic, which usually doesn't reflect reality or pay off as expected. However, since an opposition calls for balance, in principle these two should actually work toward a well-thought-out, possibly even inspired solution.

Venus/8th/Cancer sqr Uranus/5th/Aries

Challenges and crises are coming, all of which also relate to the DACA issue. Sudden transformational change will affect families, finances, and possibly life itself.

Venus/8th/Cancer sqr Jupiter/11th/Libra

These monumental changes will face huge resistance.

Jupiter/11th/Libra sqr Pluto/2nd/Capricorn

Pluto suggests the power of money and wealth pushing back against what legislative bodies may attempt to achieve.

Now let's take a look at what Chiron and the Trans-Neptunians add.

Cupido/1st/Sagittarius sqr Chiron/4th/Pisces

Cupido relates to merging, which also fits the concept of something going "viral" while Chiron, the "wounded healer," denotes injury or harm.

Chiron in Pisces, sign of the savior as well as the martyr, suggests these changes will be harmful to some, perhaps those who are most vulnerable, or affect family policies, the opposition party, and even history or historical self-perception.

Again, this easily applies to the DACA debacle.

Chiron tends to leave wounds and scars that never entirely heal. When he's retrograde, processing any injuries incurred do not proceed, but are internalized. For example, in natal astrology those with Chiron retrograde tend to have a hard time getting over offenses, trauma, or injuries, much less forgiving those responsible. Proper processing involves getting past it, then reaching out to help others similarly affected.

Vulcanus/8th/Leo, Kronos/8th/Virgo, and Hades/8th/Virgo with the Vertex/8th/Leo

The simplest delineation of this quartet in the house of transformation, death, and National Debt is that of a fated display of great power done in a masterful way will nonetheless invite disaster.

It's not much of a stretch to place Trump's attempt to "Make America Great Again" in this category.

Admetos/6th/Gemini sxtl Vulcanus/8th/Leo (anaretic)

A fresh perspective is coming that has plenty of energy, which will be compressed with Gemini-instilled logic. Leaders will be working more with numbers and statistics than considering the people's emotional reaction.

This likewise fits Trump's actions based on hard data without regard to individuals impacted by such decisions.

Admetos/6th/Gemini qnx Apollon/11th/ Scorpio

The issue is clear and requires a change of direction. Many agree that change is called for, but doing so peacefully is preferred. This is unlikely, given all the energy out there that suggests otherwise.

This is where the Mercury - Neptune opposition could help find humane as well as logical solutions, but their energies are overwhelmed by controversy and contention coupled with strong emotional reactions.

Kronos/8th/ Cancer tri Poseidon/11th/Scorpio

Issues will be clear, emotionally driven, and involve groups and legislative bodies.

Hello, protests.

DACA is still in effect. In September 2023 with Biden in office the Senate introduced SB 365 to issue permanent resident status to all DACA members along with various other benefits. At this writing (January 2024) it has not yet been passed into law.

Speaking of protests, they actually began earlier that year. There was a massive Women's March on the day Trump was inaugurated, then another on May Day, as recounted in an article in USA Today.

(https://www.usatoday.com/story/news/nation/2017/04/30/thousands-expected-for-may-day-protests/101132580/)

This was three and a half months before the eclipse, so what activated Sibly Eris at 08:08 Capricorn?

New Moon December 29, 2016 (7:59 Capricorn)

A quick check of the Ephemeris shows it was clearly lunations. The December New Moon was only nine minutes of arc from an exact hit. This was between the election and inauguration, giving dissatisfied factions time to plan protests.

New Moon January 28, 2017 (8:15 Aquarius)

The January New Moon gave it another irritating nudge.

Lunar eclipse February 11, 2017/Leo ssxtl Sibly Neptune/9th/Virgo

A lunar eclipse in February stirred up more idealism regarding other cultures.

Solar Eclipse February 26, 2017, 8:12 Pisces sxtl Sibly Eris/1st/Capricorn

The *coup de gras* was the solar eclipse on February 26 discussed in the previous section that further stirred up immigration issues.

Zeus/10th/Libra sqr Pluto/2nd/Capricorn

Zeus and his thunderbolts are pushing back against the transformational change Pluto favors. Pluto suggests that these changes will have an effect on finances, resources, and the treasury. This relates to both the oil situation and immigration, both topics hot with contention.

AUGUST 2017 ECLIPSE INTERACTION WITH THE SIBLY CHART

The eclipse alone certainly described what was occurring to say nothing of plenty of fodder for a stark division among the people, which was symbolized by the path itself.

The house structure of the two charts is similar, both with Sagittarius ascendants, though the eclipse ascendant is in the Sibly 12th house of hidden enemies, suggesting one of the areas that will be most active.

The eclipse itself occurs in the 9th in both the Washington D.C. and Sibly Charts. That house includes ambassadors, courts, religious institutions, and the media. In natal astrology the 9th represents beliefs, expectations, and philosophy of life as well as legal matters, higher learning, other cultures, and long-distance travel.

With both the eclipse chart and biwheel zeroing in on this specific area, it packs a double-whammy.

ERIS AND TRANS-NEPTUNIAN EFFECTS

Eclipse Eris is further activated by her aspects to the Sibly chart combined with several lunations, as previously noted.

Marcha "Whobeda" Fox

Inner Wheel:
U.S. Sibly Chart
Philadelphia, PA
Time Zone: 0 hours West

July 4, 1776
39N57'08" 75W09'51"
Tropical Placidus
NATAL CHART

5:10 PM
Local Mean Time

Outer Wheel:
Solar Eclipse Aug 21 2017
Washington, D.C.
Time Zone: 5 hours West

August 21, 2017
38N53'42" 77W02'12"
Tropical Placidus
Total Solar Eclipse (astrological) Saros Cycle 145 # 22

2:30:06 PM
Daylight Saving Time

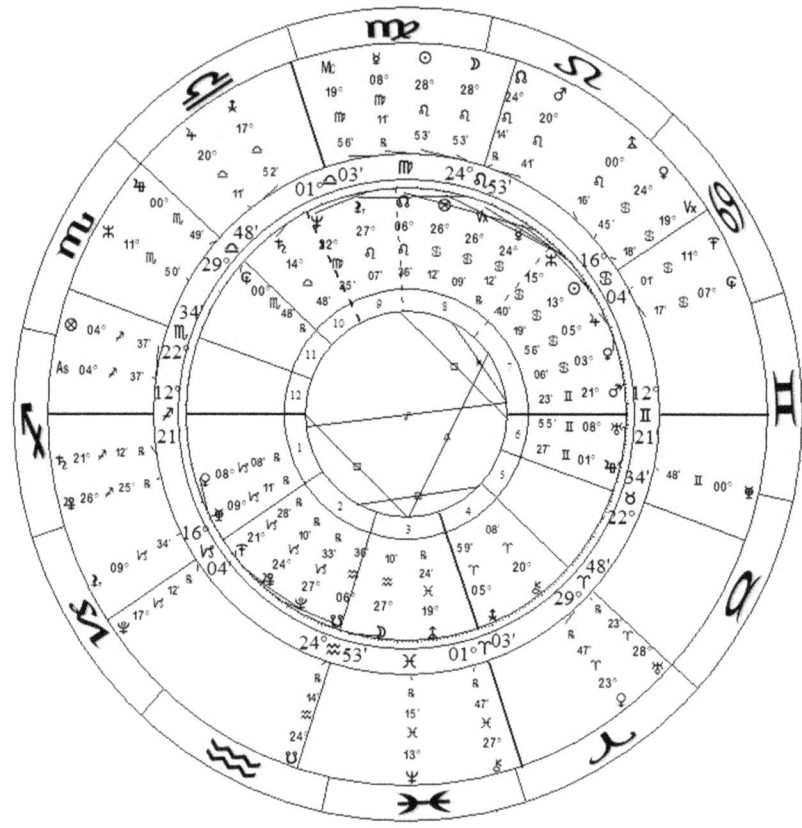

Marcha Fox
B.S. Physics, Dipl. IAA   whobeda@valkyrieastrology.com   ValkyrieAstrology.com   "Timing is Everything"

Remember that Eris and Uranus are quincunx in the Sibly chart, an aspect that calls for a change of direction though sometimes a Catch-22 is the result. Whenever something occurs at approximately 8 degrees, they'll be activated.

E-Eris cnj E-Uranus/4th/Aries (4:36 deg orb - wide)

Both troublemakers fall in the Sibly 4th house of endings and new beginnings, the same house as the eclipse chart.

E-Mercury/9th/Virgo tri Sibly Eris/1st/Sagittarius

Mercury retrograde triggers a careful review of existing legislation (and Obama's EO), which stirs up immigration issues in general.

E-Mercury/9th/Virgo sqr Sibly Uranus/6th/Gemini

This policy review that could institute new legislation creates a firestorm related to jobs. Immigrants and their proponents are not the only ones upset by looming restrictions. Numerous industries take advantage of cheap labor provided by immigrants. They are likewise unhappy about the potential impact to their workforce and its financial implications.

E-Eris/4th/Aries sqr Sibly Cupido/2nd/Capricorn

Financial impact to the corporate workforce is bad news for corporate profits, making stockholders and CEOs both opposed to change as well. Trump's plans are now annoying Republicans as well as Democrats.

Admetos/6th/Gemini (anaretic 00:48 Gemini)

Admetos in the house of work precipitated issues relevant to the working class and healthcare. The anaretic position likens it to his first day on a new battlefield. Gemini thrives on data and information, so this new environment suits his purpose.

Admetos/6th/Gemini sxtl Vulcanus/8th/Leo (anaretic 00:16 Leo)

Vulcanus injects great power and energy into what he touches. As a fire sign, Leo is no stranger to drama or demanding attention by whatever means necessary. Like Admetos, he's anaretic, but comfortable in his new Fire sign environment.

An expert at making mountains out of mole hills, Vulcanus is poised to elevate any issues to catastrophic levels. From his placement in the 8th house it's a simple matter to summon the dogs of hell to his bidding.

Easy-peasy.

The 8th house brings urgency to what occurs there. As the house of mortality and life-changing events, caution flags fly everywhere. Admetos' concentrated information fueled by Vulcanus' influence can turn the smallest spark into an apocalypse.

Apollon/11th/Scorpio sqr Vulcanus/8th/Leo (anaretic 00:49 Scorpio)

Squares bring tension and conflict. Apollon's super power is to spread the word and recruit multitudes to the cause with anaretic enthusiasm. This will include various groups with an interest in the outcome including congress, clubs, associations, and Wall Street.

While he prefers peace, Apollon's recent ingress to passion-driven Scorpio incites him to get the masses riled up and organized to present their grievances to whomever listens.

This eclipse triad works together synthesizing the essence of various issues to major importance, then organizing groups to take them forward or resist them, as applicable.

E-Uranus/6th/Aries

The spirit of rebellion against the status quo is strong, particularly the common worker or servant who feels oppressed. One ongoing argument against immigration is that these individuals take jobs away from U.S. citizens. Obamacare is also in Trump's crosshairs. Uranus will also bring upsets and innovation to the healthcare industry, for good or evil.

Will their energies bring fireworks? Or fizzle out?

E-Apollon/11th/Scorpio qncx Sibly Apollon/6th/Gemini

Adjustments and compromises are needed to come to an agreement on these smoldering issues. In this case, the result is to present the data with passion.

That is how data gets skewed. You have an Air Sign and a Water Sign clashing, which produces choppy waters.

But we're still not done with action at those energetic anaretic degrees.

E-Apollon/11th/Scorpio cnj Sibly Hades/11th/Scorpio

As the Publicist and Destroyer collide, all hell is about to break loose.

Cupido/1st/Sagittarius qncx PoF and VX/8th/Cancer

The general populace is all fired up about the policies they voted for. They're seeking answers to problems as like-minded people gather to find solutions.

E-Uranus/4th/Aries tri Eclipse/9th/Leo

Sibly Zeus/4th/Aries (no aspect)

There's a lot of explosive energy for change occupying the Sibly 4th house, which incidentally also represents the opposition party. In the eclipse chart Uranus is stirring up the eclipse itself by trining it, giving it incendiary potential. These was no way this eclipse was going to pass quietly without visible effects, even as the cosmic phenomena itself appeared over a large portion of the United States.

Can the nation remain "united" in view of the passion-infused controversy rattling multiple sectors?

E-Lilith/1st/Capricorn cnj Sibly Admetos/1st/Capricorn (0.23 deg. orb)

Trust me when I say that Lilith conjunct Admetos is not going to result in peaceful solutions that take time to resolve. Their influence is infusing the populace with serious, ambitious Capricorn energy not about to back down without results.

E-Poseidon/11th/Scorpio tri E-Kronos/7th/Cancer

Passion to bring forth truth seeks clarity before internalizing it at the emotional level. Embracing an issue with your heart is far more powerful than accepting or believing information alone. Needless to say, countries influenced by upcoming decisions are paying attention.

E-Vulcanus/8th/Leo qncx Sibly Hades/11th/Scorpio

Vulcanus in fiery Leo is gathering his weapons while Hades in emotion-driven Scorpio is procuring the ammo. No easy solutions to please both sides are evident and these two in Fixed signs aren't going to budge.

Is it any wonder ominous vibes emanated from this eclipse?

WHAT ACTUALLY HAPPENED IN 2017?

Donald Trump won the 2016 election in a landslide, much to the surprise of many, particularly those out of touch with the overall discontent of most Americans following eight years of the Obama administration.

Many factions were still in shock that they lost. Hillary Clinton was supposed to win! What went wrong? Trump made no secret of the fact he planned to "Make America Great Again" with a huge blast of Nationalism.

The opposition is not going to go peacefully into the night as he proceeds with his plans to "drain the swamp."

The alligators and water moccasins are armed for war.

Consider that the eclipse itself was in the 9th house which rules mass media.

What better weapon?

Here are some of the top 2017 news stories per https://www.cbsnews.com/news/17-stories-that-defined-2017/

1. Trump's tweets. (E-Zeus/10th/Libra)

2. Women's March (E-Lilith/1st/Capricorn cnj S-Admetos)

3. Harvey Weinstein #MeToo (Cupido/1st/Sagittarius qnx PoF/VX/8th/Cancer)

4. Hurricanes Harvey, Irma, & Maria (E-Jupiter/10th/Libra sqr E-Mars/Leo/8th)

5. Russian Investigation (9th house eclipse/Leo; (Neptune/3rd tri Sun/7th)

6. James Comey firing and testimony (Eclipse/9th/Leo qnx S-Pluto/2nd/Capricorn)

7. White House Hiring/Firing (Apollon - Hades conjunction/11th house/Scorpio)

8. Solar Eclipse ;-) (9th House/Leo)

9. Violent Rally in Charlottesville, VA by white supremacists (Apollon cnj Hades/11th/Scorpio)

10. NFL players continue to "take a knee" for National Anthem (Apollon cnj Hades/11th/Scorpio)

11. Tensions with North Korea, Trump's "Little Rocket Man" tweet (9th house eclipse/Leo)

12. Mass shootings in Las Vegas and Sutherland Springs, TX. (Vulcanus/8th sqr Apollon-Hades/11th)

13. Terror attacks around the world (9th house eclipse/Leo; Vulcanus/8th sqr Apollon-Hades/11th)

14. Trump's Travel Ban from Muslim countries (9th house eclipse/Leo)

15. Major votes on healthcare and tax reform (Apollon cnj Admetos/6th/Gemini)

16. Fake News (Neptune/3rd tri Sun/7th)

[NOTE:--Eclipses are known to reach back in time, however, weird though that may sound. I suspect much of that, as we've seen, is due to quieter lunations lighting the fuse that the eclipse ultimately detonates.]

The Dark Side of Eclipses

Trigger Points

Often the trigger point for an eclipse occurs when Mars conjoins the eclipse degree. For this eclipse, that occurred a few weeks later on September 3, 2017. Here are a few examples of news stories on that day from The Week:

https://theweek.com/10things/721491/10-things-need-know-today-september-3-2017

1. North Korea claims hydrogen bomb test *(E-Vulcanus/8th/Leo sqr S-Hades/11th/Scorpio; E-Zeus/10th/Libra sqr E-Pluto/1st/Capricorn)*

2. Trump says 'talk of appeasement' with North Korea 'will not work' *(E-Saturn/1st/Sagittarius sqr S-Neptune/9th/Virgo)*

3. Trump visits Harvey victims, declares they're 'really happy with' relief efforts *(E-Jupiter/10th/Libra sxtl E-Mars/8th/Leo)*

4. DOJ: No evidence of Obama wiretap on Trump Tower *(E-Neptune/3rd/Pisces tri S-Sun/7th/Cancer)*

5. Trump mulls canceling South Korean trade deal *(9th house Eclipse/Leo)*

6. Toxic waste sites flooded in Houston *(E-Apollon/11th/Scorpio cnj S-Hades/11th/Scorpio)*

7. Russian diplomats vacate 3 outposts on U.S. order *(9th house Eclipse/Leo)*

8. Record Los Angeles La Tuna fire forces hundreds of evacuations *(E-Zeus/10/Libra sqr E-Pluto/1st/Capricorn; E-Vulcanus/8th/Leo sqr S-Hade/11th/Scorpio)*

9. Hurricane Irma expected to escalate, won't strike Houston *(E-Jupiter/10th/Libra sqr E-Mars/Leo/8th)*

9. December 26, 2019 Solar Eclipse

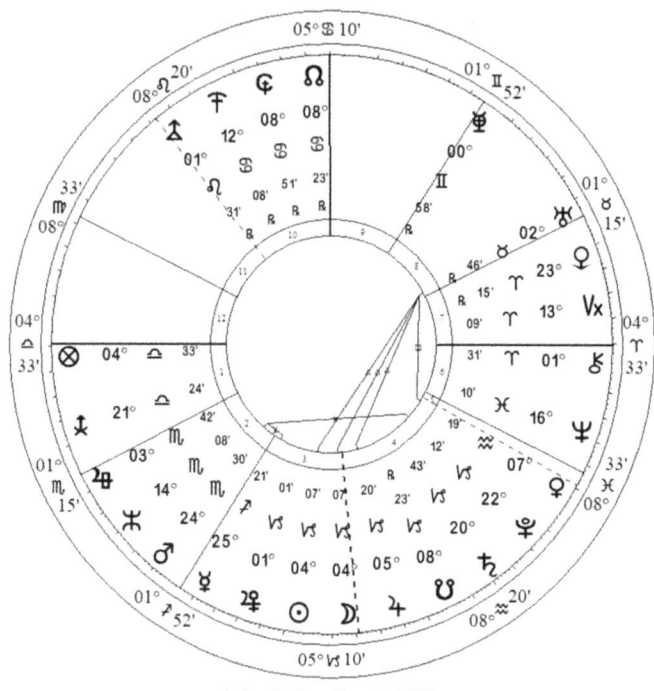

Solar Eclipse Dec 26 2019
Annular Solar Eclipse (astrological) Saros Cycle 132 # 46

The path for this eclipse was not visible in the USA, but extended from the Middle East, across India, Singapore, and island nations in the Pacific.

Bernadette Brady suggests that this family of eclipses heralds the ending of a relationship, perhaps with a younger person. She notes a large emotional component and a sense of traumatic transformation which could come through news or related to a short trip.

Think back to the end of 2019 and into 2020. Did any of those situations manifest for you?

I'll give you a hint: *COVID-19!*

This eclipse occurred in the 3rd house, which represents roads, mail, communications and physical infrastructures, primary education (K - 12), blogs, and your immediate neighborhood.

How was your neighborhood affected by the events following this eclipse? What about public schools?

Note that much of the chart for this eclipse is devoid of planets. Aries, Gemini, Cancer, Leo, Virgo, and Libra are either empty or contain Trans-Neptunians. Furthermore, all the planets except Uranus (in the 8th house of death) are beneath the horizon, suggesting much is going on in the dark.

This applies not only to lockdowns but all the underhanded activities in play between the end of 2019 and into 2020.

Eclipse/3rd/Capricorn sqr Ascendant/1st/Libra

The populace will be affected in their daily life. The effects will touch everyone in some way.

Eclipse/3rd/Capricorn cnj Jupiter/4th/Capricorn

Jupiter tied in with the eclipse, albeit in a different house, suggests its effects will be huge for families, history, and the opposition party.

I don't think anyone can argue that Trump's enemies used the pandemic to its advantage during an election year.

Neptune/6th/Pisces

Neptune, significator of deception as well as viruses, is in the 6th house of health. (Imagine that.)

Eclipse/3rd/Capricorn tri Uranus/8th/Taurus

The eclipse forecasts sudden and unexpected death, transformation to our way of life, and financial impact.

Mars/2nd/Scorpio sxtl Pluto/4th/Capricorn

Collaboration between Mars and Pluto further indicate financial troubles, resource issues (remember the great toilet paper shortage?) and difficult changes to our way of life.

In natal astrology the 2nd house includes your income, finances, possessions, needs, comforts and pleasures. Individuals will be affected in these areas. This aspect hints at job losses as well as lockdowns. Mars is in Scorpio, the sign that rules death.

Mars and Pluto are in a slight variation of a condition called *mutual reception*, making this aspect stronger. Mars, the exalted ruler of Capricorn, is in dignity in Scorpio as its traditional ruler. Pluto, the modern ruler of Scorpio, is in Capricorn. The energy exchange between them is strong and very malefic.

Venus/4th/Aquarius sqr Uranus/8th/Taurus

There will be abrupt and unanticipated deaths as well as financial impacts to families.

Mars/2nd/Scorpio ssxtl Mercury/3rd/Sagittarius

Information will be profuse, disconnected, cause friction, and much will be withheld in an underhanded secretive manner. The economy will be damaged, especially retail trade.

Saturn/4th/Capricorn cnj Pluto/4th/Capricorn

Saturn and Pluto are not a friendly combination. Both are in Capricorn, which relates to structure, government, corporations, and leadership. Saturn rules authority while Pluto represents power and control.

This conjunction as well as the eclipse's boost from Jupiter describe what followed to the proverbial "T."

How much did bureaucrats overstep their bounds in the months following this eclipse? Facts about the COVID-19 pandemic continue to emerge and they're not pretty.

As noted earlier, Judicial Watch published an entire report on the shenanigans that went on worldwide from the lies about a "lab leak" to denying the effectiveness of Ivermectin and hydroxychloroquine as treatments, to the usefulness of masks.

Trans-Neptunians Influence

Cupido/3rd, Chiron/6th, Admetos/8th, and Vulcanus/10th are all anaretic. Cupido/3rd/Capricorn sqr Chiron/6th/Aries

This combination of Trans-Neptunians, all in anaretic degrees, suggests illness and healthcare issues that will affect and unite many in the resulting suffering.

Cupido/3rd/Capricorn tri trine Uranus/8th/Taurus

A sudden transformational situation that brings people together and results in sudden or unexpected death for many, some of whom may be your family and neighbors.

Does that sound even a tiny bit like the COVID-19 pandemic?

Admetos/8th/Gemini sxtl Vulcanus/10th/Leo

Admetos suggests intense, concentrated transformational change that relates to mortality while Vulcanus implies a great power play coming from those in authority. These two are working together.

Cupido/3rd/Capricorn qncx Admetos/8th/Gemini and qncx Vulcanus/10th/Leo

Now add Cupido at the eye of a yod, a.k.a. Finger of God. His cosmic job is to bring multitudes together based on what they have in common from Admetos and Vulcanus. In other words, these three Trans-Neptunians indicate the fated nature of what was coming.

Chiron/6th/Aries sqr Cupido/3rd/Capricorn; sxtl Admetos/8th and tri Vulcanus/10th/Leo

Chiron, the "wounded healer," is in the house that rules health causing a crisis for many. He's also adding his injurious vibes to Admetos and Vulcanus as noted above, while yielding additional information about the nature and scope of what's coming. Lots of people will suffer, much of it due to the overstepping of bounds by leaders exercising despotic control that violates the Constitution.

Zeus/1st/Libra sqr Saturn-Pluto/4th/Capricorn midpoint

Zeus is directing his thunderbolt directly toward Saturn and Pluto, two malefics already in cahoots in the house of endings/new beginnings or the opposition party; take your choice.

I doubt anyone will argue that the pandemic introduced changes that haunt us to this day, whether you lost someone to death or have suffered the side-effects of the toxic vaccines.

Speaking of the vaccines, back when they became available I was learning a little about numerology. I'd met a very talented numerologist years before so was already impressed with its capabilities, that parallel astrology.

I used Chaldean numerology (slightly different than the Western version most use) to see what it could tell me about the vaccines. The number turned out to be 6 and there were three at the time--Pfizer, Moderna, and Astra-Zeneca. Which brought it to the dreaded "666," the "mark of the beast."

Coincidence? *Maybe.*

But it was enough to keep me away. Was I surprised when their ill-effects became apparent? Of course not. I personally know one person who contracted COVID from the vaccine and at least two others who are permanently affected by them. Just about everyone I know who got one is not the same person they were previously due to health or psychological/neurological issues.

Why?

Apollon/2nd/Scorpio sxtl Eclipse/3rd/Capricorn

Apollon in the 2nd of finances and resources sextiles the eclipse, showing the financial effects would involve many. Those in retail were especially hit hard during the lockdowns. How many have closed never to reopen?

Apollon/2nd/Scorpio opp Uranus/8th/Taurus

Everyone's way of life and comfort level, whether financial, physical, or emotional, would change suddenly with things never the same again.

Hades/10th/Cancer cnj North Node/10th/Cancer

Destruction is on the way and will be seen by all. Its scope will be pervasive and change life as we know it.

The South Node in the 4th tells us families are the ones relinquishing the most.

Now let's see how the eclipse interacts with the Sibly Chart.

December 2019 Eclipse Interaction with Sibly Chart

The eclipse itself falls in the Sibly 1st house, which relates to the national identity and populace, both of which will suffer the effects.

The Dark Side of Eclipses

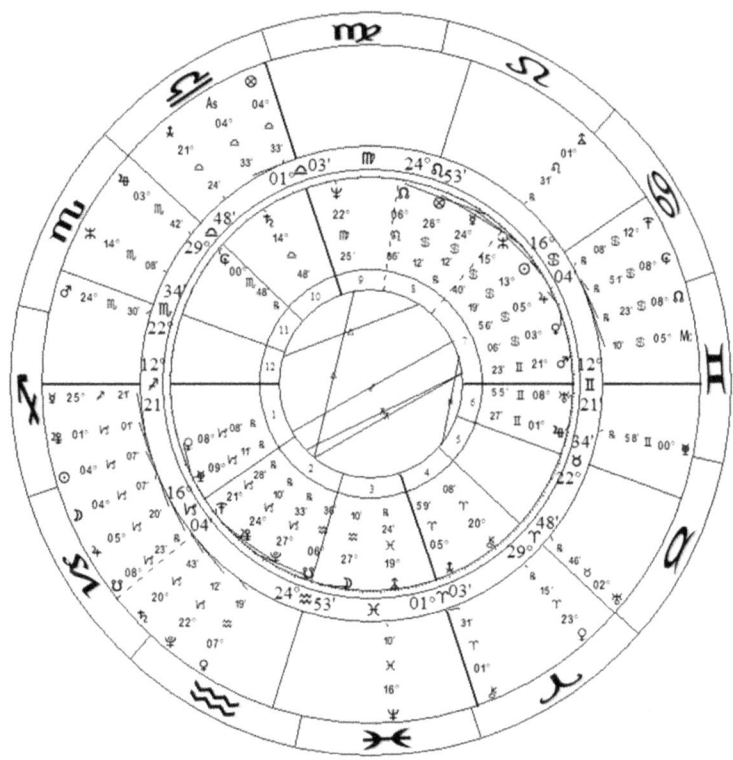

E-Saturn cnj E-Pluto/2nd/Capricorn qncx Sibly Mars/7th/Gemini

Heavy handed control over resources and living standards effects a change to our relationship with other countries. This could relate to travel restrictions during COVID.

E-Jupiter/1st/Capricorn opp Sibly Jupiter/7th/Cancer

The eclipse occurs while the U.S. is also experiencing a Jupiter-Jupiter opposition, which further exacerbates its effects on the nation.

E-Midheaven/7th/Cancer cnj Sibly Jupiter/7th/Cancer

The events incident to the eclipse will have a global effect. While each country will deal with the pandemic in its own way, all will have their eye on how the U.S. handles it.

E-Pluto/2nd/Capricorn tri Sibly Neptune/9th/Virgo

Here we have Pluto, the planet that rules death, and Neptune, the one that rules deception, liquids, and viruses collaborating. Global effects are indicated again.

E-Mars/12th/Scorpio tri Sibly Mercury RX/8th/Cancer

Attacks by a hidden enemy are indicated that is likely to result in death. Information will be subject to numerous revisions due to inaccurate and even deadly advise not only disseminated but enforced through deceit and censorship.

E-Saturn-Pluto Midpoint/2nd/Capricorn cnj Sibly Kronos/2nd/Capricorn

The government is in the drivers' seat. What Kronos touches is raised to higher levels. In this case, its power, control, and authority are elevated beyond Constitutional levels.

E-Admetos/6th/Gemini cnj Sibly Apollon/6th/Gemini (anaretic)

Admetos is conjunct Sibly Apollon in the house that includes healthcare, showing the pervasive nature of a specific issue.

E-Admetos/6th/Gemini qncx Sibly Hades/11th/Scorpio

Sibly Hades, which brings corruption and destruction, is in the 11th house of legislative bodies, clubs, and associations. This house also includes goals. Did this placement clear back in 1776 forecast that America would self-destruct? He's quincunx Apollon in the house of health, which multiplies the effects. This already ominous aspect is activated by the eclipse's Admetos, which distills issues to their essence. This points toward the destruction of many.

E-Cupido/1st/Capricorn sxtl Sibly Hades/11th/Scorpio both quincunx E-Admetos/S-Apollon/6th/Gemini (yod) (anaretic)

Here we have Cupido, the minor planet that draws people together, collaborating with the one that brings destruction, then connecting to the Admetos/Apollon conjunction in the house of health. This creates a fate-driven yod that once again reinforces the dire message of this eclipse as one that will bring destruction through health issues to many in a single focused effort.

E-Saturn/2nd/Capricorn sqr Sibly Chiron/4th/Aries

There will be injurious financial implications for families that paint the current economic picture with one of restriction and difficulty created by those in authority.

This eclipse effectively set the stage for the next one in June 2020.

10. Anthony Fauci and the December 26, 2019 Eclipse

Pardon the digression, but it's interesting to note that Anthony Fauci, who is essentially the (ugly) face of the pandemic, is a Capricorn, the sign where the eclipse occurred, the day after his birthday, no less.

Let's take a quick look at his natal chart to see how the eclipse affected him.

Eclipse Effects on Anthony Fauci's Natal Chart

Eclipse/5th/Capricorn cnj Sun/5th/Capricorn

The eclipse conjoined Fauci's natal Sun in the house that rules ego, speculations, and creativity. I don't think anyone can argue that his ego got a tremendous boost as he was allowed to dictate flawed information to the entire country that he claimed as "the science" yet was later proven to be false.

It's interesting that his 6th house, which includes healthcare, is empty. Its ruler, Saturn, also his sign ruler, is in the 9th which includes education and the media. No indicators that he's a brilliant physician qualified to make the decisions he was allowed to dictate. A simple delineation of his Sun, Moon, and Ascendant tells us he's ambitious, ruthless, and determined. Let's see how the eclipse influenced his actions.

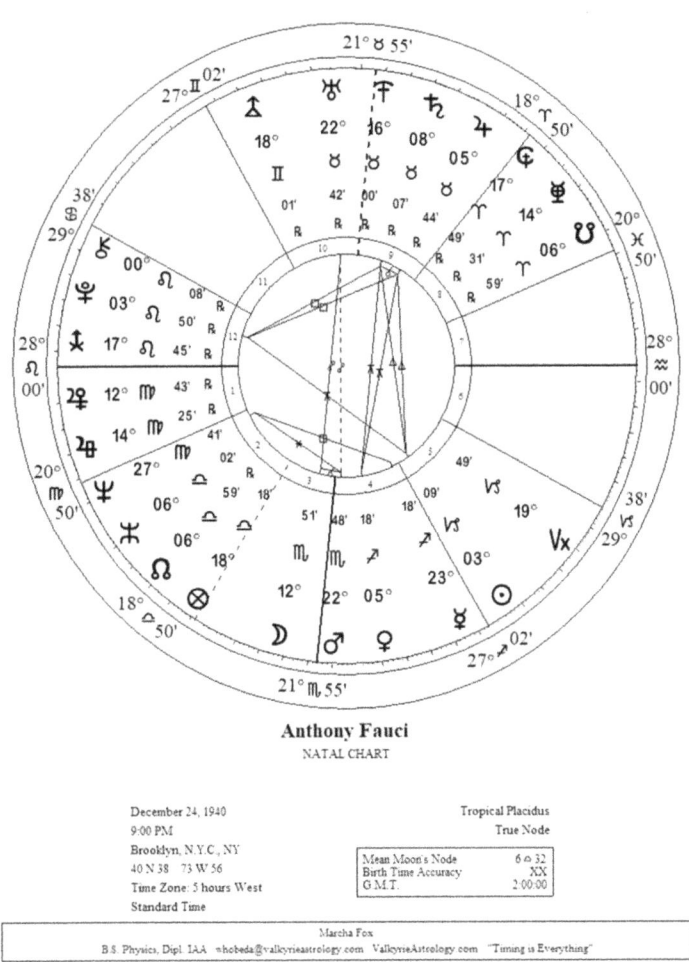

Anthony Fauci
NATAL CHART

Marcha "Whobeda" Fox

Anthony Fauci's Natal Chart with December 25, 2019 Eclipse

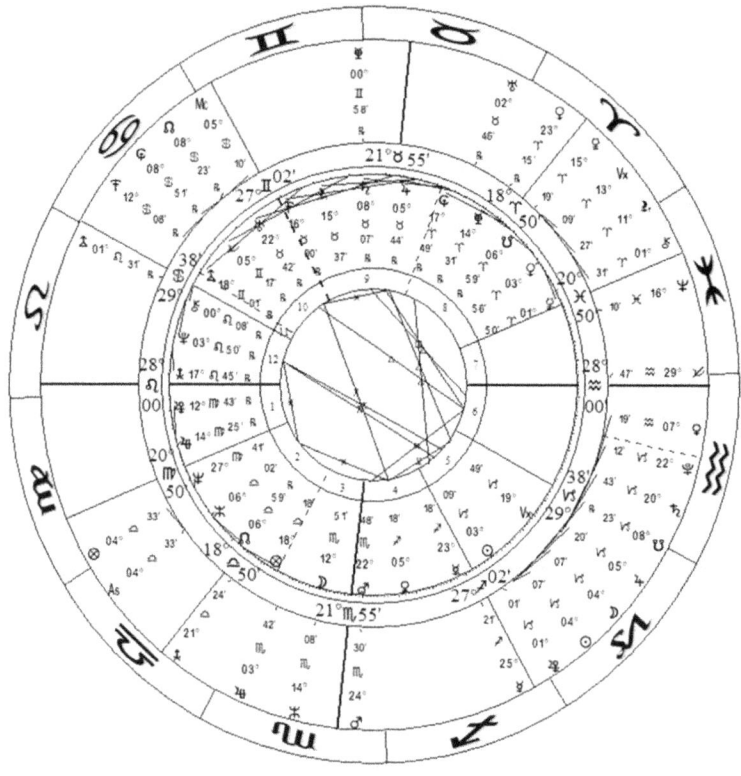

Eclipse/5th/Capricorn qncx Pluto/12th/Leo

The eclipse triggered a change of direction, unleashing his need to assume power and control. He could essentially ascend to new levels beyond his wildest dreams.

E-Mars/4th/Scorpio cnj N-Mars/4th/Scorpio

His Mars return had just occurred a day or so before the eclipse. Its location indicates it instituted a new period of ambition that he would exploit in true Scorpionic fashion. Mars is the traditional ruler of Scorpio and pursues its interests with unrelenting passion, whatever it takes.

E-Ascendant tri N-Venus/4th/Sagittarius

E-Ascendant tri N-Pluto/12th/Leo

E-Midheaven/11th/Cancer qncx N-Venus/4th/Sagittarius

Opportunities to profit were inviting and pervasive such that his Scorpio Moon couldn't resist.

I laughed out loud when I saw this. If any of you remember Flip Wilson, a comedian from decades ago, one of his favorite lines was, "The devil made me do it." If you believe astrology is deterministic, then you could believe Fauci is innocent of all blame, right? Those influences explain a lot but nonetheless don't fly with me. He saw an opportunity and jumped on it like a duck on a June bug.

E-Hades/11th/Cancer cnj North Node sxtl N-Saturn/9th/Taurus

The coming destruction would work to his advantage along with his connections overseas to create a massive windfall.

E-Saturn cnj Pluto/5th/Capricorn cnj N-Vertex/5th/Capricorn

The control and power vibes from the eclipse landed in his house of ego right on top of the Vertex, a chart energy point, that relates to fated events.

E-Saturn cnj Pluto/5th/Capricorn tri N-Uranus/10th/Taurus

Taking control through the authority he had by virtue of his position with the National Institute of Health he could effect a sudden change to his status.

E-Vulcanus/12th/Leo cnj N-Chiron/12th/Leo qncx E-Cupido/5th

Underhanded control of a situation that would injure many would feed his ego by making his name and face a household word and assure notoriety he'd only dreamed of achieving.

I recently read an article based on a talk given by Senator Rand Paul about the pandemic and Fauci's role as reported in Hillsdale College's newsletter, Imprimis, (Vol. 52, Number 12, December 2023). One statement sums it up such that I can't resist including it. To wit:

> "In addition to the fact that he was the highest paid employee of the federal government, his own net worth is estimated to have doubled to more than $12.5 million during the pandemic. This is an insult to the American taxpayer and the American ideal. We should not allow this kind of obvious corruption."

That sums it up pretty well, I would say.

11. June 21, 2020 Solar Eclipse

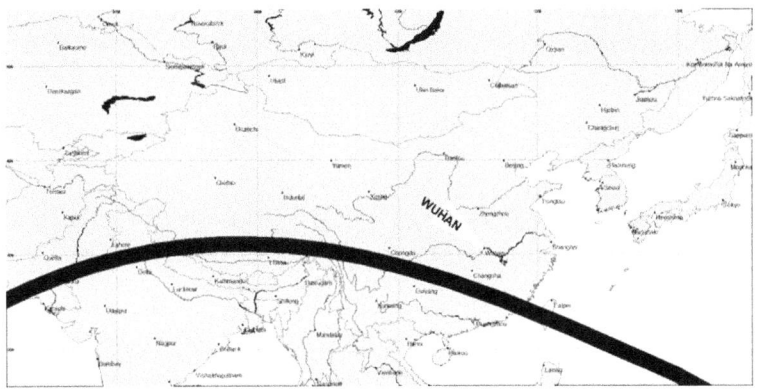

The path for this solar eclipse was over China, not far from Wuhan.

Big surprise, right?

Bernadette Brady characterizes this eclipse family as "difficult."

A gross understatement, don't you think?

She prognosticates "restriction, inhibition, restraint, separation, and illusions" as inherent to this entire eclipse family. She further notes that events could occur which "seem to block" the individual, who is likely to misjudge how to react to the situation and should wait until the eclipse passes before taking action.

If you think I'm making this up you can find this description on page 313 of her book, *Predictive Astrology: The Eagle and the Lark,* first published in 1999--roughly 20 years before the COVID pandemic.

Did she nail it or what?

Now let's take a look at the eclipse chart to see what else comes out. The outer planets and Trans-Neptunians in the December 2019 eclipse did their part, loading the bases, so to speak. Then this one came along six months later and scored a grand slam.

June 2020 Total Eclipse

This eclipse took place in an anaretic degree of the cardinal sign, Cancer, which is also a "world point," making it applicable to the entire world.

It occurred moments following the summer solstice, typically a chart that signifies the flavor of the coming season. Cancer relates most strongly to family while the 3rd house relates to local travel, your neighbors, and familiar places on the personal level; and infrastructure, K-12 education and blogs on the mundane.

I doubt anyone will argue that the events of 2020 definitely affected families, their livelihoods, schools, local travel, and relationships far and wide.

How did COVID affect you, your loved ones, and friends?

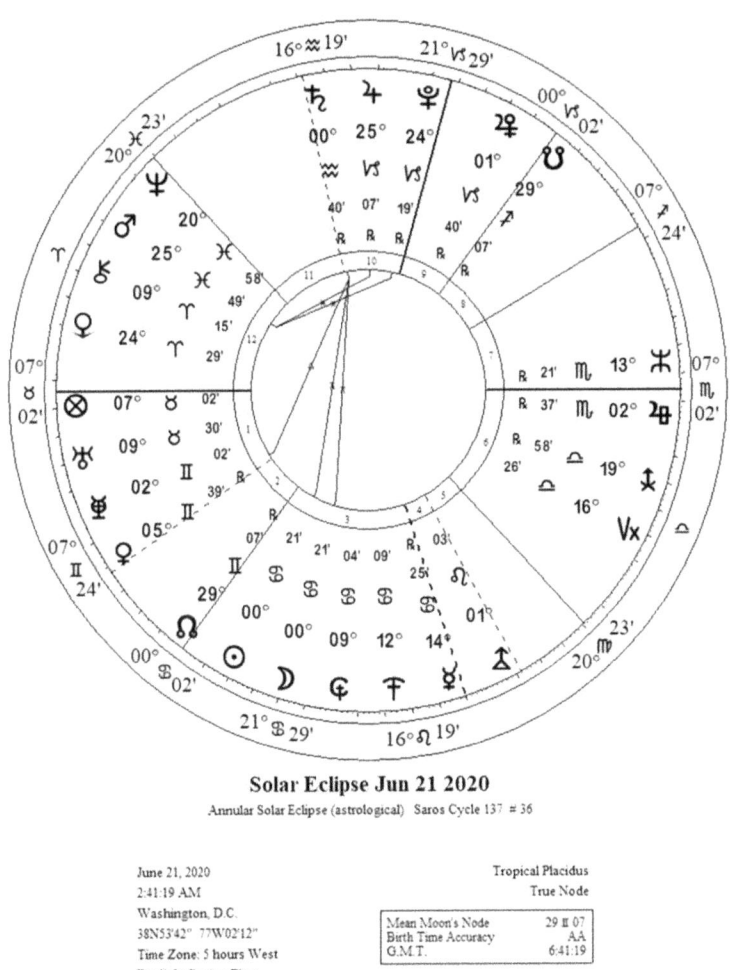

Solar Eclipse Jun 21 2020

Annular Solar Eclipse (astrological) Saros Cycle 137 #36

June 21, 2020
2:41:19 AM
Washington, D.C.
38N53'42" 77W02'12"
Time Zone: 5 hours West
Daylight Saving Time

Tropical Placidus
True Node

Mean Moon's Node 29 II 07
Birth Time Accuracy AA
G.M.T. 6:41:19

Marcha Fox
B.S. Physics, Dipl. IAA whobeda@valkyrieastrology.com ValkyrieAstrology.com "Timing is Everything"

Was your job affected? Were you able to work from home? Or were you unemployed as a result? What about your business? Did it close, never to reopen? Did you lose a loved one through faulty hospital protocols? Was someone close to you harmed or killed by a toxic vaccine? How much emotional, academic, and social damage was done to youth through school closures, religious institutions forbidden to congregate, social distancing and the like? How would you feel if you knew it was no accident?

Eclipse/3rd/Cancer qncx Saturn/10th/Aquarius (anaretic) (World points)

The eclipse's impact will change the way of life for public figures as well as individuals. Lockdowns and restrictions, both Saturnian trademarks, were imposed on millions, causing a shift in our daily routines.

The eclipse empowered unelected officials to overstep the bounds of their authority as they presented themselves as attempting to protect the masses, while in reality it was a blatant power grab and financial feeding frenzy.

Jupiter/10th/Capricorn cnj Pluto/10th/Capricorn

The effects will be massive and coupled with a huge power play by those in authority.

Jupiter/10th/Capricorn cnj Pluto/10th/Capricorn sxtl Mars/12th/Pisces

These massive power plays facilitate hidden enemies who impose extensive death and destruction within hospitals as well as social and psychological damage from imposed seclusion from lockdowns and social distancing. Vaccine mandates fall under these influences as well.

Neptune/12th/Pisces and Chiron/12th/Aries

Neptune in the 12th shows deception and delusions related to medical treatments in hospitals along with the presence of Chiron, the wounded healer, indicating permanent damage.

Chiron/12th/Aries ssxtl Uranus/1st/Taurus

The sudden upset caused by the pandemic falls on just about everyone. Everyone's sense of physical and financial security is threatened.

Hades/3rd/Cancer sxtl Uranus/1st/Taurus

Chiron/12th/Aries sqr Hades/3rd/Cancer

There will be a destructive impact on neighborhoods, retail trade, and primary education.

This triad of destruction involving Chiron, Uranus, and Hades, each at 9 degrees of its respective sign, describes the eclipse's dire effects:

There really sums it up by showing a cosmic clash between the wounded healer and hell.

Apollon/6th/Scorpio; Zeus/6th/Libra; Vertex/6th/Libra

A massive and deadly situation directly related to health was coming forth with great power that has an element of fate.

Eclipse/3rd/Cancer opp Cupido/9th/Capricorn (anaretic)

Its affect splashed on millions worldwide as well as through the media, which entered an entirely new level of faulty reporting.

Cupido's placement in Capricorn suggests authority wielded through the media as well as unelected bureaucrats wielding power they shouldn't have had (*e.g.* Anthony Fauci).

Cupido/10th/Capricorn qncx Admetos/1st/Gemini (anaretic)

The populace was driven to obsess on the situation and blindly follow what was later proven to be poor advice, such as the use of masks, all reflected in the wide but viable sextile between Pluto's power and control and Neptune's deception.

Zeus/6th/Libra qncx Neptune/12th/Pisces

Thunderbolts prevailed in the healthcare industry. The vaccine debacle as well as ineffective and potentially devious hospital procedures exacerbated rather than improved a patient's chances of recovery. Hospitals profited greatly from $48,000 government subsidies for each patient who succumbed to COVID.

Furthermore, how many deaths were falsely attributed to COVID to collect those payments?

While the eclipse itself carries an incredible view of the situation, let's see what effect it had on the U.S. as a country by linking the eclipse with the Sibly chart.

June 2020 Solar Eclipse Interaction with Sibly Chart

Eclipse/7th/Cancer

The eclipse falls in the Sibly house that includes alliances as well as open enemies. Anyone who's unaware that China is an avowed enemy of the United States has not been paying attention. Why we've been playing footsies with them for years by borrowing money to cover our explosive National Debt certainly should throw a red flag.

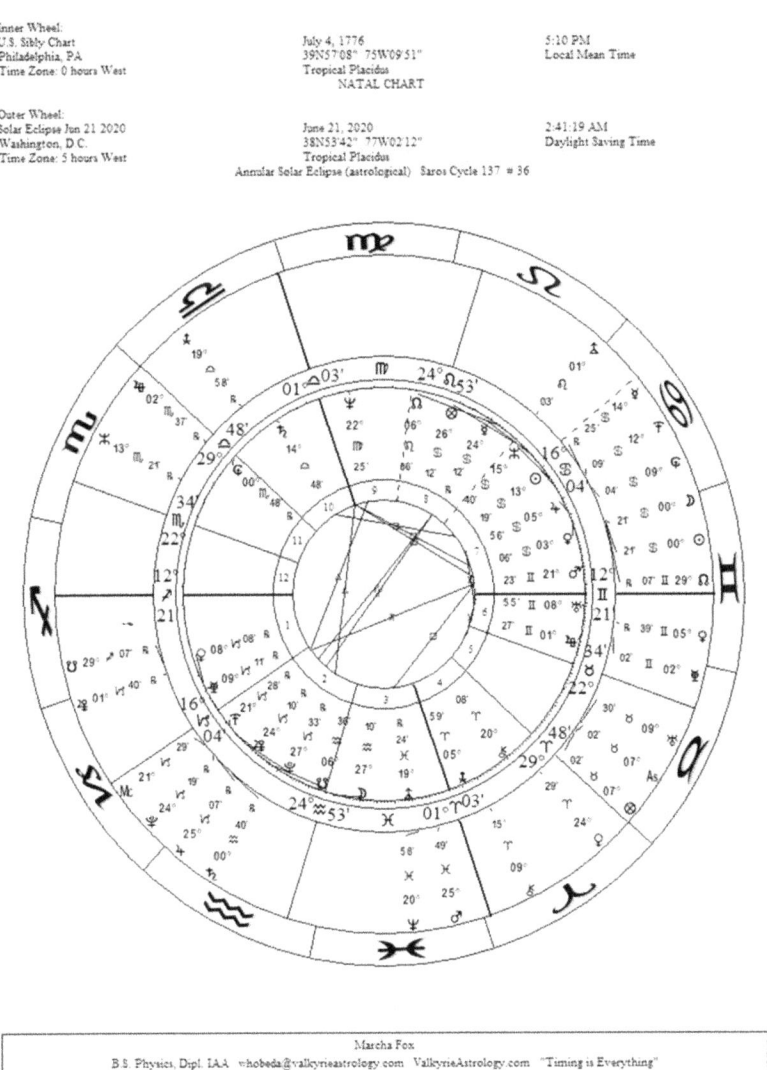

Eclipse/3rd/Cancer sqr Sibly Midheaven/10th/ Libra

The eclipse squares the Sibly Midheaven showing a detrimental effect on the country and its public image as a whole.

Saturn/2nd/Aquarius tri Sibly Midheaven/10th/Libra

Taskmaster Saturn's trine to the Sibly Midheaven indicates hard times ahead for the nation and its reputation. Saturn brings hard times and these will be known to all.

E-Midheaven cnj Kronos/2nd/Cancer and tri Sibly Neptune/9th/Virgo

Finances and the economy as well as the well-being of the people will be influenced by government's role and be integrated with the country's reputation.

Media coverage will be heavy and potentially unrealistic or unclear. With Neptune significator of both the virus and deception, no doubt both will manifest. The 9th house being involved also pulls in the media, foreign countries and their involvement.

With the Sibly Midheaven at 01:03 Libra, it is also being hit by the three anaretic Trans-Neptunians.

Cupido/1st/Cancer sqr Sibly Midheaven/10th/Libra

The populace as a whole will be affected and how it's handled reflect in a negative way on the country's image.

Apollon/11th/Scorpio ssxtl Sibly Midheaven/10th/Libra

Friction and annoyances with various groups, including lawmakers, will be pervasive.

Vulcanus/8th/Leo sxtl Sibly Midheaven/10th/Libra (exact)

Transformational change is coming down on the nation like a runaway freight train.

E-Midheaven/2nd/Cancer qncx Sibly Mars/7th/Gemini

Adjustments are required with regard to other countries. Given the context as we look at this with 20:20 hindsight, that easily relates to China and the fact that is where the virus came from and not from a lab leak as initially stated.

E-Neptune/3rd/Pisces sqr Mars/7th/Gemini

Early confusion and deception regarding the information addressing whether the virus was engineered in a lab or naturally evolved. Authorities flip-flopped on this with subsequent investigations showing they knew all along it was not natural. Whether the "leak" was deliberate or an accident is also another question, especially with Mars involved. A covert attack by a known enemy perhaps?

E-Jupiter cnj Pluto/2nd/Capricorn cnj Sibly Cupido/2nd/Capricorn

People come together with shared concerns and exaggerated fear for the future.

E-Jupiter cnj Pluto/2nd/Capricorn cnj Sibly Cupido/2nd/Capricorn opp Sibly Mercury RX/8th/Cancer

A multitude of influences are staring down Sibly Mercury, retrograde in the house that includes death, the national debt, and transformations. Everyone, including other countries, is watching America, its bad decisions out in the open.

Eclipse/7th/Cancer tri Sibly Hades/11th/Scorpio

Destructive effects on groups of all description are indicated and even hints at legislative bodies being shoved aside based on the opinion of bureaucrats.

E-Hades/7th/Cancer opp Sibly Admetos/1st/Capricorn

There will be concentrated dire effects on the populace as a whole from COVID upending everyone's life.

E-Vulcanus/8th/Leo sqr Sibly Hades/11th/Scorpio

These explosive effects will include massive destruction and death due to the actions of certain groups, bureaucrats, and sundry elected officials.

3Ignoring the truth does not change the truth.

12. July 5, 2020 Lunar Eclipse

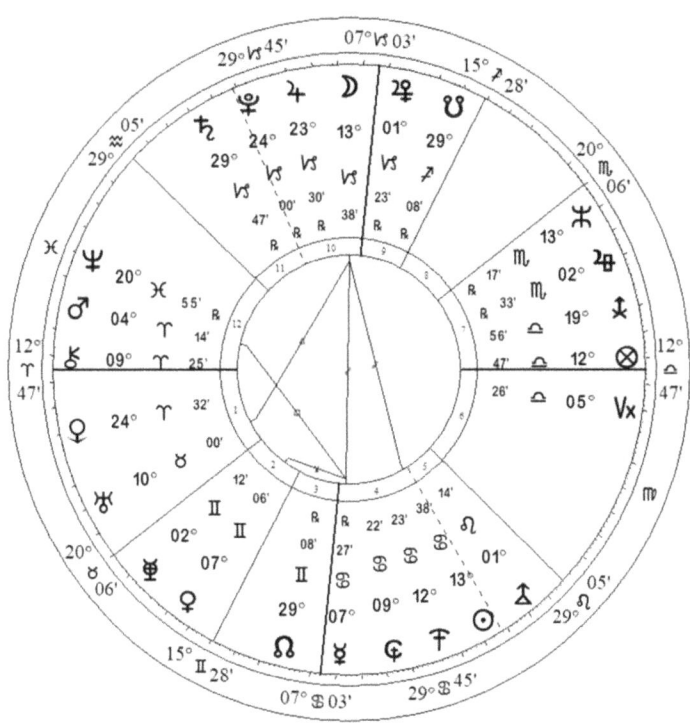

Lunar Eclipse Jul 5 2020
Lunar Eclipse (astrological)

July 5, 2020
12:44:16 AM
Washington, D.C.
38N53'42" 77W02'12"
Time Zone: 5 hours West
Daylight Saving Time

Tropical Placidus
True Node

Mean Moon's Node	28 II 23
Birth Time Accuracy	AA
G.M.T.	4:44:16

Marsha Fox
B.S. Physics, Dipl. IAA   whobeda@valkyrieastrology.com   ValkyrieAstrology.com   "Timing is Everything"

For the most part I've focused on Solar Eclipses, which tend to be stronger than their lunar counterparts, but this one fell directly opposing the Sibly Sun. Given the unprecedented events of 2020, it needed to be included.

When I first decided to write this book I planned only to cover eclipses that had paths of visibility in the United States. However, as I tore apart the ones that occurred in 2017, 2023, and 2024 in the context of current events, more and more kept joining the list.

Indeed, history evolves over time with eclipses offering key markers of where it's been and where it's headed. During such critical times it would be irresponsible to leave information out where shifts in the status quo, subtle and otherwise, set the country off in an entirely new direction.

Lunar eclipses tend to have a stronger emotional component than the solar variety. Some astrologers have noted that solar eclipses generate events while the lunar version describes the reaction to it. The previous solar eclipse described the COVID-19 pandemic quite well.

This eclipse occurred a day after the nation's "birthday." It's part of the same "family" as the last one, which Brady describes as "difficult."

Lunar Eclipse/10th/Capricorn

The 10th house placement of the eclipsed Moon suggests an emotional reaction to heads of government, which would include Trump. The Sun is in the polar sign, Cancer, in the 4th house that includes families and the policies that affect them as well as the opposition party.

Jupiter/10th/Capricorn cnj Pluto/10th/Capricorn, Saturn/11th/Capricorn

The powers that be have shackled the people with a plethora of restrictions intended to help stop the spread of COVID. While most understand the necessity, time and research have shown the dictatorial policies and overreaction were not only inappropriate, but damaging.

Capricorn is the sign that rules government and corporations. Its ruler, Saturn, Pluto and Jupiter all accompany the eclipsed Moon in the house that represents the president or head of state. Saturn drives authority, boundaries and restrictions as well as being referred to as the lord of karma. Pluto has been discussed earlier as the god of the Underworld who thrives on power and control. Jupiter expands everything he touches. This certainly captures the flavor of the times.

Mars/12th/Aries sqr Mercury RX/4th/Cancer; Neptune/12th/Pisces

Communications are suspect as inaccurate, given that Mercury is retrograde. The square from Mars, ruler of the 8th house of death, is in the house of hidden enemies. This hints at deception while Neptune in the 12th confirms it. There are too many unknowns.

Or are they secrets?

Eclipse/10th/Capricorn tri Uranus/1st/Taurus

Surprises and upsets have besieged the people for months with no end in sight. This "blood moon" reflects the death and destruction that appears to have overtaken the planet.

Eris/1st/Aries sqr Pluto/10th/Capricorn

The pandemic offers the necessary rationale to limit immigration.

Hades/4th/Cancer sextile Uranus/1st/Taurus

Upsets, disturbances, and the unexpected wreak destruction on families, particularly those who lose loved ones to COVID.

Poseidon/7th/Scorpio sxtl Moon/10th, Capricorn and tri Sun/4th/Cancer

Poseidon brings a strong political flavor to the eclipse through an aspect pattern known as a Triangle of Potential. What opportunities does the pandemic offer politically? Will propaganda, Poseidon's lowest vibration, be part of it?

Chiron/12th/Aries sqr Hades/4th/Cancer (orb 0:03 deg)

The "wounded healer" is butting heads with pervasive destruction. In the house of seclusion, the healing process is yet to begin.

July 5, 2020 Lunar Eclipse with Sibly Chart

The eclipsed Moon falls in the 1st house that represents the populace and country's image. It's within less than a third of a degree from an exact opposition with the Sibly Sun, which represents the president. He's going to receive a lot of push back from the people. Furthermore, this implies that the nation's solar return, which will be in effect for the coming year, will have nearly identical placements. This does not bode well for the nation much less Trump.

E-Jupiter RX/2nd/Capricorn cnj Pluto RX/2nd/Capricorn opp Sibly Mercury RX/8th/Cancer

There are few things more volatile than a Jupiter - Pluto conjunction. Both are retrograde, which internalizes their energy. Pluto's retrograde behavior is reminiscent of the phoenix, that burns everything to a crisp before rising from the ashes.

Jupiter retrograde tends to focus on ethics issues, which was a target-rich environment. This easily represents what Trump was trying to drain from the swamp, especially in the house of finances, which were clearly involved.

This Jupiter-Pluto conjunction reminds me of years ago when I lived in a small rural town that was the location of seven dairy farms (until most were forced to close by policies instituted by Ronald Reagan, but that's another story.) A common sight was local farmers driving tractors pulling manure spreaders on their way out to the field, dropping cow excrement along the way.

Yeah, that pretty much sums it up.

Both are in the 2nd house of finances, the treasury, and resources in general. Speaking of resources and excrement, once again the great toilet paper shortage comes to mind as well as various other commodities that were difficult to find due to industry shutdowns and supply chain issues.

The opposition to Sibly Mercury retrograde in the house of death shows this effort was doomed.

Mercury rules the house that includes treaties, alliances, and open enemies. That points at corrupt foreign powers who definitely didn't want to be exposed, either.

Marcha "Whobeda" Fox

Inner Wheel:
U.S. Sibly Chart
Philadelphia, PA
Time Zone: 0 hours West

July 4, 1776
39N57'08" 75W09'51"
Tropical Placidus
NATAL CHART

5:10 PM
Local Mean Time

Outer Wheel:
Lunar Eclipse Jul 5 2020
Washington, D.C.
Time Zone: 5 hours West

July 5, 2020
38N53'42" 77W02'12"
Tropical Placidus
Lunar Eclipse (astrological)

12:44:16 AM
Daylight Saving Time

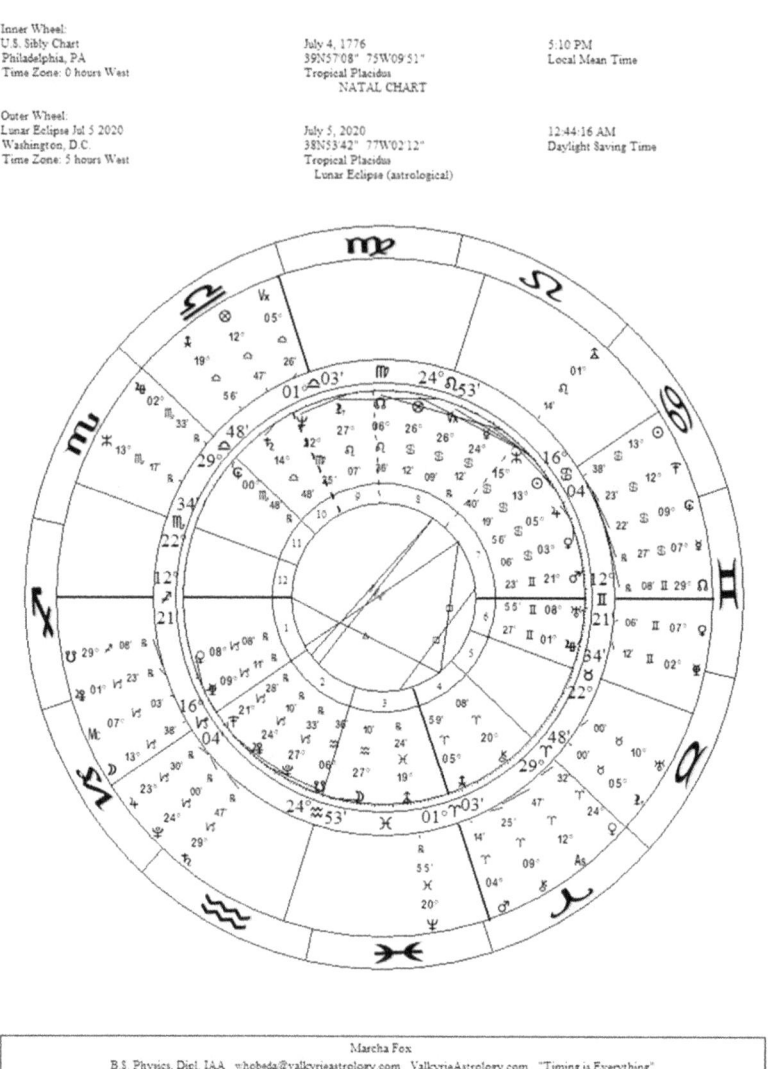

Marcha Fox
B.S. Physics, Dipl. IAA whobeda@valkyrieastrology.com ValkyrieAstrology.com "Timing is Everything"

Election interference was no doubt anticipated by Section 8 (f) of Executive Order 13848 issued September 12, 2018. It defined "foreign interference" with respect to an election as *"any covert, fraudulent, deceptive, or unlawful actions or attempted actions of a foreign government, or of any person acting as an agent of or on behalf of a foreign government, undertaken with the purpose or effect of influencing, undermining confidence in, or altering the result or reported result of, the election, or undermining public confidence in election processes or institutions."*

Dominion Voting Systems is owned and controlled by foreign entities. The electronic information from these machines went to Germany, Barcelona, Serbia, and Canada.

A forensic report directed at the programming of these machines stated "the Dominion Voting System is intentionally and purposefully designed with inherent errors to create systemic fraud and influence election results." (*The Deep Rig*, Chapter 3.)

Bingo.

S-Pluto cnj E-Pluto/2nd/Capricorn cnj E-Saturn/2nd/Capricorn midpoint opp Sibly Vertex/8th/Cancer

This increases the Plutonian energy and tinges it with Saturn's propensity for shortages, restrictions, boundaries, and hard times. Opposing the Sibly Vertex in the house of death and destruction again illustrates the fated nature of this debacle.

E-Venus/6th/Gemini cnj Sibly Uranus/6th/Gemini

Venus, is in the house of healthcare, which she rules, and conjunct the planet that causes disturbances and upsets, *i.e.* Uranus. Anyone who wasn't upset by the pandemic wasn't paying much attention.

E-Pluto/2nd/Capricorn cnj Sibly Cupido/2nd/Capricorn and opp Sibly Mercury/8th/Cancer

Pluto, god of the Underworld, is affecting multitudes who are receiving unreliable information. Bear in mind that the Underworld in this case is far more literal than you may realize.

E-Neptune/3rd/Pisces cnj Sibly Vulcanus/3rd/Pisces sqr Sibly Mars/7th/Gemini

Vulcanus magnifies what he touches, similar to Jupiter, but in a more explosive way. Neptune, master of deception and illusions, is directly under his influence. While there is no question the pandemic was bad, much of it was deliberately blown out of proportion or exacerbated by poor leadership and deadly hospital protocols.

The square to Mars in the house of open enemies points an accusing finger at a foreign country, whom we know was China.

The 3rd house represents less powerful communication outlets than the mainstream media, such as blogs and podcasts. Some of these were questioning policies and leaking truth bombs that were then debunked or censored as "conspiracy theories."

Sorry, folks. The tin-foil hat crowd was right as indicated as the truth continues to emerge.

E-Ascendant/4th/Aries tri Sibly Ascendant/1st/Sagittarius

The populace in general and families in particular are at the forefront of those affected most by government policies.

E-Poseidon RX/11th/Scorpio tri Sibly Sun/7th/Cancer

This aspect appeared in the eclipse chart, but now it's plowing into the Sibly Sun from the house of groups, which includes Congress. Poseidon's energy relates to clarity, politics, education, and philosophy with its lowest vibration the dissemination of propaganda. (Hello, H.R. 4310.)

Until the pandemic hit with full force, the country itself was faring reasonably well. Now it was chaotic. How could certain groups use that to their advantage?

Let's filter this 4th house action as representing the opposition party. They have been doing everything possible to undermine Trump since his election nearly four years before. It's now another election year and they are more determined than ever to be rid of him. What opportunities does the pandemic offer to do just that?

E-Eris/4th/Aries sqr Sibly Mercury RX/8th/Cancer and sqr Sibly Cupido/2nd/Capricorn opp Sibly Mercury RX/8th/Cancer (Cardinal T-square)

Eris in the house of endings and new beginnings is immersed in Aries, the sign of the warrior, a volatile combination. She's not alone with Mars, Chiron, and the eclipse ascendant also in that sign, each projecting their own sparks. Eris-ruled minorities and immigrants are particularly in a state of unrest.

E-Mars/4th/Aries cnj Sibly Zeus/4th/Aries and sqr Sibly Jupiter-Venus midpoint/7th/Cancer

Mars is at his peak of aggressive power in Aries where he's gathering ammo from Sibly Zeus. This is squared off with the Jupiter/Venus midpoint in the house of foreign relations and open enemies. Jupiter's energy in Cancer is exalted and saturated with emotion.

The social climate created by fear of getting sick, lockdowns, social distancing, and wearing masks was not conducive to a contented population. Reactions vary, but while some express their frustration and anger in blogs and social media, others do so via protests and riots. According to Google, these occurred in 2020:

1. Breonna Taylor protests, May 2020 – August 2022.

2. George Floyd protests, May 2020 – May 2023.

3. Capitol Hill Autonomous Zone, June–July 2020.

4. Kenosha unrest and American athlete strikes, August 2020.

5. Minneapolis false rumors riot, August 2020.

6. Red House eviction defense protest, December 2020.

Naturally, all of this was dumped on the White House lawn and decidedly Trump's fault.

13. December 14, 2020 Solar Eclipse

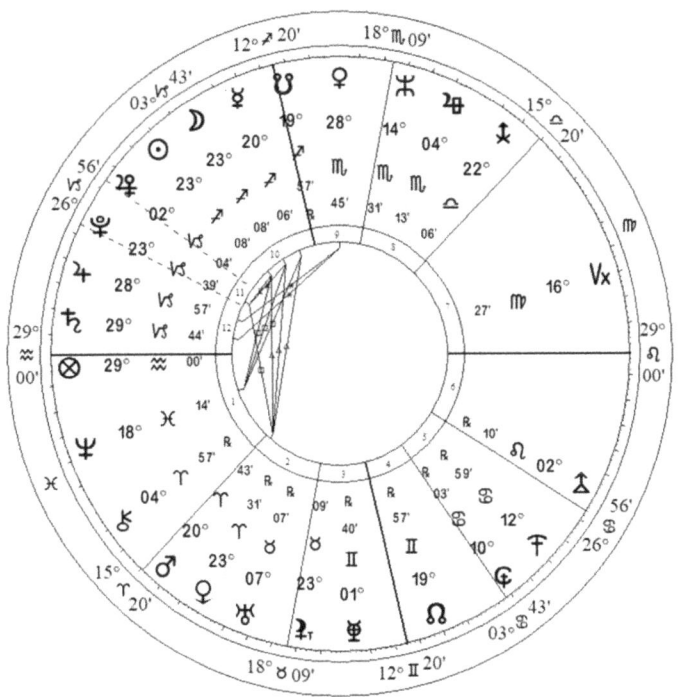

Solar Eclipse Dec 14 2020
Total Solar Eclipse (astrological) Saros Cycle 142 ≈ 23

December 14, 2020
11:16:25 AM
Washington, D.C.
38N53'42" 77W02'12"
Time Zone: 5 hours West
Standard Time

Tropical Placidus
True Node

Mean Moon's Node	19 ♊ 47
Birth Time Accuracy	AA
G.M.T.	16:16:25

Marcha Fox
B.S. Physics, Dipl. IAA   whobeda@valkyrieastrology.com   ValkyrieAstrology.com   "Timing is Everything"

This solar eclipse occurred following the 2020 election. The truth of what happened with that is one of the biggest cover-ups of all times. Anyone who questioned the results was automatically labeled a conspiracy theorist.

The COVID pandemic provided conditions to institute new election procedures that included mail-in ballots that facilitated absentee voting. It also facilitated election fraud on a scale never before seen.

It was a sick but viable joke that Hillary Clinton couldn't even win a rigged election in 2016. The powers-that-be were making sure that didn't happen again. This is another reason many believe the pandemic was indeed a "plandemic" to facilitate these unique, exploitable conditions.

Much of this cheating was in plain sight and explained in detail by Patrick Byrne in his book, "The Deep Rig: How Election Fraud Cost Donald J. Trump the White House, By a Man Who did not Vote for Him."

Free elections are the foundation of the United States. When they no longer exist, we're all in deep, Pluto-ruled excrement.

So let's see if any of this shows up in the eclipse that occurred a few weeks later. Will it carry shades of the January 6 demonstration? That was the most blatant example ever that we're living under a regime that bears no resemblance whatsoever to the Constitution. Black Lives Matter (BLM) riots were labeled "peaceful" while those protesting a stolen election were thrown in jail and are still there, since they're unable to get a fair trial.

Accusing your enemy of crimes of which you're guilty is one of the first rules of war. Sadly, too many just don't get it.

Brady's take on this eclipse family states, "Restriction, inhibition, restraint, separation and illusions are the trademarks of this family of eclipses. Events can occur which seem to block the individual. In this blocking the individual is very prone to misjudge his or her strengths or the situation and is best advised to wait until the eclipse passes before taking any real action. This is a difficult Saros Series."

So let's see what the cosmos has to say about this disgraceful time in U.S. history.

Eclipse/10th/Sagittarius cnj Mercury/10th/Sagittarius tri Mars/2nd/Aries

An eclipse in the 10th house suggests once again that the president is being "eclipsed." It took place in Sagittarius, the sign that represents the zodiacal 9th house and rules politics, religion, academia, the legal system, and philosophy in general.

Mercury in the sign where he's in debility conjunct the Sun/Moon implies information is obscured. Furthermore, in Sagittarius he's inclined to go off in so many different directions that simple truth gets lost or buried in rhetoric.

This eclipse trio trined by Mars operating from his home base of Aries indicates an attack.

This is coming from the house that relates to resources, finances, treasury, the economy, and standard of living which had been upended by the pandemic. It also implies that financial interests were behind the loss.

Eris/2nd/Aries tri Eclipse/10th/Sagittarius

Eris is likewise trining the eclipse from the money house. This brings in minorities, immigrants, and all those protesters who were likewise interested in dumping the president.

If you saw the documentary "2000 Mules" now you know which groups the "mules" were hailing from. The usual sources debunked this film as expected. What the film demonstrated using cell phone tracking is entirely possible and done on a regular basis.

Eris/2nd/Aries sqr Pluto/11th/Capricorn

Pluto in the house of groups suggests underhanded dealings. For a moment let's think about the BLM "mostly peaceful protests." Did you know the protesters were paid? Who funded them? If you think any of BLM's wealth goes back to the black community, think again.

Mars/2nd/Aries sqr Pluto/11th/Capricorn

The attack was funded by seditious groups with an agenda to finish destroying the country.

Eclipse ascendant 29:00 Aquarius cnj Saturn

It's generally acknowledged that the last degree of a fixed sign relates to a permanent ending. Aquarius in general relates to the people and equality. You know, like the "Age of Aquarius," right? This symbolizes the end of the populace having a say in who runs their country. Saturn on the ascendant shows hard times or restrictions.

Neptune/1st/Pisces sqr Eclipse and Mercury/10th/Sagittarius

4 Burnet, Texas, February 16, 2021

Neptune in the 1st tells us the people are being duped. It also represents socialism, idealism, pollution, oil, and pharmaceuticals, all hot issues at the time as the populace struggled to get through the health and economic effects of COVID.

Chiron's presence in the 1st tells us the people are under assault and being hurt. A few months later in Texas, a severe winter storm killed 136 and caused 9.9 million power outages. This was not a naturally occurring storm, but part of the geoengineering agenda.

Been there, done that, got the T-shirt in Central Texas in February 2021. We had an unheard of 9 degrees Fahrenheit accompanied by a power failure followed by rolling blackouts caused by frozen up wind turbines. You can see how overflow from my water collection tank flash-froze.

Jupiter cnj Saturn/12th/Capricorn sxtl Venus/9th/Scorpio

Jupiter and Saturn in the house of hidden enemies, spies, prisons, charities, and non-profit organizations suggest massive planned subversion.

Venus is in debility in Scorpio, where she tends to be self-serving and selfish. She's operating from the house where mainstream media resides along with other cultures, academia, religious institutions, and the courts.

This implies perpetrators colluded with the press and most likely the courts, which definitely didn't show any support toward hard evidence of election fraud. Conversely, they criminalized those who so much as mentioned it.

Judicial Watch issued a special report entitled "The Militant Left's Plan to Disrupt the 2020 Presidential Election" in September 2020, two months before it occurred. You can read it on their website:

https://www.judicialwatch.org/wp-content/uploads/2020/09/JWElectionBulletin21Sept2020-1.pdf

Judicial Watch has facilitated the removal of over four million names of individuals who were either dead, moved out of the district, or otherwise ineligible from voter roles across the country. This was done by taking specific counties to court. How many have not yet been audited and forced to clean up their voter roles, which is a legal requirement?

https://www.youtube.com/watch?v=nj0kw28cOZs

Lilith/3rd/Taurus ssxtl Eris/2nd/Aries; tri Pluto/11th/ Capricorn; qncx Eclipse

Dark Moon Lilith, who's often associated with women's rights and feminism, was particularly active. This aspect indicates an opportunity that requires effort, but can turn in your favor. This contact with Eris, plus being in cahoots with Pluto, makes me think this relates to the woman who was about to become Vice President of the United States.

North Node/4th/Gemini opp South Node/10th/Sagittarius

The South Node shows something going out of the 10th, which includes the president and government, while the North Node shows the opposition party coming in.

Pluto/11th/Capricorn ssxtl Eclipse/10th/Sagittarius

Corrupted groups and legislative bodies are taking advantage of the chaos caused by the pandemic. Numerous issues that deserved Congressional investigation were dismissed.

WHO-China investigation claims COVID wasn't caused by a lab leak, but evolved naturally, which is later proven false.

Hades cnj Kronos/5th/Cancer

Hades and Kronos have antithetical energies where one represents destruction and the other excellence. In the house that relates to children, the Senate, and how the nation views itself, this combination denotes the perfect destruction of what had been the United States.

"Difficult" indeed.

December 14, 2020 Eclipse with Sibly Chart

Now let's see how the December 14, 2020 eclipse interacts with the Sibly chart. The eclipse chart alone said a lot. What other details will be revealed?

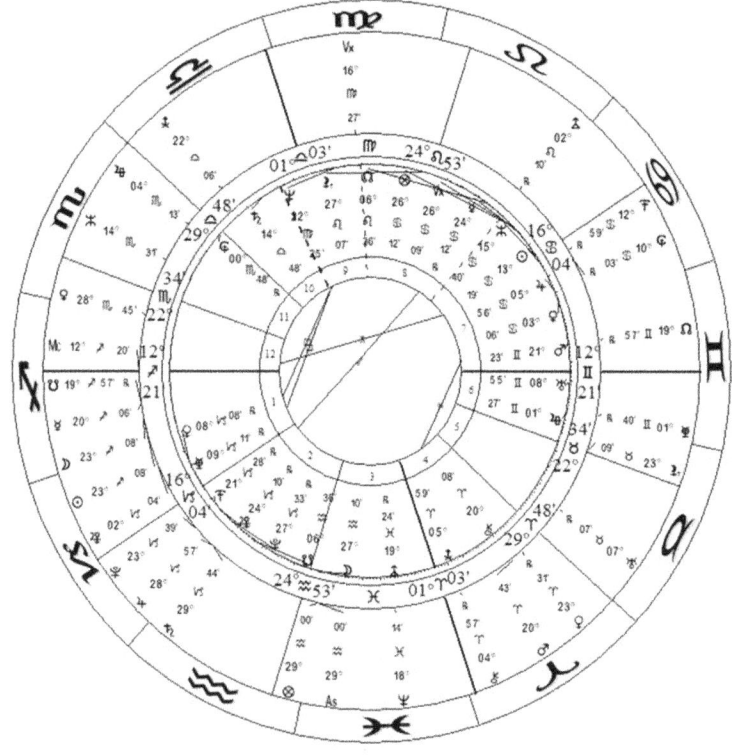

Eclipse/1st/Sagittarius sqr Sibly Neptune/9th/Virgo

The eclipse landed in the 1st house of the Sibly chart, suggesting the will of the people is being eclipsed. Its square to Neptune in the 9th indicates the people are being duped by the media. Foreign countries are also involved.

Existing law is crumbling, facilitated by the pandemic. This applied especially to election law, which states are allowed to define. Making it easier to vote via absentee ballot came about due to the pandemic. "Ballot harvesting" was also widely practiced. These were addressed in the documentary "2000 Mules" as previously noted.

9th house entities include the press, courts, academia, and even religious institutions. This aspect tells us deception is pervasive in all of them.

E-Mars cnj E-Eris/4th/Aries sxtl Sibly Mars/7th/Gemini

Immigrants, minorities, various Left Wing factions, and other countries collaborated to influence the election.

E-Pluto/2nd/Capricorn opp Sibly Mercury RX/8th/Cancer

Pluto in the house of finance, the economy, treasury, and resources indicates corruption or something being hidden. Or does it represent financial gain for a chosen few? Mercury in the 8th, which includes secrets, reflects information being suppressed or rewritten.

With the COVID pandemic in full-swing, this indicates its financial impact as the government subsidizes hospitals and dictates ineffective protocols for patients.

E-Pluto cnj Sibly Kronos - Cupido Midpoint/2nd/Capricorn

Kronos represents the law while Cupido draws like-minded people together. Pluto caught between them brings to mind all those "conspiracy theorists" and people who protested the election results on January 6, pushed back on COVID restrictions, and refused to take the toxic vaxx.

E-Neptune cnj Sibly Vulcanus/3rd/Pisces

Deception increases, particularly via the communications and social media infrastructure. According to the comprehensive report prepared by Judicial Watch, the government conducted psychological operations to frighten the American public about COVID; suppressed safe, effective, and inexpensive drugs to treat COVID; and hid reports of injuries and deaths caused by the vaccines.

E-Chiron cnj Sibly Zeus/4th/Aries

The "wounded healer" gains additional energy from Zeus as COVID cases and deaths continue to rise.

E-Mars cnj Sibly Chiron/4th/Aries sxtl Sibly Mars/7th/Gemini

The pandemic is injurious to many, particularly families, but provides benefits to other countries. Consider all the medical equipment such as masks and test kits imported from China (who caused the pandemic in the first place).

E-Admetos cnj Sibly Apollon/6th/Gemini and qncx Hades/11th/Scorpio

COVID continues to infect multitudes. Vaccine mandates are causing controversy as many refuse to be injected. So far government efforts to control or reduce the destruction are not effective and need to change.

E-Kronos RX/7th/Cancer cnj Sibly Sun/7th/Cancer

Kronos backing away from the Sibly Sun shows the president's methods are ineffective.

E-Hades/7th/Cancer opp Sibly Admetos/1st/Capricorn

Hades in the house of other countries, including known enemies, does not bode well. His opposition to Sibly Admetos in the house that includes the populace implies a deliberate attack. Did our enemies have some hand in what occurred with the pandemic? (Obviously so.)

What about the election? This further points toward foreign interference, which also showed up in the July eclipse described earlier.

E-Midheaven/12th/Sagittarius qnx Sibly Sun/7th/Cancer

The Midheaven represents the Sun's location at noon and signifies status due to its highest location on a horoscope. It marks the 10th house cusp, which includes the president and government.

The eclipse's Midheaven falling in the 12th of the Sibly chart quincunx the Sun suggests the president's status is changing due to hidden forces. The eclipse Midheaven was nearly exactly conjunct, *i.e.* within 1/60 degree, of the Sibly ascendant. One way to look at this is that the president has been "downgraded" to a member of the populace.

14. June 10, 2021
Annular Solar Eclipse

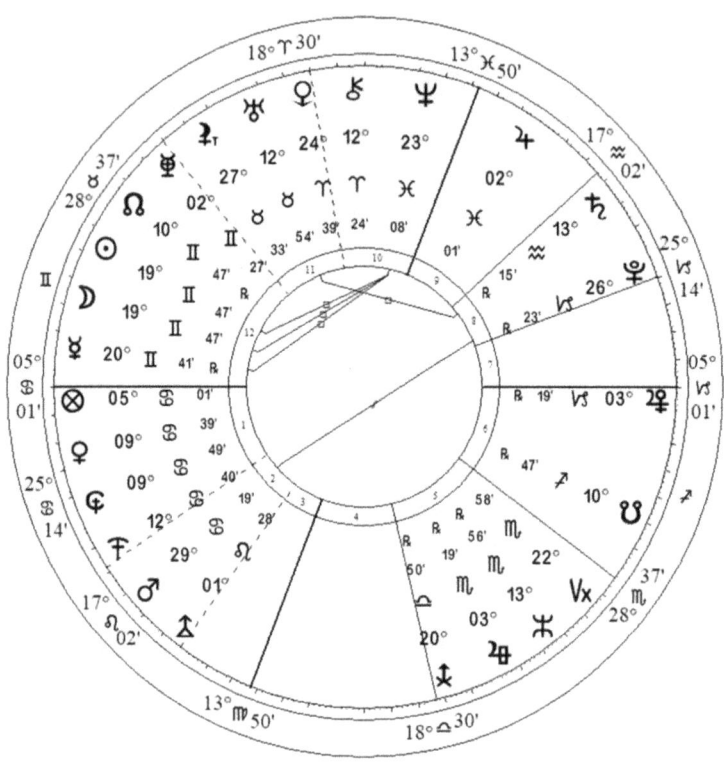

Solar Eclipse Jun 10 2021
Annular Solar Eclipse (astrological) Saros Cycle 147 # 23

June 10, 2021 — Tropical Placidus
6:52:29 AM — True Node
Washington, D.C.
38N53'42" 77W02'12"
Time Zone: 5 hours West
Daylight Saving Time

Mean Moon's Node	10 II 22
Birth Time Accuracy	AA
G.M.T.	10:52:29

Marcha Fox
B.S. Physics, Dipl. IAA whobeda@valkyrieastrology.com ValkyrieAstrology.com "Timing is Everything"

This eclipse was visible from Canada, Greenland, the North Pole, and the Russian Far East.

Brady described it as "very unusual" with "sudden flashes of ideas that seem to have a psychic or unconscious flavor.... A truly creative series which should leave the individual enriched."

Eclipse/12th/Gemini cnj Mercury sqr Neptune/10th/Pisces

The eclipse's Gemini placement conjunct Mercury in the 12th house suggests covered up information. The trifecta's collective square to Neptune indicates that anything revealed by government is likely to be inaccurate or deceptive. The truth comes out in time, and almost three years later we're finding out more and more about the lies.

Less that two weeks later world leaders gather for a conference on Climate Change to celebrate Earth Day. The U.S. agreed to reduce greenhouse gas emissions 40% by 2030, undoubtedly a goal of U.N. Agenda 2030.

Neptune in the 10th suggests some of this deception is "overhead." If you're unfamiliar with chemtrails, you can learn about them on this website, *https://www.geoengineering.org*. Climate change is indeed manmade, but not related to cow farts or volcanoes. Our extreme weather is being engineered, not the result of natural climate cycles.

Mars/2nd/Cancer opp Pluto/8th/Capricorn (Mars anaretic/fall)

Mars, ruler of the house that includes health and healthcare, the army, working class, and farmers is in the house that relates to our standard of living. Pluto in the 8th suggests more subversive activities that relate to death.

Mars is anaretic in the last degree of emotionally-driven Cancer where he's prone to "temper tantrums." In other words, his aggression is often impulsive and misdirected.

COVID was still raging. Vaccine mandates were profuse. Many sacrificed their jobs when they refused. By the end of June those who'd received the vaccines worldwide exceeded three billion. Deaths reached four million from COVID itself with worldwide cases over 200 million by summer.

The withdrawal of American troops from Afghanistan after a two-decade war that took the lives of over 2,400 U.S. service personnel was a total disaster. Many were left behind, including U.S. citizens and Afghan citizens who aided the war effort. $7.12 billion worth of military infrastructure was left in the hands of our enemies.

All the sordid details, including the fact all of this quickly fell into the hands of the Taliban and is being used to violate human rights, can be found here:

https://foreignpolicy.com/2022/04/28/the-u-s-left-billions-worth-of-weapons-in-afghanistan/

In August the United States launches an airstrike that it claims killed the Islamic State member who was believed to have planned the Kabul airport bombings. However, the U.S. Defense Department later acknowledged that the strike instead killed ten civilians, including seven children, and that no terrorists were killed.

Ironically, in December the U.S. announces a diplomatic boycott of the 2022 Winter Olympics in Beijing in response to China's human rights record, after facilitating just that by its clumsy withdrawal from Afghanistan.

Saturn/8th/Aquarius sqr Uranus/11th/Taurus

Saturn in the house of death squaring Uranus in the house of groups and goals relates to the wave of "sudden deaths" that began to occur among youth, sports participants, and working age individuals. These were publicized as "unexplainable" when they were clearly associated with COVID vaccines. In spite of all the evidence, official sources still refuse to admit it. This includes, of course, your doctor who told you to get injected.

The U.S. Vaccine Adverse Event Reporting System (VAERS) database (*https://vaers.hhs.gov*) indicated huge spikes in vaccine reactions following the rollout of the COVID injections.

Cupido/6th/Capricorn sxtl Jupiter/9th/Pisces

Many are united in opposing the vaxx mandates and questioning what they're being told (or not told) by the media.

This could also relate to a Minneapolis jury finding former police officer Derek Chauvin guilty of murdering George Floyd a year earlier.

Zeus/5th/Libra, Apollon/5th/Scorpio, Poseidon/5th/Scorpio and Vertex/5th/Scorpio

This cluster of Trans-Neptunians in the house that includes children suggests they're under attack but it's being covered up with propaganda.

Venus/1st/Cancer cnj Hades/1st/Cancer (partile, orb 1/6 deg)

Venus rules the house that includes children. Her conjunction with Hades further supports the destruction imposed on the nation's youth.

Kronos/1st/Cancer sxtl Uranus/11th/Taurus

Kronos, which instills excellence, combined with Uranus, the planet the rules technology, fits the successful splashdown of the first operational spaceflight by a private company, Elon Musk's SpaceX.

Jupiter/9th/Pisces trine Apollon/5th/Scorpio

The implementation of the Texas Heartbeat Act bans abortions after roughly six weeks. The Supreme Court declines to block the law, saying it's a question for lower courts.

Admetos/12th/Gemini sqr Jupiter/9th/Pisces

Hidden enemies, most of whom represent views unpopular with the general public will focus their attention and protests on legislation that is contrary to what they support.

June 10, 2021 Eclipse with Sibly Chart

This eclipse occurred in the 7th house of foreign relations accompanied by a vast entourage that included Mercury, the eclipse Ascendant, Venus, Hades, and Kronos.

The eclipse chart itself indicated various incidents involving foreign countries as previously described. What appears in this bi-wheel further emphasizes those events.

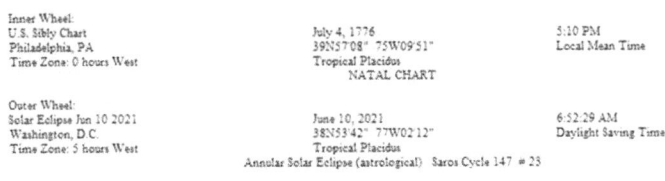

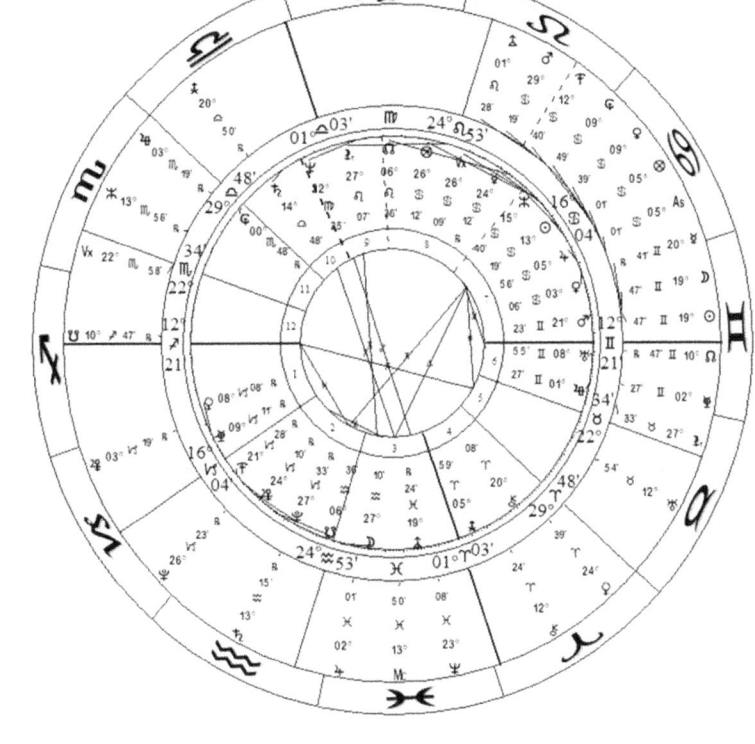

The following aspects relate to the military debacles in Afghanistan and destroying the wrong target in retaliation for the Kabul Airport bombing:

Neptune/3rd/Pisces opp Sibly Neptune/9th/Virgo

Deception in media relative to other countries.

Mercury RX/7th/Gemini cnj Sib Mars/7th/Gemini

Total debacle in foreign relations.

Pluto/2nd/Capricorn cnj Pluto/2nd/Capricorn

Deadly power related to finances and resources. (Military equipment left in Afghanistan.)

Hades/7th/Cancer opp Sibly Admitos/1st/Capricorn

Death and destruction overseas due to deliberate actions such as Afghanistan and Kabul airport bombings.

Cupido/1st/Capricorn opp Sibly Venus/7th/Cancer

People drawn together opposed to foreign relations issues.

Zeus/10th/Libra tri Sibly Mars/7th/Gemini

Power strike related to presidential actions, *i.e.* Afghanistan and Kabul.

Vulcanus/8th/Leo sxtl Sibly MC/10th/Libra

Death and destruction affects reputation.

The following relate to conditions associated with the COVID pandemic:

E-MC/3rd/Pisces tri Sibley Sun/7th/Cancer

Attention drawn to communications related to president's edict for continued restrictions due to COVID.

Uranus/5th/Taurus qncx Sibley Asc/1st/Sag

Upsets and changes for children such as encouraging vaccines and those that "died suddenly" without admitting the cause.

Uranus/5th/Taurus sxtl Sibley Sun/7th/Cancer

Upsets related to children due to presidential action. Could relate to school closures.

Venus/7th/Cancer ssxtl Sibly Uranus/6th/Gemini

Friction with other countries related to health issues, such as immigration restrictions.

Mars/8th/Cancer (anaretic unaspected)

Mortality issues such as COVID, vaxx, "died suddenly" events.

Chiron/4th/Aries sqr Sibly Sun/7th/Cancer

Family trouble and challenges due to presidential policies.

Chiron/4th/Aries tri Sibly Asc/1st/Sagittarius

Populace having health or psychological issues related to pandemic.

Eris/4th/Aries sqr Sibly Mercury/8th/Cancer

Minority and immigrant mortality issues. Fits people left behind in Afghanistan and border issues over COVID.

Admetos/6th/Gemini cnj Sibly Apollon/6th/Gemini

Concentration of COVID issues that affect many members of the working class.

Lilith/6th/Taurus sqr Sibly Moon/3rd/Aquarius

Health issues affect national mood and cause confrontations with family, friends, and neighbors over restrictions, masks, etc.

Lilith/6th/Taurus tri Sibly Pluto/2nd/Capricorn

Could relate to women's fertility issues induced by vaccine.

Vulcanus/8th/Leo qncx Sibly Hades/11th/Scorpio

Death and destruction related to agency directives from National Institute of Health, *i.e.* vax mandates, "died suddenly" syndrome, cover-ups regarding effective cures, etc.

Zeus/10th/Libra opp Sibly Chiron/4th/Aries

Abuse of power by government officials (*e.g.* Fauci) causes permanent injury to families and their way of life.

Jupiter/3rd/Pisces qncx Sibly MC/10th/Libra

E-MC/3rd/Pisces qnx Sibly Saturn/10th/Libra

Status change with neighboring countries related to government authority. Applies also to school shutdowns.

Saturn/2nd/Aquarius sxtl Sib Asc/1st/Sag

Pluto/2nd/Capricorn ssxt Sibly Moon/3rd/Aquarius

Saturn/2nd/Aquarius qncx Sibly Sun/7th/Cancer

These relate to changes in comfort level/living conditions due to COVID restrictions and shortages, which generate an emotional reaction.

More than 175 million third stimulus payments, totaling over $400 billion, were sent out starting in March 2021 as part of the American Rescue Plan Act. Money was being funnelled overseas, mostly to China, for COVID test kits and masks.

Poseidon/11th/Scorpio tri Sibly Sun/7th/Cancer

Legislative action has a favorable affect on President.

T-square with Eris/4th at apex sqr Sibly Cupido/2nd opp Sibly Mercury/8th

Minorities band together in BLM protest of George Floyd's death.

Lilith/6th/Taurus sqr Sibly Lilith/9th/Leo

Protests to Texas "heartbeat" law that banned abortion after six weeks gestation. (Lilith often represents feminists and women's issues activists.)

15. December 4, 2021 Solar Eclipse

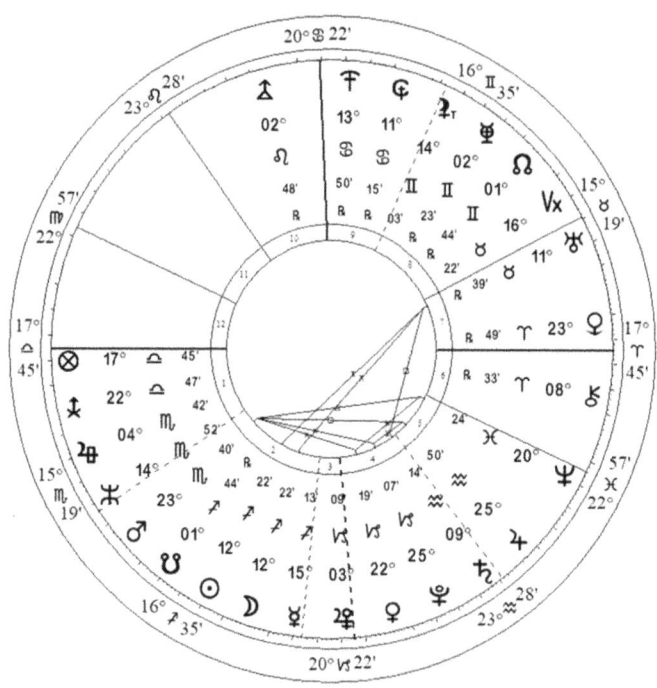

Solar Eclipse Dec 4 2021
Total Solar Eclipse (astrological) Saros Cycle 152 # 13

December 4, 2021
2:42:51 AM
Washington, D.C.
38N53'42" 77W02'12"
Time Zone: 5 hours West
Standard Time

Tropical Placidus
True Node

Mean Moon's Node   1 ♊ 00
Birth Time Accuracy   AA
G.M.T.   7:42:51

Marsha Fox
B.S. Physics, Dipl. IAA   whobeda@valkyriaastrology.com   ValkyriaAstrology.com   "Timing is Everything"

The Dark Side of Eclipses

Six months later, the next eclipse occurred in the 2nd house of finances, the treasury, resources, the economy, and standard of living. Brady claims this one is "A very joyful, happy family of eclipses. ...a sense of good news, falling in love, a peak experience that is joyful. Benefits that appear can be expected to continue..."

I don't know about you, but that's not how I remember that period of time....

Sorry, Bernadette. You win some, you lose some.

Eclipse/2nd/Sagittarius qncx Uranus/7th/Taurus

Russia invaded Ukraine two months later on February 24, 2022. The U.S. established diplomatic relations with Ukraine in 1991 and stepped in to assist. The financial impact escalates considerably over the next few years as the war drags on.

Eclipse/2nd/Sagittarius qncx Hades/Kronos midpoint/9th/Cancer

Polar opposites Hades and Kronos both occupy the house that includes the media, courts, and other countries. A quincunx from the eclipse indicates a Catch-22, showing a widening chasm between destruction and growth. Interest rates are increased in an attempt to control inflation. Relations with other countries will likewise have a financial impact.

Uranus/7th/Taurus sxtl Hades/9th/Cancer

The situation with Ukraine will be destructive. Combining this with the previous two aspects constitute a yod, which indicates a fated situation.

Ukraine has a rather sordid reputation for corruption, one factor which has precluded being admitted to NATO. The situation is going to be costly, infuriate the Russians, and get the U.S. back into a war.

This sextile forms the base of a yod with the eclipse at the eye, showing its importance.

Saturn/4th/Aquarius sqr Uranus/7th/Taurus

Financing the Ukraine war is reigniting a precarious situation with Russia. Conservatives, represented by Saturn, point out connections between Biden, the Clintons, and Ukraine that have suspicious financial implications.

Saturn/4th/Aquarius sextile Chiron/6th/Aries

A record number of COVID cases (more than 300 million worldwide) shows the pandemic is still raging. Vaccines are still being pushed with mandates still in effect. Side effects of the vaccines are becoming more obvious than ever along with more cases of "died suddenly."

Venus/4th/Capricorn cnj Pluto/4th/Capricorn

Venus rules the 8th house of transformations. Her conjunction with Pluto in the house of endings/new beginnings points toward radical, major change and undercover money dealings. Accusations that the Ukraine War is being used for money laundering fit this aspect.

Neptune/5th/Pisces tri MC/10th/Cancer

Deception unleashed on children reflects on U.S. image.

Venus/4th/Capricorn sxtl Neptune/5th/Pisces

Economic issues create dire conditions for families that drive them to government programs or charitable organizations for help. The huge COVID vaccination campaign active during 2021 ultimately endangered millions of children.

Pluto/4th/Capricorn ssxtl Jupiter/5th/Aquarius (partile)

Mars/2nd/Scorpio sxtl Venus cnj Pluto/4th/Capricorn

Policies that affect families cause friction and a jaded view of where the country is headed. High inflation is especially challenging. Societal changes instituted due to the pandemic are affecting children.

Mars/2nd/Scorpio tri Neptune/5th/Pisces

Attacks from the financial sector that drive the standard of living are eroding how Americans feel about their country and its leadership. Deception/propaganda is being unloaded on children as well in the form of Critical Race Theory and the Woke agenda.

Mars/2nd/Scorpio sqr Jupiter/5th/Aquarius

Mars in Scorpio squaring Jupiter is another indicator of high inflation and rising debt. How U.S. citizens see their country is worsening.

Mars/2nd/Scorpio qncx Eris/7th/Aries

Financial impact of illegal immigration requires a change of direction.

Saturn/4th/Aquarius sqr Uranus/7th/Taurus

Families are stressed financially by assistance to Ukraine. Aquarius is a zodiac sign that believes in helping others and being involved, but not when it jeopardizes America's own wellbeing with runaway debt.

Zeus/1st/Libra sqr Venus/4th/Capricorn (partile)

Venus rules the chart as well as the 8th house of death. The populace is likely to protest heavy handed leadership policies.

Vulcanus/10th/Leo sxtl Admetos/8th/Gemini both Qnx Cupido/3rd/Capricorn

This was a tough one to identify. The 3rd house relates to both primary education (K-12) and social media. There are two that seem to fit, both listed in the top news for the months in 2022 covered by this eclipse.

First is the bill signed by Governor Ron DeSantis of Florida that banned certain discussions about sexual orientation and gender identity in school classrooms from kindergarten to third grade.

The other is Elon Musk's agreement to acquire Twitter, which he rebranded as X. Musk opened up the files that revealed censorship and corruption, especially during the early days of COVID, and various other issues that had been covered up.

Venus/4th/Capricorn sqr Eris/7th/Aries

The open border is causing trouble in small border towns saturated with illegal immigrants. Criminal activity is a major problem.

Vulcanus/10th/Leo qncx Cupido/3rd/Capricorn

Radical policies are being forced on primary education such as Critical Race Theory and the Woke agenda. Concerned parents who protest are labeled domestic terrorists by a government out of touch with the average citizen.

December 4, 2021 Eclipse with Sibly Chart

This is another Eclipse-Sibly biwheel that's a "hot mess." The lines shown in the chart relate only to the interactions between planets and doesn't show those involving the Trans-Neptunians, Eris, or Chiron. Clearly there's a lot going on. Events suggested by this eclipse will occur over the next several months until the next one in April 2022.

Eclipse/1st/Sagittarius cnj Sibly Ascendant/Sagittarius

An eclipse within 1/60 degree of being exact on the Sibly ascendant indicates the populace and people's will are being eclipsed by current policies.

Eclipse/1st/Sagittarius qncx Sibly Sun/7th/Cancer

A change of direction is required of the president whose actions and policies (and position) do not represent the will of the people.

E-Uranus/5th/Taurus qncx Sibly Ascendant/1st/Sagittarius

This indicates numerous upsets and disturbances relate to children. Critical Race Theory and the Woke agenda are being imposed on public schools, which Florida passed legislation against.

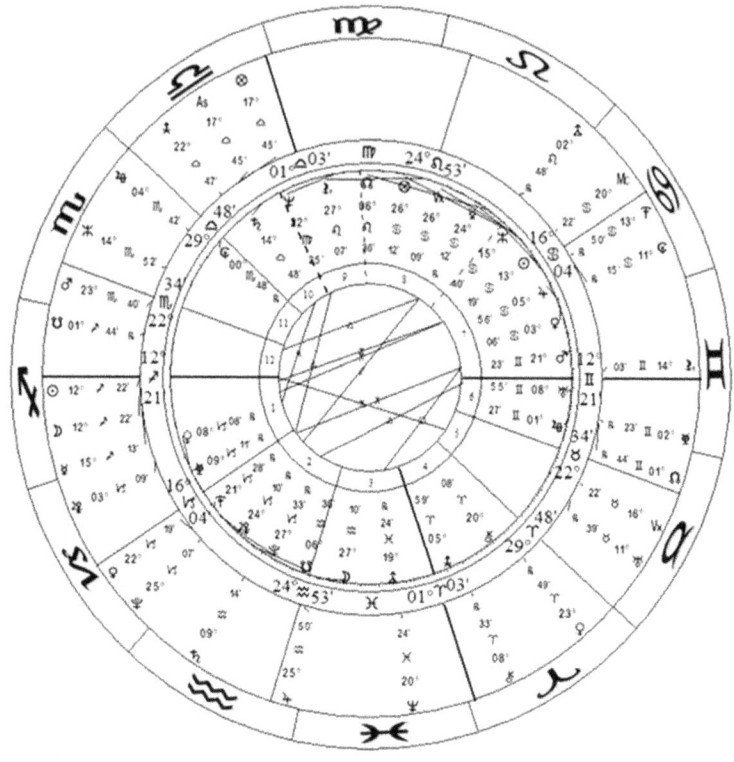

Inner Wheel:
U.S. Sibly Chart
Philadelphia, PA
Time Zone: 0 hours West

July 4, 1776
39N57'08" 75W09'51"
Tropical Placidus
NATAL CHART

5:10 PM
Local Mean Time

Outer Wheel:
Solar Eclipse Dec 4 2021
Washington, D.C.
Time Zone: 5 hours West

December 4, 2021
38N53'42" 77W02'12"
Tropical Placidus
Total Solar Eclipse (astrological) Saros Cycle 152 # 13

2:42:51 AM
Standard Time

Marcha Fox
B.S. Physics, Dipl. IAA whobeda@valkyrieastrology.com ValkyrieAstrology.com "Timing is Everything"

COVID vaccine side-effects are responsible for a huge number of cases of life-threatening problems like myocarditis, especially in young, otherwise healthy boys and men. The latter is the elephant in the room where everyone can see the connection, but it's not being acknowledged or reported.

E-Mercury/1st/Sagittarius sxtl Sibly Saturn/10th/Libra

Retail trade is suffering as a result of high-inflation caused by flawed government policies and out of control congressional spending.

E-Mars/12th/Scorpio tri Sibly Mercury/8th/Cancer

Hidden forces are undermining retail merchants to the point many are closing down. This in turn increases unemployment.

This also relates to another massive winter storm in February 2022.

E-Jupiter/3rd/Aquarius cnj Sibly Moon/2rd/Aquarius

This aspect suggests a large emotional response to issues related to primary education. This points to the Woke agenda to which parents are protesting and being labeled "domestic terrorists."

It also suggests people connecting with blogs and podcasts as more accurate sources of news than the mainstream media.

E-Venus/2nd/Capricorn tri Sibly Neptune/9th/Virgo

Media reports relative to finances and the economy are inaccurate.

E-Venus/2nd/Capricorn qncx Sibly Mars/7th/Gemini

Financial assistance to other countries is causing economic chaos. Billions of dollars funneled to Ukraine is jeopardizing the U.S.'s stability and wellbeing of its own citizens.

E-Pluto/2nd/Capricorn opp Sibly Mercury/8th/Cancer

The financial well-being and standard of living is dying with the country's fiat currency. It can't be sustained in view of escalating debt and waning reserves.

E-Neptune/3rd/Pisces sqr Sibly Mars/7th/Gemini

Undermining the public education system with deception benefits our enemies. Our communication infrastructure is being attacked by foreign entities, including via cell phone apps such as Tik Tok.

E-Neptune/3rd/Pisces cnj Sibly Vulcanus/3rd/Pisces

Social media as well as the communications infrastructure that includes blogs and podcasts have a major affect on everyday life. It also functions as a vehicle of propaganda, distraction, and deception. In April Elon Musk cuts a deal to obtain Twitter, which also showed up in the eclipse itself, illustrating its importance for liberating truth about censorship and other issues.

There's also the escalating drug problem with Fentanyl, which comes into the U.S. via the Mexican border.

E-North Node/6th/Gemini cnj Sibly Apollon/6th/Gemini

The placement of the North Node suggests something coming into this area that will affect many. The 6th house includes the working class, farmers, labor unions, and healthcare. Admetos is there, too, compressing the issue. The COVID pandemic is still in effect, but vaccine mandates are being reduced as the Supreme Court disallows the federal mandate except for providers to Medicare and Medicaid recipients.

E-Chiron/4th/Aries sqr Sibly Admetos/1st/Capricorn

In December a late season tornado outbreak occurs in the Southern and Midwestern United States, causing major damage and killing at least 94 people. One of the longest-tracked tornadoes in history occurred, which impacted western Kentucky, particularly Mayfield.

E-Chiron/4th/Aries sqr Sibly Eris/1st/Capricorn

Issues with land, such as the open border policy, are at crisis levels. Immigrants are also suffering.

E-Eris/4th/Aries sqr Sibly Cupido/2nd/Capricorn

The border and immigration issue bring many together who oppose this policy.

E-Eris/4th/Aries sqr Sibly Mercury/8th/Cancer

Death and destruction related to the immigration issue require policy change.

E-Eris/4th/Aries qncx Sibly Neptune/9th/Virgo

A change of direction is required at the border where most illegal drugs including Fentanyl enter the country.

E-Poseidon/11th/Scorpio tri Sibly Poseidon/7th/Cancer and

E-Apollon/11th/Scorpio tri Sibly Jupiter/7th/Cancer

Coming from the 11th house, which includes the House of Representatives, this suggests financial support for Ukraine and political agendas.

E-Midheaven/8th/Cancer sqr Sibly Chiron/4th/Aries

The placement of the Midheaven indicates where public attention will be directed. Involvement of Chiron in the 4th implies this will involve injuries or damage such as COVID, the vaccine side effects, or another disaster. This could also indicate the February 2022 winter storm.

16. April 30, 2022 Solar Eclipse

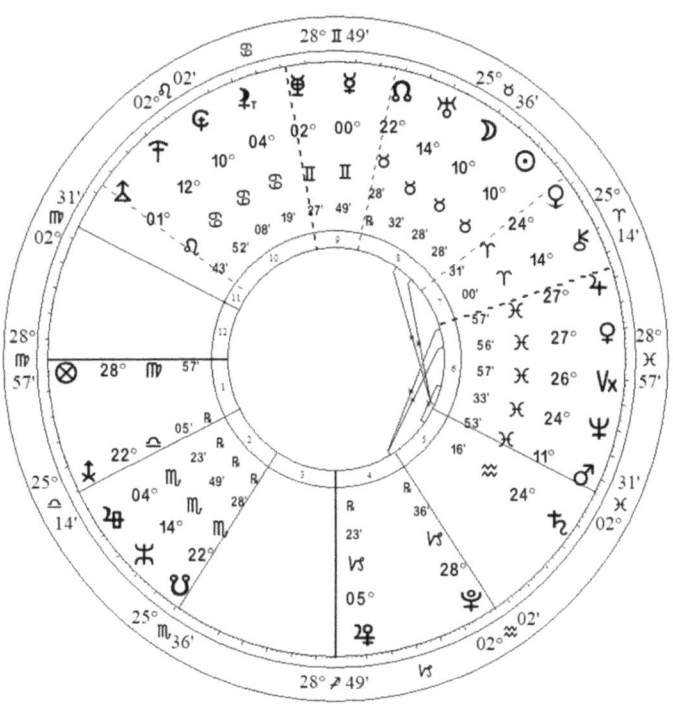

Solar Eclipse Apr 30 2022
Partial Solar Eclipse (astrological) Saros Cycle 119 # 66

Brady's description of this one is interesting to say the least. She states it's "concerned with the individual's relationship to father figures, authority figures, or the need to take responsibility and control...A time to accept the commitments presented, commitments which could occur due to another person's illness or unreliability."

What comes to mind for me as a "father figure" is Joe Biden and his illustrious relationship with his son, Hunter. As they say, "No life is ever wasted. You can always serve as a bad example."

Eclipse/8th/Taurus sxtl Mars/6th/Pisces and sxtl Hades/10th/Cancer (sextile pattern) as well as Zeus/1st/Libra qncx North Node/8th/Taurus and Ascendant/1st/Virgo tri Pluto/4th/Capricorn

This eclipse includes a lethal triad of ominous energies. It occurs in the house of death and transformations, Mars is seldom friendly, and of course Hades represents destruction as well. This combined with some of the other aspects implies numerous deadly events will occur during this eclipse's reign.

There were numerous mass shooting during this period, including three in April a few weeks before the eclipse. These occurred in Sacramento, California; A New York City subway attack; and a shooting in Pittsburgh.

In May a shooting occurred in a grocery store in Buffalo, NY, and another in a church in Laguna Woods, California. In that same month, a gunman stormed Robb Elementary in Uvalde, Texas, killing 19 children and two teachers in the deadliest school shooting in the U.S. in nearly a decade.

Also in May the official death toll from COVID-19 in the U.S. exceeded 1 million people since the start of the pandemic.

Mercury cnj Phaethon/9th/Gemini (anaretic)

Vulcanus/10th/Leo sxtl Mercury and Admetos/9th/Gemini

Phaethon wasn't in all these charts, but he showed up in this one for some lucky reason in partile conjunction with Mercury. I refer to Phaethon as the "crash and burn" asteroid.

This could relate to a literal "crash" in September when NASA's DART crashes into the asteroid Dimorphos in a first test of potential planetary defense.

It also applies to fallout in October since Musk obtained Twitter and instituted numerous changes. He fired half the staff, axed contract content moderators and disbanded a council of trust and safety advisors.

He dropped enforcement of COVID-19 misinformation rules and called for criminal charges against Dr. Anthony Fauci, the top U.S. infectious disease expert. Information revealed in the "Twitter Files" definitely resulted in the "crash and burn" of numerous policies and individuals enforcing them.

Venus cnj Jupiter/6th/Pisces as well as Pluto/4th/Capricorn sxtl Jupiter/Venus/6th/Pisces

This is a powerful conjunction between two fortunate planets. Venus is exalted in Pisces while Jupiter is in dignity as its traditional ruler. What did they facilitate in the house of health and the working class?

Many may disagree, but could it possibly relate to the June Supreme Court decision to overrule Roe vs. Wade? This is considered one of the court's most consequential decisions in decades. The court's conservative majority ruled that abortion is not a constitutional right, which led to abortion bans in more than a dozen states.

On May 18 Biden invoked the Defense Production Act of 1950 to address a shortage of baby formula across the country. Supposedly the shortage was due to shipments sent overseas.

Saturn/5th/Aquarius sxtl Eris/7th/Aries

These imply an issue related to the children of immigrants and may relate to DACA.

Saturn/5th/Aquarius ssxtl Neptune/6th/Pisces ssxtl Eris/7th/Aries (partile)

This minor aspect triad that usually indicates friction or an annoyance involves planets in the 5th, 6th, and 7th houses. The involvement of Eris implies this relates to the children of illegal immigrants and therefore to DACA.

It appears this was when the issue came under discussion. As it turns out, six months later, following the next eclipse, it was resolved. Per a web search, "On October 31, 2022, the DACA Rule rescinded and replaced the 2012 DACA memo. All current grants of DACA and advance parole issued under the 2012 DACA memo remain valid. Applications to renew DACA are now governed by the DACA Rule."

Apollon/2nd/Scorpio tri Lilith/10th/Cancer

With Lilith involved, this fits the thousands who protest over the Supreme Court decision to overrule Roe vs. Wade.

Poseidon/2nd/Scorpio qncx Chiron/7th/Aries

Poseidon relates to politics. This aspect involving the house of finances fits the U.S. giving financial help to Ukraine.

Poseidon/2nd/Scorpio opp Uranus/8th/Taurus

With Uranus conjunct the eclipse in the 8th house, this implies that all the death and destruction in the U.S. and otherwise is going to have an impact on the U.S. economy and finances. It could also relate to the Federal Reserve raising its benchmark interest rate by half a percentage point from a range between 0.25 percent and 0.50 percent to a range between 0.75 percent to 1 percent, the biggest increase since May 2000, which definitely impacted the cost of living.

To whom do you think Brady's reference to "father or authority figures" apply? Keep that in mind as we see what's going on with the Sibly chart.

APRIL 30, 2022 SOLAR ECLIPSE WITH SIBLY CHART

This eclipse fell in the 5th house of the Sibly chart but didn't aspect any Sibly planets or Trans-Neptunians. Its presence in the house that includes children and the Senate, as with the eclipse chart, could relate to DACA.

E-Uranus/5th/Taurus qncx Sibly Saturn/10th

E-Lunar North Node/5th/Taurus tri Sibly Neptune/9th/Virgo

Issues related to children facilitate a change of direction from the government. This relates to the new DACA ruling as well as bipartisan gun control legislation passed following the Uvalde, Texas school shooting.

E-Neptune/3rd/Pisces tri Sibly Mercury/8th/Cancer

E-Neptune/3rd/Pisces sxtl Cupido/2nd/Capricorn

E-Saturn/2nd/Aquarius qncx Sibly Mercury/8th/Cancer

E-Jupiter cnj E-Venus/3rd/Pisces sxtl Sibly Pluto/2nd/Capricorn

These reflect actions related to elementary schools and communications, particularly that related to shootings as

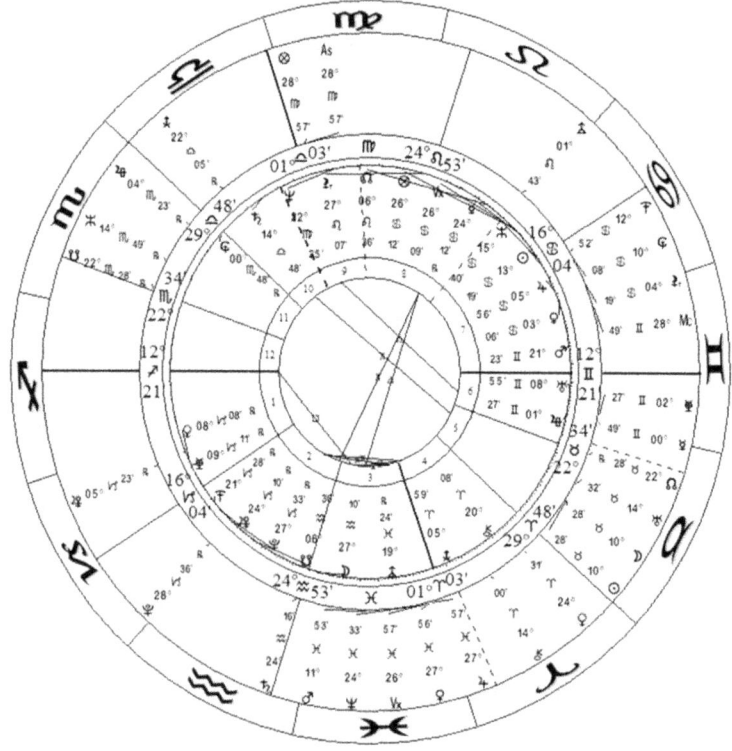

well as the Woke and transgender agendas, topics that were banned by legislation in Florida. The number of relevant aspects shows its importance.

E-Saturn/2nd/Aquarius ssxt Sibly Cupido/2nd/Capricorn

This implies that a lot of people are concerned with the economy, inflation, and the cost/quality of living.

E-Mars/3rd/Pisces sqr Sibly Ascendant/1st/Sagittarius

E-Kronos/7th/Cancer cnj Sibly Sun/7th/Cancer qncx Sibly Asc/1st/Sagittarius

The ascendant represents how the U.S. is seen by other countries. Mars in Pisces is wishy-washy, if you'll excuse the technical term. Those in other countries are wondering what happened to what used to be the most powerful nation on Earth.

The president needs to change his policies to improve the U.S. image.

E-Cupido/1st/Capricorn opp Sibly Jupiter/7th/Cancer

E-Chiron/4th/Aries opp Sibly Saturn/10th/Libra

Large numbers of the populace are questioning all the aide going to Ukraine and its affect on inflation, the National debt, and economy in general. Too many people in the country legally are suffering and deserve help. The government is not following the will of the people but following their own political agenda.

E-Eris/4th/Aries sqr Sibly Mercury/8th/Cancer

Immigrants are coming into the country faster than they can be accommodated. Most are not properly screened which allows criminals to enter causing an increase in crime and danger to U.S. citizens, especially through drug and human trafficking.

E-Mercury/6th/Gemini qnx Sibly Hades/11th/Scorpio

E-Mercury/6th/Gemini cnj Sibly Apollon/6th/Gemini

This appears to relate to the Farm Bill, which helps farmers with subsidies and crop insurance. It also includes SNAP (Supplemental Nutrition Assistance Program, formerly known as food stamps), which requires more than half of the budget. It's in force for five years and was due to expire in 2023 so was under review. An excellent explanation of the Farm Bill can be found here:

https://kansasreflector.com/2022/08/13/farm-bill-season-arrives-whats-the-outlook-for-2023/

Various changes and adjustments needed to be made to cover problems due to droughts and severe weather, market disruptions, and inflation. Agribusiness groups, environmental organizations, climate change experts, poverty and hunger groups and religious organizations all provide input to the farm bill.

The fact it showed up in the eclipse emphasizes its importance, not only to farmers but everyone since it affects the food supply.

Consider the fact that farmland is being bought by foreign countries such as China. This should be a major concern.

E-Lilith cnj Sibly-Venus - Jupiter midpoint/7th/Cancer

E-Apollon/11th/Scorpio tri Sibly Jupiter-Venus midpt/7th/Cancer

Both the eclipse and Sibly chart have Venus-Jupiter conjunctions. Lilith in the middle of the Sibly pair suggests the women's rights movement that began with #MeToo in 2006.

Women's rights worldwide were being pursued by numerous groups. The worst country for women's rights is Afghanistan with Syria on the list as well as several countries in Africa.

E-Vulcanus/8th/Leo sxtl Sibly Apollon/6th/Gemini

E-Vulcanus/8th/Leo sqr Sibly Hades/11th/Scorpio

This aspect indicates the concern of many related to life-threatening issues. This is not surprising with COVID still infecting millions and the increasing number of serious and lethal side-effects from the vaccines surfacing.

E-Zeus/10th/Libra ssxtl Sibly Neptune/9th/Virgo

Zeus and Neptune point toward the government and Biden administration's heavy hand with regard to the press and the fake news epidemic facilitated by Obama in 2012. Trust in the mass media was in freefall.

E-Zeus/10th/Libra tri Sibly Mars/7th/Gemini

This indicates government support of Ukraine and other foreign conflicts.

17. October 25, 2022 Solar Eclipse

Solar Eclipse Oct 25 2022
Partial Solar Eclipse (astrological) Saros Cycle 124 # 55

October 25, 2022
6:48:31 AM
Washington, D.C.
38N53'42" 77W02'12"
Time Zone: 5 hours West
Daylight Saving Time

Tropical Placidus
True Node

Mean Moon's Node	13 ♉ 47
Birth Time Accuracy	AA
G.M.T.	10:48:31

Marsha Fox
B.S. Physics, Dipl. IAA whobeda@valkyrieastrology.com ValkyrieAstrology.com "Timing is Everything"

This eclipse family is described by Brady as relating to "being forceful and taking power. It has a manic flavour about it, with great force or strength manifesting."

It occurs in the 1st house, bringing attention to the populace. Conjunct Venus, who's debilitated in Scorpio, suggests a sense of entitlement for damages.

Eclipse/1st/Scorpio cnj Venus/1st/Scorpio qncx Jupiter/6th/Aries

The triple quincunx to Jupiter suggests the people want something to change with respect to healthcare or labor unions.

Venus/1st/Scorpio sxtl Cupido/3rd/Capricorn and qncx Admetos/8th/Gemini (Yod)

Venus sextile Cupido in the 3rd suggests numerous people working together who have concerns regarding K-12 education, infrastructure, or social media issues. Both connect with Admetos in the house of death, forming a fate-laden yod. This implies an issue(s) gaining momentum.

A Freedom of speech issue in Llano County, Texas occurred where a Federal judge ordered schools to put books that related to LGBT+ and transgenderism back on their shelves. Release of ChatGPT or Montana's TikTok ban also fit.

On a more positive note, in October 2022 Congress passed the Speak Out Act, which limits how employers can use nondisclosure agreements in the case of a claim or dispute regarding sexual harassment.

Cupido/3rd/Capricorn qncx Admetos/8th/Gemini sxtl Vulcanus/10th/Leo (Yod)

This yod overlaps with the previous one, sharing the quincunx between Cupido and Admetos. Thus, both involve a group of like-minded people and an escalating concern related to transformation, National debt, insurance, or mortality issues. Its difference lies in Vulcanus in the 10th house, suggesting government involvement that affects the masses.

Mercury/12th/Libra cnj Zeus/12th/Libra qncx Neptune/5th/Pisces sqr Mars/9th/Gemini

Mercury/12th/Libra sqr Pluto/3rd/Capricorn qnx Mars/9th/Gemini

(2 Course Adjustment Loops)

These suggests Montana's TikTok ban. The app originated in China and has been accused of spreading propaganda focused on children or spying on Americans. This many aspects pointing to the same thing indicate its seriousness, which apparently only one state recognized as a threat.

Mercury cnj Zeus/12th/Libra tri Mars/9th/Gemini

The balloon suspected to be of Chinese origin is tracked across the U.S. and finally shot down off the coast of South Carolina. Three other "high altitude objects" were also shot down by the U.S. Military.

Chiron/6th/Aries qncx South Node/1st/Scorpio

This implies job losses or other damage to the working class or involving healthcare. Labor union membership dropped to an all-time low, which could be related to unemployment.

Mercury/12th/Libra tri Saturn/4th/Aquarius sqr Uranus/7th/Taurus cnj Phaethon

This combination, especially with "crash and burn" Phaethon involved, relates to shooting down the Chinese balloon and other three "high altitude objects."

Mercury cnj Zeus/12th/Libra opp Eris/7th/Aries

The ongoing immigration crisis is reflected here.

October 25, 2022 Solar Eclipse with Sibly Chart

Not that much showed up in the eclipse chart alone. Let's see what we can find when it's integrated with the Sibly chart.

Eclipse cnj Venus/11th/Scorpio trine Sibly Venus/7th/Cancer

The eclipse in the 11th brings attention to groups, lobbyists, and the House of Representatives. Republicans gained control of the House in the Midterm elections less than a month following the eclipse. The trine to Venus suggests financial support for Ukraine.

E-Cupido/1st/Capricorn opp Sibly Venus/7th/Cancer

A multitude of like-minded people are pushing back against money going to Ukraine, seeking equal consideration for domestic issues such as controlling immigration.

As I researched news events for the sake of these delineations rarely did immigration show up, illustrating how the press ignores certain issues. The only mention was of Biden visiting the border for the first time during his administration in January. The lack of reporting is suspect in view of the fact 16.8 million illegal immigrants now reside in the U.S. per the Heritage Foundation. That seems news-worthy to me.

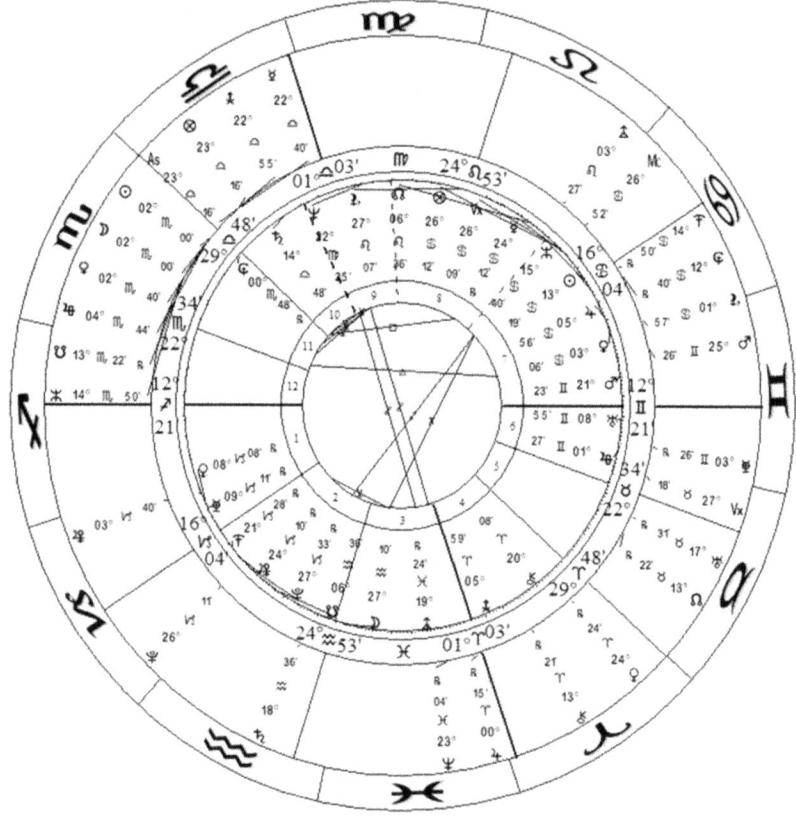

Inner Wheel:
U.S. Sibly Chart
Philadelphia, PA
Time Zone: 0 hours West

July 4, 1776
39N57'08" 75W09'51"
Tropical Placidus
NATAL CHART

5:10 PM
Local Mean Time

Outer Wheel:
Solar Eclipse Oct 25 2022
Washington, D.C.
Time Zone: 5 hours West

October 25, 2022
38N53'42" 77W02'12"
Tropical Placidus
Partial Solar Eclipse (astrological) Saros Cycle 124 = 55

6:48:31 AM
Daylight Saving Time

Marcha Fox
B.S. Physics, Dipl. IAA whobeda@valkyrieastrology.com ValkyrieAstrology.com "Timing is Everything"

The Dark Side of Eclipses

E-Pluto/2nd/Capricorn opp Sibly Vertex/PoF/8th/Cancer (partile)

E-Midheaven/8th/Cancer cnj Sibly Vertex/PoF/8th/Cancer

E-Midheaven/8th/Cancer qncx Sibly Moon/3rd/Aquarius

Pluto in the house that includes the treasury and resources opposite the Sibly Vertex and Part of Fortune in the house of foreign debt, banking, reserves, and mortality shows the country's financial problems.

Interest rates continued to rise and a rash of bank failures occurred during March, including the Silvergate Bank, Silicon Valley Bank, First Republic Bank and Signature Bank.

The Eclipse Midheaven in the 8th indicates this would draw significant attention. The Silicon Valley Bank in particular held the accounts of numerous celebrities that created a large emotional reaction.

Another event that fits with these energies is the Norfolk Southern train derailment while carrying dangerous chemicals outside of East Palestine, Ohio, which created a large environmental disaster.

Several deadly winter storms occurred as well as a rash of shootings.

There was the winter storm in December 2022 (which I witnessed first hand from northwestern New York State. Do I attract these things somehow?)

It hit the northern U.S. as well as southern Canada and killed at least 91 people.

5 Gasport, NY, Dec. 26, 2022. These extreme weather events seem to follow me. At least this time the power stayed on for us.

E-Neptune/3rd/Pisces opp Sibly Neptune/9th/Virgo

This Neptune opposition was in effect from May 2021 until January 2023. An opposition demands balance. The two principles involved in polar signs, Virgo and Pisces, are reality and idealism. Neither taken to the extreme is viable, but a practical, realistic approach to accomplish a dream can succeed.

When the U.S. was founded, practicality reigned. Now it's a world of delusions and illusions. The challenge is to find that sweet spot between them.

The release of ChatGPT fit this admonition. Artificial intelligence has tremendous power to provide both valid information and spread propaganda or create illusions.

E-Jupiter/3rd/Aries opp Sibly Midheaven/10th/Libra

Jupiter is retrograde in Aries and heading back into Pisces, where his energy changes significantly. Remember, Jupiter's function is to increase and inflate what he touches. In Aries he promotes action, retrograde he promotes investigating corruption and ethics issues. In Pisces he promotes ideals, dreams, and unfortunately, delusions and deception.

Opposing the Sibly Midheaven is an admonition to take action to improve the U.S. image and status. As the Ruler of the ascendant, which represents the U.S. image as well as the people, he's telling communities to take action. Every flood begins with a single drop.

E-Jupiter/3rd/Aries qncx Sibly Hades/11th/Scorpio

Jupiter's quincunx with Sibly Hades indicates the need for a change of direction from the destructive path the U.S. is currently pursuing. Corruption in various groups is pervasive and needs to be exposed, which Pluto has been working on as part of his return cycle.

E-Eris/4th/Aries sqr Sibly Mercury/8th/Cancer

Another indicator of the ongoing immigration crisis.

E-Eris/4th/Aries sqr Sibly Cupido/3rd/Capricorn

Many oppose the open border and uncontrolled immigration.

E-Vertex/6th/Taurus tri Sibly Pluto/2nd/Capricorn

The vertex relates to fated events. This trine with Pluto suggests the need to purge factors causing economic chaos manifested as bank failures to help the working class.

E-Admetos/6th/Gemini ssxt Sibly Venus/7th/Cancer

Foreign policy is causing friction with the working class as more concern is shown for other countries and illegal immigrants than our own poor much less veterans who fought for this country.

E-Mars/7th/Gemini ssxtl Sibly Mercury, Vertex, PoF/8th/Cancer

This suggests the U.N. Biodiversity Conference held where nearly 200 countries agree to a landmark deal to protect a third of the planet for nature by 2030. This relates to U.N. Agenda 2030 which actually doesn't bode well for humans.

E-Kronos/7th/Cancer sqr Sibly Saturn/10th/Libra

Kronos relates to excellence and this square to Saturn, which represents government authority, indicates it's failing miserably in its international policies.

E-Chiron/4th/Aries sqr Sibly Sun/7th/Cancer

Families are being harmed by foreign policy promoted by the president, such as an open border. This is particularly true of those who live in border states and towns.

E-Vulcanus/8th/Leo ssxt Sibly Venus/7th/Cancer

This suggests the explosion in the national debt that relates to helping Ukraine as well as illegal immigrants.

E-Mercury, Zeus/PoF and Asc/10th/Libra qncx 6th cusp

This convention of energy in the house that represents the country's public image and reputation suggests the working class wants things to change.

E-Poseidon/11th/Scorpio tri Sibly Poseidon/7th/Cancer

Poseidon in its lowest form, which is likely in Scorpio, relates to propaganda about foreign policies. Foreign aid is often accused of facilitating money laundering as well as providing corrupt governments with inflows of cash that never benefit their citizenry.

18. April 20, 2023 Solar Eclipse

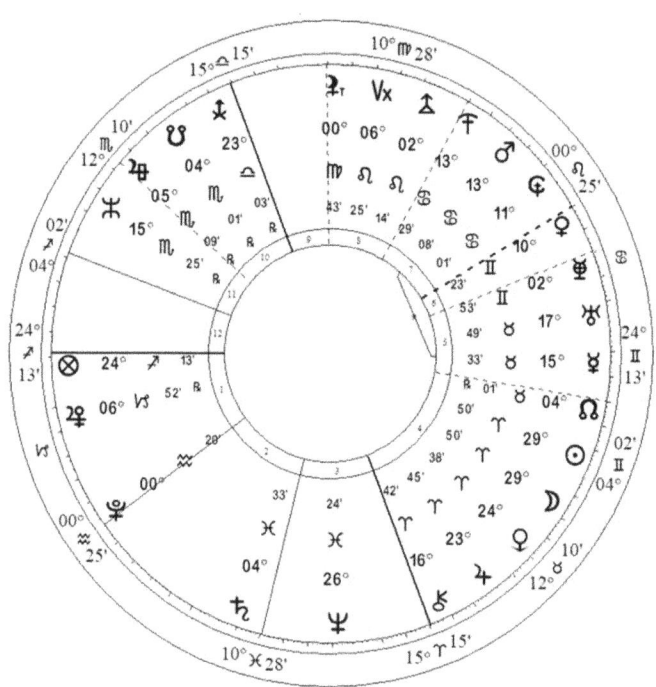

Solar Eclipse Apr 20 2023
Total Solar Eclipse (astrological) Saros Cycle 129 = 52

April 20, 2023
12:12:19 AM
Washington, D.C.
38N53'42" 77W02'12"
Time Zone: 5 hours West
Daylight Saving Time

Tropical Placidus
True Node

Mean Moon's Node   4 ♉ 25
Birth Time Accuracy   AA
G.M.T.   4:12:19

Marcha Fox
B.S. Physics, Dipl. IAA whobeda@valkyrieastrology.com ValkyrieAstrology.com "Timing is Everything"

This eclipse in the last degree of Aries and only 1/6 of a degree from Taurus has some interesting aspects to investigate.

According to Brady it's "very sensual" and "Not subtle, and can catch people off guard and confront them with their own very deep passion which may have been hidden for many years."

Eclipse/4th/Aries (anaretic)

An eclipse in the last degree of a Cardinal sign in the 4th house suggests an ending. In mundane astrology this is the house of the opposition party, land values, family policies and historical self-perception.

I'm sure my "historical perception" of the U.S. is far different from that of my younger grandchildren. I was in high school when JFK was assassinated while they experienced COVID school closures and watch Tik Tok.

What is your perception? How has it changed? How does it relate to the report that in 2022 the U.S. recorded its highest number of suicides (49,449) since World War II?

Mercury cnj Uranus cnj Phaethon/5th/Taurus

Mercury/5th/Taurus opp Poseidon/11th/Scorpio

There are numerous events during this time period that fit this triple conjunction and their opposition to Poseidon, but one really stands out. The presence of Phaethon, the "crash and burn" asteroid, fits so well. You can't make this stuff up.

Four days after the eclipse and within minutes of each other, two mainstream media news figures were fired.

Fox News ditched Tucker Carlson for comments related to the Dominion voting machine lawsuit settlement. CNN canned Don Lemon because of numerous misogynistic comments made in the past.

In a more literal sense, the day after the eclipse Elon Musk's SpaceX first test flight of Starship ended in an explosion following launch.

The Writers Guild of America goes on strike, stopping the production of most movies and TV shows.

Hello, reruns.

Mercury/5th/Taurus sxtl Mars/7th/Cancer

Since the 5th relates to children and the entertainment industry, it fits that Disney filed suit against Ron DeSantis for his "Florida's Parental Rights in Education Act." Disney had enjoyed a special arrangement with the state for years allowing it to be self-governing, which was also revoked. This should raise a huge red flag as to why Disney would object. Are foreign influences involved as well?

Mars cnj Kronos/7th/Cancer (partile)

Kronos typically indicates excellence and this occurs in the house of foreign relations. It could relate to the Biden administration recognizing the Cook Islands and Niue as sovereign states, establishing formal relations between both Pacific island countries.

This could also indicate the trilateral pact between America, Japan, and South Korea.

Venus/6th/Gemini ssxtl Hades/7th/Cancer

The 6th includes the military, so combined with the involvement of destructive Hades, the deployment of a carrier strike group that includes an aircraft carrier, a cruiser and four destroyers in response to terror attacks on civilians in Israel by Hamas to the Eastern Mediterranean seems to fit.

Jupiter cnj Eris/4th/Aries

Eris/4th/Aries tri Asc/1st/Sagittarius

Increased immigration on our southern border, plain and simple. In May the Title 42 expulsion policy expired necessitating a new immigration policy. Naturally this occurred as a surge of migrants gather at the U.S southern border. Can you guess what that new policy was?

Saturn/2nd/Pisces sxtl NN/4th/Taurus and tri SN/10th/Scorpio (TOP)

House Republicans and the White House reach a deal to raise the debt ceiling and prevent the United States from defaulting.

The national debt rises to $33 trillion.

Interest rates are the highest they've been since 2001, which no doubt relates to the U.S. debt rating being downgraded from AAA to AA+ by Fitch Ratings citing "deteriorating standard of governance."

Well said, Fitch.

Another bank failure, the second largest in U.S. history, when First Republic Bank goes under and is seized by the FDIC.

Pluto/1st/Aquarius qncx Lilith/8th/Virgo (anaretic)

Mercury/5th/Taurus ssxt Chiron/4th/Aries

These subtle but ominous aspects fit the ongoing abortion question. A few days after this eclipse occurred, the Supreme Court rules that pending trial, mifepristone can remain on US markets, which constitutes a victory for the national abortion-rights movement.

In May, North Carolina's state legislature bans nearly all abortions after twelve weeks, overriding a veto by governor Roy Cooper.

Along similar lines, the FDA announced that the birth control pill Norgestrel, also known as Opill, will be available without a prescription.

Jupiter/4th/Aries opp Zeus/10th/Libra

Cupido/1st/Capricorn qncx VX/8th/Leo

Apollon/10th/Scorpio cnj South Node/10th/Scorpio

These fit the ongoing mass shootings, literal train wrecks, and extreme weather events affecting thousands. The worst is undoubtedly the wildfire in Hawaii that destroyed the entire town of Lahaina.

In August, wildfires supposedly caused by high winds from Hurricane Dora struck Maui. It killed at least 115 people, 67 injured, over 380 people missing, and 2,207 buildings destroyed. It marks the deadliest wildfire in the last 100 years.

There are a lot of conspiracy theories out there about this wildfire. There are questions on why buildings were destroyed, but much of the vegetation was not. Walls were built around the area and no one allowed in.

What actually started the fires? Witnesses claim they were started by an airborne or space-based laser weapon, which is why destruction was so severe and selective. The temperature of wildfires is not sufficient to melt certain substances.

Investigate the incident yourself and draw your own conclusion. Zeus operating from the top of the chart directed at Jupiter in the house of land captures this scenario quite well. There are lasers available on the open market that will start a fire.

For example: *https://laser.gunnergear.com/blue/*

If this is as easy to attain as a conventional cigarette lighter, what does the military have?

Just saying.

April 20, 2023 Solar Eclipse with Sibly Chart

Numerous events that transpired during this eclipse's six month reign showed up. Let's see how many appear when setting it with the Sibly chart.

The eclipse and Sibly charts have similar house structures with both having Sagittarius ascendants. However, the eclipse slips into the 5th which includes children, entertainment, sports, gambling, speculation, the Senate, and the country's "self-awareness."

I'll avoid being redundant as much as possible and only give brief reference to those items already covered in the eclipse chart alone.

Inner Wheel:
U.S. Sibly Chart
Philadelphia, PA
Time Zone: 0 hours West

July 4, 1776
39N57'08" 75W09'51"
Tropical Placidus
NATAL CHART

5:10 PM
Local Mean Time

Outer Wheel:
Solar Eclipse Apr 20 2023
Washington, D.C.
Time Zone: 5 hours West

April 20, 2023
38N53'42" 77W02'12"
Tropical Placidus
Total Solar Eclipse (astrological) Saros Cycle 129 # 52

12:12:19 AM
Daylight Saving Time

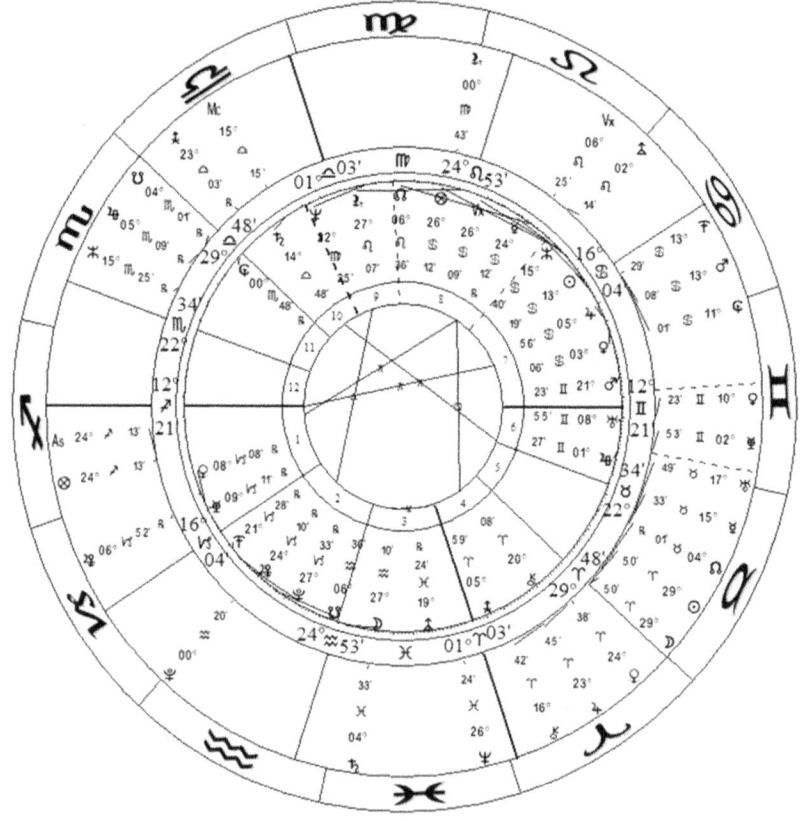

Marcha Fox
B.S. Physics, Dipl. IAA whobeda@valkyrieastrology.com ValkyrieAstrology.com "Timing is Everything"

Eclipse/5th/Aries

E-Lilith/9th/Virgo sxtl Sibly Hades/11th/Scorpio

The various events related to abortion noted for the eclipse itself are reflected in this placement of the eclipse in the 5th house that includes children. The approval of the abortion drug fits the Lilith aspect.

E-Jupiter cnj Eris/4th/Aries sqr Sibly Mercury/8th/Cancer

E-Ascendant/1st/Sagittarius qncx Sibly Mercury/8th/Cancer

Immigration issues are not being addressed and getting out of hand. The people are demanding that something be done but it falls on deaf ears.

Regarding other factions, the masses are pushing back. For example the City Council of Hamtramck, Michigan passed a resolution prohibiting the display of all flags except the American flag and "nations' flags that represent the international character of [the] City." This was perceived as targeting the rainbow flag on city property and sidewalks, which had been the source of controversy. Following three hours of public comment, the Council passed the resolution unanimously.

E-Cupido cnj Sibly Eris/1st/Capricorn

Many are concerned with the immigration issue.

E-Mercury cnj E-Uranus cnj E-Phaethon/5th/Taurus qnx Sibly Saturn/10th/Libra

This house placement reinforces the firing of Tucker Carlson and Don Lemon as well as the Disney issues. The connection with Saturn in the 10th shows the public nature as well as authority demonstrated.

E-Jupiter/4th/Aries sqr Sibly Cupido/2nd/Capricorn

E-Pluto/2nd/Aquarius tri Sibly Midheaven/10th/Libra

E-Pluto/2nd/Aquarius tri Sibly Apollon/6th/Gemini

Many are affected by financial debacles like bank failures, inflation, and increasing interest rates. As families struggle to make ends meet, they rely more on credit, which will be more costly.

The country's financial problems are public knowledge and reflect on its reputation as shown by its debt rating being downgraded. Many of the working class are affected. Pluto's involvement indicates the transformational nature of the financial crisis and potential death of the dollar.

E-Mars/7th/Cancer qncx Sibly Ascendant/1st/Sagittarius

E-Mars cnj E-Kronos/7th/Cancer cnj Sibly Sun/7th/Cancer

The people are demanding that the President change his immigration policies. His rating has been slipping as conditions in the U.S. continue to deteriorate.

E-Pluto/2nd/Aquarius sqr Sibly Hades/11th/Scorpio

Corrupt financial dealings of various government officials (elected and otherwise) are being exposed.

E-Neptune/3rd/Pisces tri Sibly VX/PoF/8th/Cancer

Deception via the communications infrastructure and social media is fated and relates to America's demise as the people are duped and true agendas hidden.

The 3rd house relates to neighbors, which for the U.S. would be Mexico and Canada. Obviously there's the immigration issue, but this also points toward wildfires in

Quebec that caused air quality to be so bad in the Northeast and parts of the Midwest that millions were advised to wear N95 masks.

E-Neptune/3rd/Pisces qncx Sibly Lilith/9th/Leo

E-Mercury/5th/Taurus sxtl Sibly Poseidon/7th/Cancer

This suggests deception being imposed on Primary Education with the Woke agenda and foreign influence such as apps like Tik Tok.

E-Vertex/8th/Leo cnj Sibly North Node/8th/Leo

E-Zeus/10th/Libra sqr Sibly Cupido/2nd/Capricorn

More fated and likely destructive events are coming that will have a transformational effect on many as well as the country.

New York bans gas stoves and propane heating in new residential constructions. The bans take effect in 2026 for smaller residential buildings and 2029 for larger residential buildings.

Even seemingly minor laws such as this move that affects consumers and restricts their freedom in the supposed cause of "climate change:"

C'mon.

If you want to know the true source of "climate change" you can find the answer here:

https://www.geoengineeringwatch.org

E-Midheaven/10th/Libra cnj Sibly Saturn/10th/Libra

E-Mercury/5th/Taurus qncx Sibly Saturn/10th/Libra

E-Midheaven/10th/Libra sqr Sibly Poseidon/7th/Cancer

How the administration handles issues related to children will reflect on the U.S. reputation and be publicly known. Deception and political games will be recognized for what they are.

What comes to mind is the January 6 debacle and prosecution of several accused of a seditious conspiracy for protesting a stolen election that was exactly that. Whichever side of the political aisle you favor (both are seriously corrupt, in case you haven't noticed), imprisoning political opponents is what dictatorships do.

E-Poseidon/11th/Scorpio tri Sibly Poseidon/7th/Cancer

Poseidon relates to politics, philosophy and in its lowest form, propaganda. This is likely to involve Congress as well as foreign policy, particularly financing the war in Ukraine.

19. October 14, 2023 Annular Solar Eclipse

This eclipse was annular, which occurs when the moon does not entirely cover the Sun, resulting in a "ring of fire," and thus the name "annular." This is the result of the Moon's orbit at apogee, *i.e.* when it appears the smallest due to being at its farthest point from Earth. (A "super moon" occurs when its at perigee, i.e., closest.)

Whether their effect is as strong as a Total eclipse is open to question. My own opinion is that they may offer more of a warning, whereas a Total eclipse proclaims the Universe has had enough.

The eclipse path of visibility crossed the American Southwest. It does not intersect that of the 2017 eclipse, but converges with it when it reaches the Pacific Ocean. It will leave its mark on Texas, New Mexico, Arizona, Utah, Nevada, California and Oregon. Some of that territory includes the Navajo Nation and other reservations, which suggests implications for Native Americans.

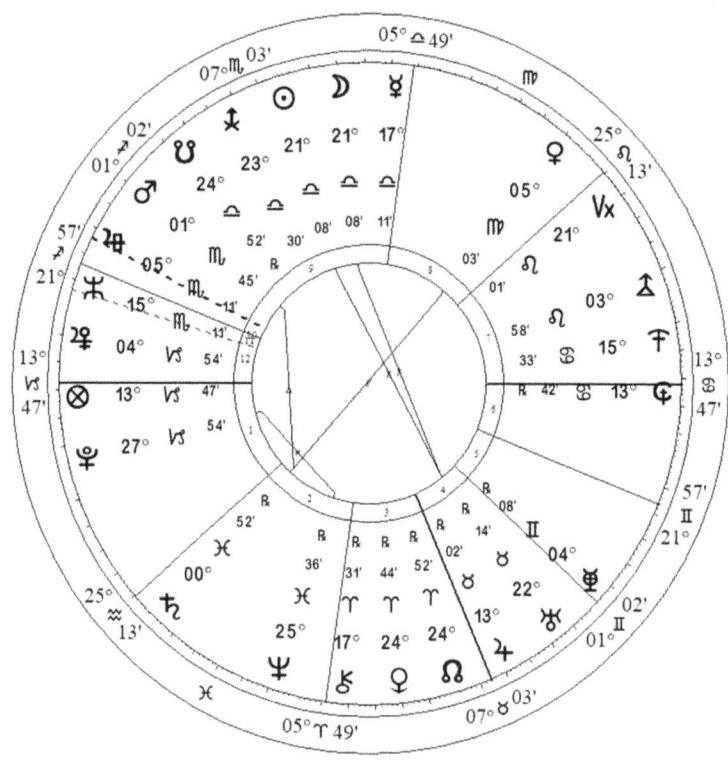

Solar Eclipse Oct 14 2023

Annular Solar Eclipse (astrological) Saros Cycle 134 = 44

October 14, 2023
1:54:55 PM
Washington, D.C.
38N53'42" 77W02'12"
Time Zone: 5 hours West
Daylight Saving Time

Tropical Placidus
True Node

Mean Moon's Node ... 25 T 01
Birth Time Accuracy ... AA
G.M.T. ... 17:54:55

Marcha Fox
B.S. Physics, Dipl. IAA whobeda@valkyrieastrology.com ValkyrieAstrology.com "Timing is Everything"

Eclipse guru, Bernadette Brady characterizes this eclipse as one that wields "immense power, anger, and force." She notes that individuals will find huge obstacles suddenly disappear, on one hand, or bring a sudden crisis out of nowhere on the other. Nonetheless, it will pass as quickly as it appeared. It will feel as if everything is moving at an accelerated speed.

Let's see how well that fits events around that time.

Sun, Moon, Mercury, Lunar South Node, and Zeus/Libra/9th and Mars and Apollon/Scorpio/9th

That's a lot of cosmic energy in the 9th. It suggests influences involving other cultures, courts, and the media.

Mars/9th/Scorpio tri Saturn/2nd/Pisces

Mars is dignified in Scorpio where he wields considerable power. His trine with Saturn, both in anaretic degrees, increases the influence. Impact to finances and our way of life from foreign sources are again implicated.

Don't think trines are always favorable. All they indicate is an easy flow of energy. Between two malefic planets, trust me when I say it's not going to be friendly. Saturn in the 2nd could indicate money wars to jeopardize the dollar, which is already in freefall.

Considering the path follows the USA's southern border and the states most affected by immigration issues, there's no telling what this could bring. It could actually indicate an invasion.

What do you call it when literally millions of illegal immigrants enter our country? If that doesn't constitute an invasion, I don't know what does.

Kronos/7th/Cancer and Vulcanus/7th Leo and Vertex/7th/Leo

As noted earlier, the 7th house includes open enemies. With Kronus (mastery) and Vulcanus (great power) in that house along with the Vertex (fate) this doesn't evoke a warm feeling.

Cupido/12th/Capricorn qncx Vulcanus/7th/Leo

Cupido in the house of hidden enemies and spies indicates many are involved from this realm.

His aspect to powerful Vulcanus in the 7th of foreign relations indicates something in this area requires an adjustment or change with charities, institutions, and prisons also part of the 12th.

Eris/3rd/Aries cnj North Node/3rd/Aries (partile)

This conjunction implies an irreversible situation coming our way related to immigrants or other factions and the country's infrastructure. Roads, bridges, communications, the neglected wall on the southern border all come to mind.

Venus/8th/Virgo opp Saturn/2nd/Pisces

Venus/8th/Virgo sextile Apollon/9th/Scorpio

Venus, natural ruler of love and money, is in Virgo, where she's in "fall." In other words, her energy is incompatible with her zodiacal environment. She opposes Saturn, ruler of the 2nd, which includes finances and resources in general, while Venus rules the 9th, which is loaded with participants such as the media and religious institutions.

The love goddess's debilitated state does not support all that activity hailing from the 9th. Pisces compromises Saturn's usual expertise at maintaining structure and discipline.

This does not bode well for the financial community with both planets that could conceivably lend support dueling from compromised zodiacal positions.

This situation will affect many in a life-changing manner.

Eclipse/9th/Libra qncx Uranus/4th/Taurus

Sudden upsets or disturbances that involve land, history, family policies, and the opposition party will impose changes.

Remember the 4th includes endings and new beginnings. Uranus's involvement indicates unexpected and disruptive events. These can range from explosions (literal or figurative) to new technology, or some sort of political action that's going to be fundamentally irreconcilable and force a shift in their current path.

Or, I might add, all of the above.

Jupiter/4th/Taurus tri PoF/1st/Capricorn (partile)

Jupiter inflates these effects even more. His trine with the Part of Fortune will affect the populace generally. While many consider Jupiter a benefic planet, in reality he's neutral, like Mercury. All he does is inflate what he touches, for good or ill. For example, in the charts for hurricanes and tornadoes Jupiter is typically involved.

Eclipses are powerful and influence the entire planet, though that's always heaviest along their path of visibility.

So what are the Trans-Neptunians doing amongst themselves that might further refine our view of what to expect?

Cupido/12th/Capricorn qncx Admetos/5th/Gemini

The 5th indicates involvement of the senate, children, sports, and/or the entertainment industry while the 12th tends to be spies and hidden enemies. Many will be affected. Both drug and child trafficking occur at the Mexican border. Fentanyl enters the U.S. through this route and is killing people in droves. Something needs to change.

Hades/6th/Cancer Cnj Descendant/7th/Cancer

Hades is retrograde and moving back into the 6th, which includes the working class, farmers, standing army, labor unions, and the healthcare industry.

In some parts of the world, especially Canada and Western Europe, a war is being conducted against farmers. If the effort succeeds in seizing their land for questionable purposes (*e.g.,* UN Agenda 2030), its natural consequence will be food shortages.

This conjunction likewise bodes badly for foreign relations. It points toward the Israel - Iran war, which occurred before the eclipse, but within its realm of influence. Three days before the eclipse occurred, this news story broke:

https://amgreatness.com/2023/10/11/hamas-leader-calls-for-global-day-of-rage-on-friday-this-is-the-time-for-jihad/

On October 7, 2023, a week before the eclipse, the Palestinian Sunni Islamist group Hamas, a U.S.-designated foreign terrorist organization, led surprise attacks against Israel.

Zeus/9th/Libra qncx Uranus/4th/Taurus

Thunderbolt wielding Zeus is further fueled by Uranus, creating an explosive situation. Besides issues at the border, this could relate to problems with U.S. interests in the Middle East, or our relationship with Russia due to our ongoing support of the war with Ukraine.

Subsequent to the eclipse issues arose with academia, another 9th house component. Scandals on Ivy League Campuses are nothing new. These are covered in detail in an article on https://www.grunge.com/1393511/biggest-scandals-to-hit-ivy-league-schools/

In this case, two hit simultaneously. Harvard University President Dr. Claudine Gay and the University of Pennsylvania President Dr. Elizabeth Magill found themselves in hot water for mishandling student demonstrations on their respective campuses regarding the war between Israel and Iran.

When Pro-Palestinian groups called for the genocide of Jewish people, neither president rebuked them in a suitable manner according to Congress, the public, and even a former Harvard president. Accused of antisemitism, Magill resigned a few days later and Gay did likewise in January 2024.

The media isn't likely to escape, either. As more lies perpetrated during the COVID pandemic emerge, news organizations could likewise find a target on its back. This would especially relate to censoring done by both mainstream and social media at government behest, revealed by the Twitter files, made public by Elon Musk.

In July 2023 the watchdog group, Judicial Watch, issued a lengthy, well-documented special investigative report on the multiple scandals associated with COVID, of which I have a copy.

I encourage you to check them out at their website judicialwatch.org.

Their report, which includes seventy-one endnotes of documentation, contains detailed information to the following issues per the report's executive summary:

> * U.S. Government involvement in and funding of gain-of-function and bio warfare research, both in the United States, China and elsewhere, and in particular, with coronaviruses, which may have led to the COVID crisis.
>
> * Government psychological operations to frighten American citizens about the "COVID pandemic."
>
> * Government officials' discussions and suppression of safe, effective, and inexpensive drugs to treat COVID illness, such as Ivermectin and hydroxychloroquine.

> *The injuries and deaths caused by COVID "vaccines," as demonstrated in both laboratory test animals prior to the authorization of COVID injections and in human beings after their roll-out under Emergency Use Authorization.*

Moving right along...

Kronos/7th/Cancer tri Poseidon/11th/Scorpio

Kronos, proponent of mastery and doing things correctly, occupies the 7th, which represents treaties, alliances, open enemies, and our relationship with other countries, friendly and otherwise.

Poseidon's purpose is to promote clarity. This ties together foreign relations with groups, the stock market, and legislative bodies. Mastery on the part of other countries directed toward our groups in the U.S. does not sound particularly favorable.

There's already too much foreign and domestic influence on our legislative bodies. Messing with the stock market is likewise playing with fire. There's a fair amount of noise out there regarding trouble on the way. If you have investments there, you should pay attention and take any necessary corrective action.

Meanwhile, to the south, this eclipse didn't do Central America any favors, either. This is where many of those illegals are hailing from.

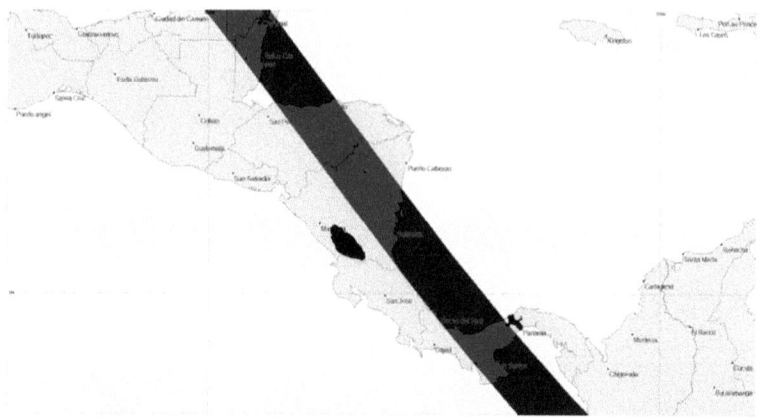

As if that's not already enough for concern, let's see how it interacts with the U.S. Sibly Chart.

October 2023 Eclipse with Sibly Chart

The biwheel integrating the October 2023 eclipse with the Sibly chart provides additional insights.

Eclipse/10th/Libra tri Sibly Mars/7th/Gemini

The eclipse is blasting the 10th house, which includes the president, ruling party, and the U.S. reputation. Is it "eclipsing" their influence?

The trine to Mars suggests aggression toward (or from) other countries. It could indicate support from an ally, though as a malefic it's hard to tell. Perhaps it simply reflects U.S. financing Ukraine (or its president, as some believe.)

E-Mars/11th Scorpio ssxtl Sibly Midheaven/10th/Libra

This suggests an annoyance or friction from a group of some description. It could indicate Congress annoyed with the president or vice versa, perhaps for not moving forward on something he wants. Either way, there's friction between them.

Congress's public image isn't the greatest, either. Their failure to act on matters that require attention is definitely annoying.

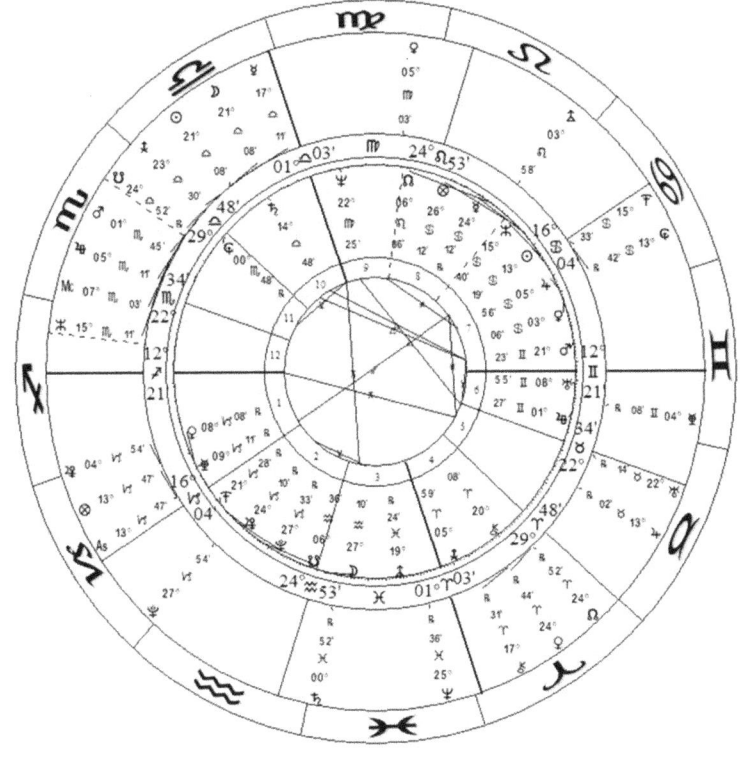

E-Vulcanus/8th/Leo ssxtl Sibly Venus/7th/Cancer

Vulcanus represents great power. His semi-sextile with Venus shows discord with our allies.

E-Venus/9th/Virgo sxtl Sibly Jupiter/7th/Cancer

Venus in the sign of her fall sextile exalted Jupiter suggests any allies with whom we negotiate have the advantage. Or are they taking advantage of the U.S.? The 9th represents other countries, but not necessarily those with whom we have a treaty or alliance.

E-Uranus/5th/Taurus tri Sibly Neptune/9th/Virgo

This aspect begs the question, "Are things as they appear?" There has been so much deception the past few years it's difficult to know fact from fiction. Uranus indicates technology is involved.

Neptune represents spies, so could this refer to the fact the U.S. was taken by surprise and claims to have had an intelligence failure by not knowing this ongoing conflict in the Middle East was about to escalate into overt war-- which occurred right around the time of this eclipse.

E-Ascendant/1st/Capricorn opp Sibly Sun/7th/Cancer (partile)

The Sun typically indicates the president with this emphasis from the 1st house suggesting the people do not agree with whatever the president is doing (or not doing).

E-Hades/7th/Cancer cnj Sibly Sun/7th/Cancer

E-Jupiter/5th/Taurus sxtl Sibly Sun/7th/Cancer

The 5th includes such a diverse group this is not easy to call. Could it be about children? Or the stock market and speculation in general? Upsets in that area, given rampant inflation and unsustainable fiscal policies, are being predicted on a regular basis. What might happen when Jupiter and Uranus station direct? Is that when all hell breaks loose?

Nothing about these aspects is good! Hades, which denotes destruction, conjunct the Sun is bad enough, but Jupiter accelerates it.

E-Pluto/2nd/Capricorn cnj Sibly Pluto/2nd/Capricorn (partile)

E-South Node/10th/Libra opp E-North Node/4th/Aries

Skipping over to the 2nd of finances and resources, the conjoined Plutos do not instill confidence for a peaceful or positive outcome. The U.S. already experienced its Pluto returns, but since he moves so slowly, he's still in the same degree following his final retrograde cycle of the return. It did not perfect and constitute part of the return, but that doesn't mean it's not powerful, lingering in that area for so long.

This concerning conjunction is even more so "at the bendings" of the lunar nodes. If a collapse of our financial system or currency occurs it will definitely incur a major shift from which there is no going back. The placement of the South Node indicates losing status as a country while the North Node suggests an ending with Pluto caught in the middle. Whatever occurs will be transformational.

E-Saturn/3rd/Pisces qncx Sibly Midheaven/10th/Libra

Saturn nudging the Midheaven shows a shift in status. The communication or physical infrastructure of the U.S. could be affected in a detrimental manner. Does this relate to that controversial wall in the south that's rather pointless, given an open border policy?

Saturn in Pisces is a good fit for a border that doesn't exist. The influx of millions over the years with as many as 300,000 in a single month undoubtedly affects U.S. status to say nothing of National Security. The Heritage Foundation believes as many as 16.8 million illegal immigrants are living in the U.S.

One of the reasons Trump objected to DACA was concerns that terrorists were using the program to stay in the country. Given the terms of DACA, this was probably unlikely. His attempt to protect the country from a legitimate threat unfortunately splashed on those who considered the U.S. home.

No easy answers exist for either issue. Presidents by virtue of their scope of responsibility sometimes make difficult and unpopular decisions. I believe Trump deserves credit for prioritizing the protection of U.S. citizens. We're last on the list with Biden.

No telling what consequences an open border will have. Everything about this eclipse and the next one suggest that issue is going to explode.

E-Mars/11th/Scorpio cnj Sibly Hades/11th/Scorpio qncx Sibly Apollon/6th/Gemini

E-Hades/7th/Cancer cnj Sibly Sun/7th/Cancer

Mars conjunct Sibly Hades is another massive energy burst, especially in Scorpio, the sign that rules death and destruction. This combined with eclipse Hades conjunct the Sun constitute ominous indicators.

Sibly Apollon is facing down this volatile conjunction vying for peace on behalf of the common man, farmers, military, and healthcare workers, but it doesn't look as if it will have much effect.

Other Factors

No single aspect defines any fated event. There are typically at least seven, usually on or around the same day, that effect the final trigger. Eclipse charts provide teasers and "watch items" that subsequent transits trigger and vice versa.

In additional to the eclipse, however, there are other preparatory astrological events to examine for clues.

Pluto completed three passes of the Sibly Pluto Return cycle December 29, 2022. Pluto "returns" occur approximately every 248 years. If democracies tend to fail around 250 years it appears that the transformational (or cleansing) effects of Pluto have a bearing.

Pluto retrograded back to 27:54 Capricorn, but didn't make it all the way to his Sibly natal placement at 27:33. Technically, this didn't count as another "return" hit, but it was short by only 21 minutes of arc, less than a half degree. In my opinion, energy wise that was another blast when he stationed at that degree on November 1, 2023. (A planet "stations" when it goes into or comes out of retrograde. For outer planets such as Pluto, it can remain in the same position for several days, dumping a lot of energy into that degree of the zodiac.)

Stations activate zodiacal degrees similar to eclipses. Subsequent contact by transiting planets, lunations, or other stations can trigger a significant event.

When Mars made it to that degree on February 10, 2024 it was expected to trigger something related to this eclipse that will also provide a preamble to the April 8, 2024 eclipse.

So what happened?

That was the date the Senate "killed" a bi-partisan immigration bill that would close the border.

Why did they kill it?

Most likely because full funding for the Ukraine war was also included in that bill!

Sounds familiar, right? Just like they hid the tidbit that made it okay to lie to the American people in a bill, they were sneaking this in to something everyone is demanding.

It's high time that these "Christmas tree" bills as they call them were outlawed. They're deceptive and loaded with pork barrel projects and other political "favors." As it stands, they are typically so long that no one reads them, so this corruption is hidden in plain sight.

I sincerely doubt this is what the Founding Fathers had in mind.

20. February 14, 2024 Mars-Pluto Conjunction

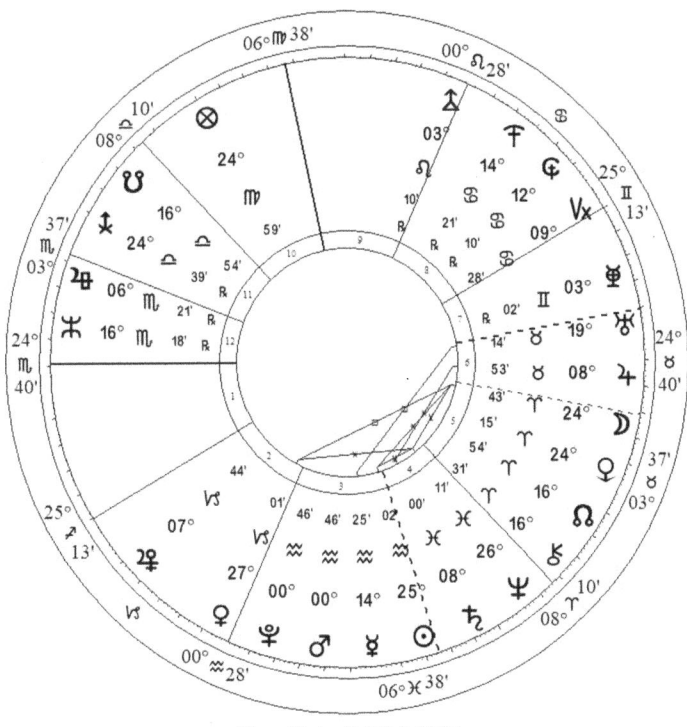

Mars-Pluto Cnj Feb 2024
NATAL CHART

February 14, 2024
1:06:35 AM
Washington, D.C.
38N53'42" 77W02'12"
Time Zone: 5 hours West
Standard Time

Tropical Placidus
True Node

Mean Moon's Node	18 ♈ 32
Birth Time Accuracy	XX
G.M.T.	6:06:35

Marcha Fox
B.S. Physics, Dipl. IAA   whobeda@valkyrieastrology.com   ValkyrieAstrology.com   "Timing is Everything"

This conjunction in Fixed sign, Aquarius, is particularly strong since it's anaretic at 00:48 Aquarius. Since this is not a Cardinal sign, it's not a "world point" so doesn't affect the entire planet. Numerous partile conjunctions add to its strength.

Mars-Pluto Conjunction/3rd/Aquarius

In general, a Mars-Pluto conjunction brings together power and aggression. Something corrupt is likely to be exposed. In Aquarius, it will relate to the people and in this House, most likely to our relationship with our neighbor, Mexico.

The house placement suggests it has a bearing on infrastructure, communications, our geographical neighbors, or primary education.

On this day, the House of Representatives impeached Alejandro Mayorkas, Secretary of the Department of Homeland Security, for his policies related to the Mexican Border. However, it may not pass the Senate, who claims there's no evidence he broke the law.

That, of course, fits the usual narrative promoted by the current administration. Protecting the border is included in the Constitution, which is clearly not being followed. How it's resolved will occur after I cut off trying to keep up with real-time events to include in this book.

Another event that followed this conjunction was the subject of a Health Ranger video that stated:

"Russia has just gone live with an orbital nuke platform that can drop nuclear warheads out of orbit at any time, detonating over key U.S. cities and military basis without warning and with zero chance of being intercepted.

Capitol Hill is in a panic, describing Russia's new technology as "destabilizing" and calling for urgent action to somehow counter Russia's military weapons advantage.

The U.S. military, meanwhile, is too busy being "woke" to build any new technology. Russia has orbital nukes, but the U.S. Navy has drag queens and trannies in charge. Do not wonder how this ends..".

Here's the video, for what it's worth:

https://www.brighteon.com/0aa1c424-7ab1-46fd-a5a4-78dcb853d791

Sun/3rd/Aquarius sqr Asc/1st/Scorpio

The Sun squaring the Ascendant is a classic indicator that the president's actions are clashing with the populace. The people have spoken and the government is not listening. The safety issues involved should be nonpartisan, but one side is operating on their own agenda, not that of the populace.

Moon/5th/Aries cnj Eris/5th/Aries

This shows immigration is an emotional issue that the Senate is committed to allow.

North Node/5th/Aries cnj Chiron/5th/Aries

This suggests that the current policy is injurious to children and is likely to continue.

Mercury/3rd/Aquarius sqr Uranus/6th/Taurus

Mercury's square to Uranus suggests this unexpected news is going to incur resistance.

Sun/3rd/Aquarius sxtl Moon/5th/Aries

The Moon in the 5th indicates the Senate's reaction is purely emotional, especially in Aries. They're angry and claim the impeachment is "partisan" as opposed to being well-deserved.

Moon/5th/Aries opp Zeus/11th/Zeus

This made me smile since it clearly shows the House taking a shot at the Senate. The opposition suggests the need for balance, which is unlikely to be attained.

Moon/5th/Aries sqr Venus/2nd/Capricorn

Financial and resource issues are likewise seeing impulsive and defensive reactions from the Senate.

Venus/2nd/Capricorn sxtl Neptune/4th/Pisces

The placements involved with Venus shaking hands with Neptune reminds me of the drug wars and the Fentanyl crisis that is a huge factor in the border situation.

Saturn/4th/Pisces sxtl Jupiter/6th/Taurus

Saturn working with Jupiter reflects this is a Conservative move that represents the opinion of families and the working class.

Sun/3rd/Aquarius ssxtl Neptune/4th/Pisces

This shows the President's annoyance and confusion. His mental state has been in question lately and his reaction to this situation may illustrate it.

Neptune/4th/Pisces ssxt Moon/5th/Aries

The Senate refusing to acknowledge the legitimacy of the charges against Mayorkas is of great concern. Shouldn't they be upholding the Constitution? Since the Senate is split with no solid majority, this is unlikely to pass since it requires a two-thirds vote.

Kronos/Hades/Vertex/8th/Cancer

Kronos conjunct Hades implies "perfect corruption." The presence of the Vertex suggests the fated nature of the situation.

This event was clearly indicated in this chart. Good job, Universe.

MARS - PLUTO CONJUNCTION WITH SIBLY CHART

Mars/Pluto conjunction/2nd/Aquarius in Sibly 2nd House

This placement in the house of resources shows this as a resource and financial issue. The cost of illegal immigration is a huge factor as well as the quality of life that's jeopardized by the drug crisis. Approximately 200 people a day die from Fentanyl per the latest statistics.

C-Mars/Pluto/2nd/Aquarius tri Sibly Midheaven/10th/Libra

The conjunction suggests this crisis and how it's handled will influence the U.S. status, which should be intuitively obvious.

C-Mercury/2nd/Aquarius tri Sibly Saturn/10th/Libra

Government responsibility is called out by this connection between Mercury and Saturn.

C-Asc/12th/Scorpio tri Sibly Mercury/8th/Cancer

The people's voices are being ignored regarding this deadly issue.

C-Midheaven/9th/Virgo sxtl Sibly Jupiter/7th/Cancer

Public attention on the immigration issue will expand its importance regarding our handling of the border.

C-Venus/2nd/Capricorn cnj Sibly Pluto/2nd/Capricorn

The deadly nature of this financial issue is reflected by conjoined Venus and Pluto.

C-Sun/3rd/Aquarius qncx Sibly Mercury/8th/Cancer

A change of direction is required from the president to address this deadly issue.

C-Saturn/3rd/Pisces sqr Sibly Uranus/6th/Gemini

Not taking responsibility for the border issue clashes with changes the working class wants that relate to health, and therefore the drug and human trafficking issues.

The Dark Side of Eclipses

Inner Wheel:
U.S. Sibly Chart
Philadelphia, PA
Time Zone: 0 hours West

July 4, 1776
39N57'08" 75W09'51"
Tropical Placidus
NATAL CHART

5:10 PM
Local Mean Time

Outer Wheel:
Mars-Pluto Cnj Feb 2024
Washington, D.C.
Time Zone: 5 hours West

February 14, 2024
38N53'42" 77W02'12"
Tropical Placidus
NATAL CHART

1:06:35 AM
Standard Time

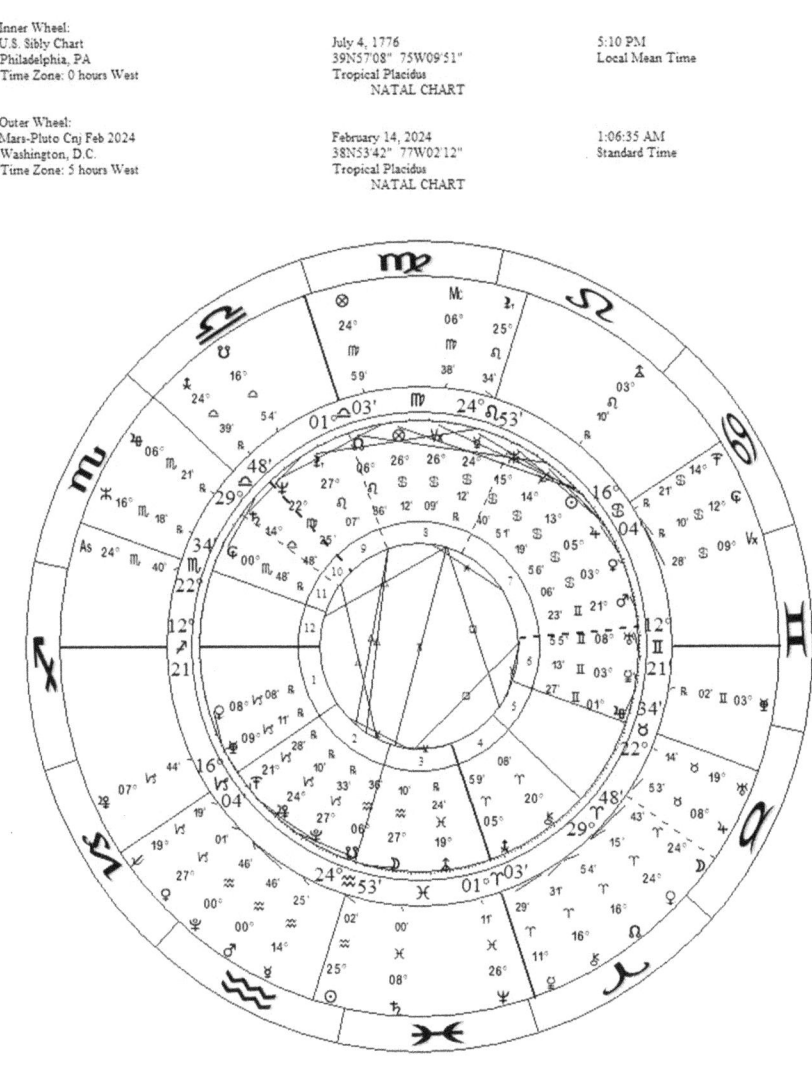

C-Moon-Eris cnj sqr Sibly Mercury/8th/Cancer

The emotional resistance to dealing with the immigration issue conflicts with information regarding the deaths, crime, and financial situations it's causing.

C-Mars-Pluto/2nd/Aquarius sqr Hades/11th/Scorpio (1/30th degree orb)

The nearly exact square between the conjunction and Hades is particularly ominous. This shows that the House of Representatives has attempted to address the situation, but is encountering resistance. The fate of Mayorkas's impeachment is going to reverberate far more than most realize.

C-Zeus/10th/Libra sqr Sibly Mercury/8th/Cancer

Power plays by the president and his supporters are exacerbating a deadly crisis that affects families, both among immigrants and U.S. citizenry.

C-Kronos/Hades/7th/Cancer

Perfect destruction looms relative foreign relations.

C-Jupiter/5th/Taurus ssxt Sibly Uranus/6th/Gemini

The senate's actions will bring considerable friction and a few surprises from the working class as well as healthcare implications.

C-Apollon/11th/Scorpio tri Jupiter/7th/Cancer

Future foreign relations depend on this action by the House of Representatives.

[NOTE:– Cosmic events are happening so fast that just when I think I've finished this book I find something else that should be included. What follows has not yet happened, so I'm only delineating the charts and speculating. Needless to say, looking at horoscopes in retrospect is far more accurate. Time will tell how well I did.]

21. February 28, 2024 Double Cazimi

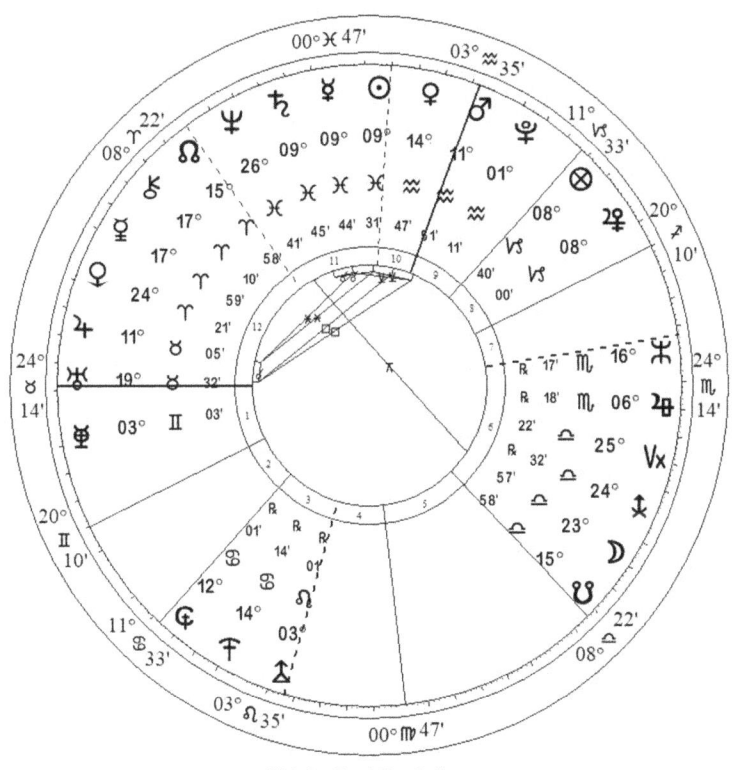

Triple Conj Peak Caz
NATAL CHART

February 28, 2024　　　　　　　　　Tropical Placidus
10:00 AM　　　　　　　　　　　　　True Node
Washington, D.C.
38N53'42"　77W02'12"　　　| Mean Moon's Node | 17 ♈ 46 |
Time Zone: 5 hours West　　　| Birth Time Accuracy | XX |
Standard Time　　　　　　　　| G.M.T. | 15:00:00 |

Marcha Fox
B.S. Physics, Dipl. IAA   whobeda@valkyrieastrology.com   ValkyrieAstrology.com   "Timing is Everything"

The future as reflected in astrology evolves over time. When I studied predictions in one of my classes at the International Academy of Astrology, the final exam comprised an unnamed person's birth chart from which we were to determine when within a period of approximately three months that something significant would happen and define what it would be.

As it turned out, the individual was Christopher Reeve and the event his crippling accident.

What was incredible about that class and its culmination in that final assignment was that the signs of that transformational event were there months before! You would think accidents came out of the blue, but there was a distinct path leading to it, leaving cosmic breadcrumbs, if you will, along the way.

The Moon and Sun do their monthly dance seen in lunar phases and eclipses. Mercury's path oscillates to and fro as reflected in his quarterly retrograde cycles. The Sun, in turn, conjoins Saturn's location every year. For the Sun, Saturn, and Mercury to converge on the same degree on the same day, however, is rare.

First, let's take a look at what those planets signify. The Sun represents the head of state or president. Mercury stands for writers, journalists, retailers, and intelligentsia in mundane while in general he represents information, as well as anything that moves or thinks. Saturn signifies the elderly, conservatives, and bureaucrats in mundane; responsibility, boundaries, and limitations otherwise.

This cosmic event takes place in Pisces. Neither Mercury nor Saturn function well in that sign. Pisces, like its modern ruler, Neptune, is out there in "deep space." It's dreamy, other-worldly, and logic has no bearing. Thus, whatever this brings is likely to be counter-intuitive. Let's hope it's inspired and not delusional, but from what we've seen so far of our leadership, logic isn't likely to manifest.

If you're unfamiliar with the term "cazimi" it's Arabic and translates "in the heart of the Sun." It refers to when a planet is within 17 arc minutes of the Sun, which signifies it's empowered by the solar blast and begins a new cycle. Two planets within that position at the same time is rare.

This dynamic event involves a triple conjunction as well as dual cazimis. The duration from when Mercury enters cazimi to when Saturn's ends is 28 hours 20 minutes. Needless to say, a lot can transpire in that amount of time.

The cazimi begins with Mercury catching up with the Sun on February 27 at 7:45 PM. The Saturn cazimi begins at 8:32 AM on February 28 when the Sun catches up with Saturn. The double cazimi lasts until 11:25 AM at which time Mercury moves on, having conjoined both the Sun and Saturn along the way.

Rather than slog through each of the charts involved, which would involve multiple house structures and interpretations, I chose the middle of the time span I call Peak Cazimi, *i.e.*, when both planets are "in the heart of the Sun." The cazimi falls in the Sibly 3rd house of infrastructure, neighbors, and K-12. Let's see how it interacts with the Sibly chart and address aspects within the Peak Cazimi chart based on their placement there.

Marcha "Whobeda" Fox

February 28, 2024 Cazimi with Sibly Chart

Inner Wheel:
U.S. Sibly Chart
Philadelphia, PA
Time Zone: 0 hours West

July 4, 1776
39N57'08" 75W09'51"
Tropical Placidus
NATAL CHART

5:10 PM
Local Mean Time

Outer Wheel:
Triple Conj Peak Caz
Washington, D.C.
Time Zone: 5 hours West

February 28, 2024
38N53'42" 77W02'12"
Tropical Placidus
NATAL CHART

10:00 AM
Standard Time

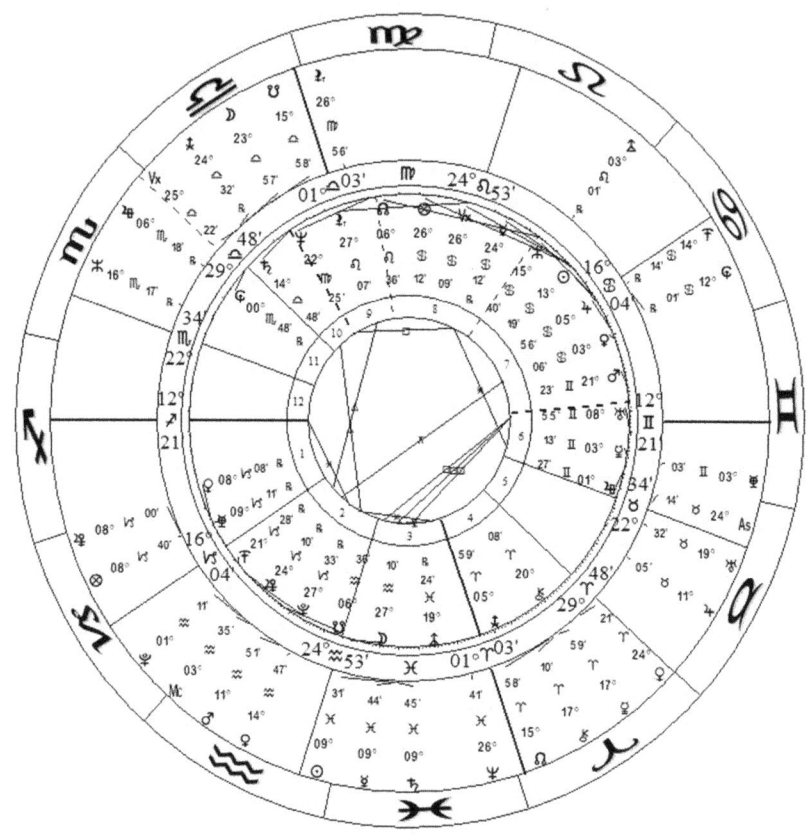

Marcha Fox
B.S. Physics, Dipl. IAA   whobeda@valkyrieastrology.com   ValkyrieAstrology.com   "Timing is Everything"

Cazimi/3rd/Pisces sqr Sibly Uranus/6th/Gemini

Our relationship with a neighboring country has brought about disruptions that affects the working class.

C-Mars/2nd/Aquarius sxtl Sibly Ascendant/1st/Sagittarius

Mars sextile the ascendant shows the people taking action to protect resources, finances, or way of life.

C-Venus/2nd/Aquarius tri Sibly Saturn/10th/Libra

C-Pluto/2nd/Capricorn tri Sibly Midheaven/10th/Libra

C-Venus/2nd/Aquarius qncx Sibly Sun/7th/Cancer

Several aspects involve the treasury and finances. As it turns out, this day is the deadline for Congress dealing with justifying the U.S. debt. Saturn's involvement suggests conservative moves. Pisces implies they'll back down.

C-Sun/Mercury/Saturn/3rd/Pisces sxtl Sibly Admetos/1st/Capricorn

The combination of the double cazimi with Admetos indicates a serious situation concentrated in its scope that impacts the populace and relates to infrastructure. The triple-square to Uranus indicates a demand by the working class to deal with a situation.

C-Pluto/2nd/Aquarius sqr Sibly Hades/11th/Scorpio

A power play related to resources or the treasury brings destruction from a group, most likely Congress.

C-Eris/4th/Aries sqr Sibly Mercury/8th/Cancer sqr S-Cupido/2nd/Capricorn (T-square)

This configuration shows a deadlock. Immigration issues are involved. Considering their impact to the budget and debt, this isn't surprising. Review of policy is demanded.

C-Moon/Zeus/Vertex/10th/Libra sqr Sibly Mercury/8th/Cancer

This triple conjunction from the Cazimi chart falls in the 10th house of the Sibly Chart, suggesting it relates to the country's status. It will be in the public view, whether the press ignores it or not. Demands to review policy are indicated.

C-Neptune/3rd/Pisces sxtl Sibly Pluto/2nd/Capricorn both qnx Sibly Lilith/9th/Leo

The drug crisis fueled by the open border is implicated by Neptune and Pluto. Their quincunxes to Lilith indicate feminist influences. Will Kamala Harris be involved in some way? Called upon to decide a tie in the Senate?

C-Admetos cnj Sibly Phaethon/6th/Gemini

C-Eris/4th/Aries opp C-Zeus/10th/Libra

C-Chiron cnj C-Phaethon/4th/Aries

A situational "crash and burn" that affects the working class has reached critical mass. Could be a border confrontation. Injuries to families are possible or something comes to an end.

C-Cupido/C-PoF cnj Sibly Eris/ Admetos/1st/Capricorn qnx Sibly Uranus/6th/Gemini

This cluster of cosmic energies indicates like-minded people from the populace demanding changes that affect them directly.

Considering the border issue making multiple appearances, news media silence notwithstanding, Uranus is being slammed by Trans-Neptunians as well as the cazimi. This suggests there will be disturbances, surprises, and perhaps sudden change.

There's potential for violence considering the Texas National Guard is defying Biden's policy of open borders, which violates the Constitution, but the feds aren't backing down. The 6th includes the military, where Uranus is being blasted by the cosmos.

Other major issues include drug and human trafficking by cartels. Perhaps a confrontation will occur. In that case, the Border Patrol would be caught in the middle.

Timeline for the cazimi in Eastern Standard Time (EST).

2/27/24 7:45 PM: Mercury Cazimi begins

2/28/24 3:45 AM Mercury - Sun conjunction exact

2/28/24 8:32 AM Saturn Cazimi begins

2/28/24 10:15 AM Mercury - Saturn conjunction exact

2/28/24 11:25 AM Mercury Cazimi ends

2/28/24 4:25 PM Sun - Saturn conjunction exact

2/29/24 12:05 AM Saturn cazimi ends

CAZIMI SUMMARY

2/28/24 8:32 - 11:25 AM Double cazimi (2 hours 53 minutes)

2/27/24 7:45 PM - 2/29/24 12:05 AM Cazimi series (28:20 hours)

2/28/24 9:58 AM Peak of double cazimi

22. March 25, 2024 Lunar Eclipse

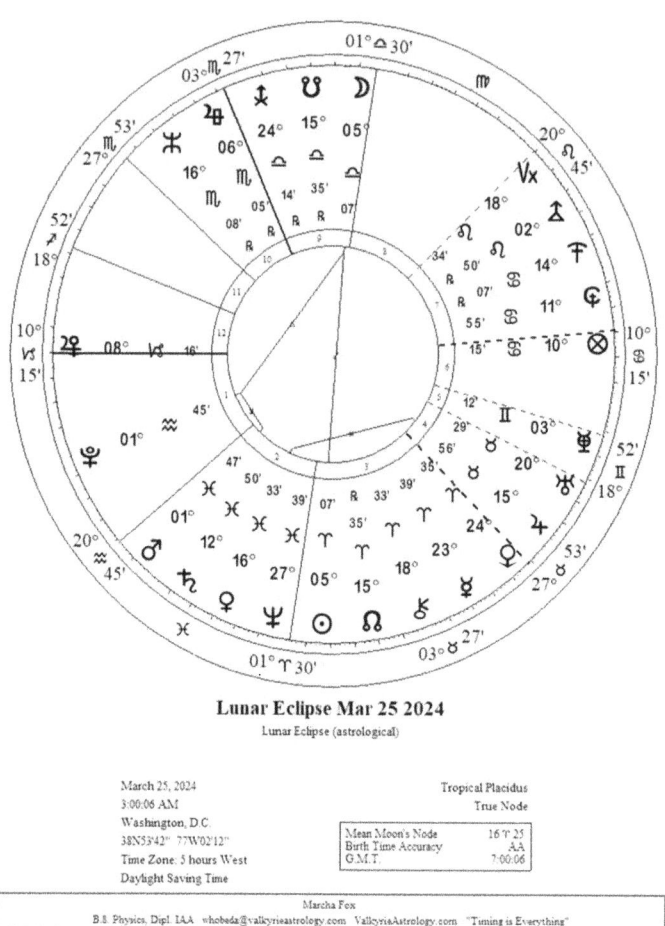

Lunar Eclipse Mar 25 2024
Lunar Eclipse (astrological)

So far I've focused on solar eclipses, but there's a reason this one is included, so bear with me. Lunar eclipses tend to bring emotional impact whereas solar eclipses precipitate events and situations. This one is in the same family as the one coming on April 8.

Brady describes it as having "inventiveness and flashes of genius...intuitive leaps, insights, good ideas, visions, or vivid dreams...a time when the person needs to be free, if only for a few weeks."

Brady's description describes a strong Uranus influence, which also include disturbances, surprises, unexpected events, rebellion, and explosions, which are more likely in view of the status quo.

The eclipse occurs in the 9th, which relates to other countries, academia, courts, religious institutions and the media.

Moon/9th/Libra tri Pluto/1st/Capricorn

The eclipsed Moon's trine to Pluto suggests a transformational event that affects the populace and relates to the 9th, as described above.

Mars, Saturn, Venus and Neptune/2nd/Pisces

There's quite a convention in Pisces in the house of finance, the treasury, and resources which includes Mars, Saturn, Venus, and Neptune. That's a rolling stellium that packs a lot of diverse planetary energy.

Venus/2nd/Pisces sxtl Jupiter/4th/Taurus (mutual reception)

Exalted Venus is sextile dignified Jupiter. They're also in mutual reception (each rules the sign the other occupies) for a strong relationship. This suggests something related to finance and new beginnings that will affect family policy, land values, and so forth.

Note that other than the Trans-Neptunians, the eclipsed Moon is alone above the horizon. The Sun and planets are concentrated in the 1st - 4th houses below. This suggests many will be "in the dark" with regard to whatever occurs. (No surprise there.)

Chiron/3rd/Aries tri Vertex/7th/Leo

There appear to be fated injuries related to infrastructure and our relationship with another country. With two Fire signs involved, sparks are going to fly.

Eris/3rd/Aries opp Zeus/9th/Libra

Mars/2nd/Pisces ssxtl Pluto/1st/Capricorn

Eris from the house that includes U.S. "neighbors" and infrastructure opposes Zeus in the house that includes other countries. This conjures up thunderbolts coming across the border, as it did for the double cazimi.

There have been numerous warnings about an attack on our infrastructure, such as an EMP. Mars, ruler of the 3rd, 10th, and 11th, is in Pisces where he's more likely to sympathize with our enemies than fight.

He's an annoying semisextile away from Pluto in the 1st, indicating his dysfunctionality irritates people who want something done.

How do military veterans view the trend to compromise our armed services to the point of making it a laughing stock? If we suffer an attack how effective will our "woke" military be defending us?

Seriously, people. Are drag queen soldiers going to beat invaders with their purse? You can't run very fast in high heels.

But with Mars in Pisces, sadly this is possible.

Mars is traditional ruler of the Midheaven, which includes our leaders, who defend Ukraine to the tune of billions of dollars yet refuse to address border issues. Recently the budget included $53 million for debit cards for illegal aliens, which was more than that allocated for veterans, many of whom are homeless and committing suicide.

People are dropping dead on the streets from the lethal influx of Fentanyl across our non-existent border. That alone should slam it shut. Estimated daily deaths from the drug provided by the CDC based on data from 2017-2018 was 150 per day. Other sources report 200 per day, with it undoubtedly far more since this problem escalated significantly in the past five years.

https://www.cdc.gov/stopoverdose/fentanyl/index.html

At this point what justification is there to leave the border open when the consequences to legitimate U.S. citizens are so grave? Furthermore, why are illegal aliens getting better treatment that veterans? Or taxpayers footing the bill?

Pluto/1st/Capricorn tri Admetos/5th/Taurus

Pluto trining Admetos suggests a lot of pressure on the Senate from an angry "had-enough" the populace. Are the people finally making their voices heard? As an election year, will Congress Critters start to listen? Or is it too late?

Vulcanus/7th/Leo opp Pluto/1st/Capricorn

Vulcanus/7th/Leo sxtl Admetos/5th/Taurus

Vulcanus opposing Pluto suggests a confrontation. Will the people themselves take matters into their own hands as some ranch owners in border states have already done? The sextile between Admetos and Vulcanus shows either the Senate is waking up or being forced to.

States such as Texas have taken action on their own and are being sued by the Federal Government.

Our government has never been our friend but now it's our enemy, expertly hidden behind a devious agenda of which too many are unaware.

This Blood Moon strikes me as a prelude to the Solar Eclipse on April 8. That is when all of this is likely to "hit the fan" and why I went to the trouble and expense to move out of Texas.

However, there's one more thing about this eclipse that's striking. It occurs at the same time as the Sibly Chart progresses to a New Moon in Pisces.

A progressed New Moon is "A Big Deal" in astrology. It marks a new emotional beginning. In synch with a lunar eclipse, this has major implications for life-changing events on the horizon.

Let's take a look.

23. Sibly Progressed New Moon

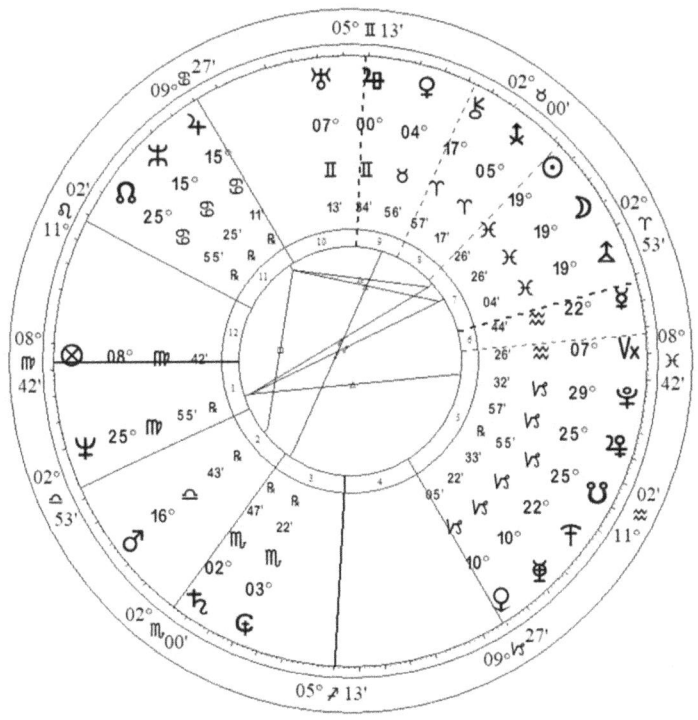

U.S. Sibly Chart
Secondary Progression, Mean Sun Method, for March 25, 2024 at 12:00 PM GMT

Calc: March 9, 1777
3:30:32 PM GMT
Philadelphia, PA
39N57'08" 75W09'51"
Time Zone: 0 hours West
Greenwich Mean Time

Tropical Placidus
True Node

Mean Moon's Node	24 ♋ 28
Birth Time Accuracy	XX
G.M.T.	15:30:32

Marcha Fox
B.S. Physics, Dipl. IAA   whobeda@valkyriasastrology.com   ValkyriaAstrology.com   "Timing is Everything"

The Pisces New Moon occurs in the 7th house which includes alliances and open enemies. Pisces is the sign of both the savior and the martyr. My impression is that we'll be at the mercy of our enemies and desperately need the help of any allies we may have left.

New Moon/7th/Pisces cnj Vulcanus/7th/Pisces

One interpretation of this placement with Vulcanus' presence, is that a foreign invader will be in charge. If that doesn't creep you out, I don't know what will.

Chiron and Zeus/8th/Aries

The 8th house of death and transformation is occupied by Zeus and Chiron, which isn't particularly good news, either, with both in Aries, sign of the warrior.

Apollon in the 9th approaching the Midheaven is vying for peace, but will he be heard?

Vertex/5th/Aquarius tri Uranus/10th/Taurus

The Vertex in the house that includes the Senate, is working with Uranus in the house that includes the president, which looks like an unexpected but fated sudden change in leadership.

Jupiter/11th/Cancer cnj Poseidon

Jupiter/11th/Cancer tri New Moon/7th/Pisces

Jupiter represents the courts while the 11th includes the House of Representatives and groups in general. Poseidon stands for clarity and politics, so this suggests there will be no mistaking what is transpiring. Jupiter is strong as he pushes for something new. This further implies new legislation that affects our relationship with other countries.

North Node/11th/Cancer opp South Node/5th/Capricorn cnj Cupido

The North Node in the 11th implies something new is on the way while the South Node in the 5th indicates a door is closing that affects many. It could also be the Senate sending a bill back to the House with revisions.

The conventional interpretation of the 5th is children, but also includes the entertainment industry, sports and recreation, the Senate, speculation and gambling. This does not seem to fit all that's going on elsewhere in this chart or the previous ones.

In natal astrology the 5th house includes a person's self-image and ego. Translating this to mundane suggests it represents our national self-identity, *i.e.*, what its citizens envision it to be. It's rather troubling to have the South Node in that house, suggesting that it will be left behind.

Eris/5th/Capricorn cnj Admetos

Cupido/5th/Capricorn cnj South Node

The 5th house is packed! Eris, Admetos, Kronos, Cupido, Pluto, and the Vertex as well as the South Node. This shows a lot going on.

Eris represents immigrants and factions while Admetos indicates a concentration. Cupido suggests a opinions merging as some 5th house element(s), perhaps the Nation's self-image, fade into oblivion.

Saturn/3rd/Scorpio cnj Hades

Taskmaster Saturn and destructive Hades are conjoined in Scorpio, the sign that rules death. This suggests destruction of our infrastructure.

For those of you who remember the movie "Red Dawn," consider how prophetic it may have been.

Two weeks after this, the April 8th solar eclipse slashes its way across the continental United States. We've already seen what the 2017 eclipse did as far as dividing the nation.

What will this double-whammy bring?

[NOTE:--Another factor, which represents a standard in mundane astrology, is the Aries Ingress. The Sun's entrance into a Cardinal signs marks a new season, literally and figuratively. With the Sun at zero degrees, it constitutes a world point that's felt across the globe. It relates to events in the three months to come with its interpretation tied to lunations with eclipses the strongest indictors.

The Ingress Chart for Washington D.C. for the Spring Equinox implied a strong push from the populace for action related to the border. It occurred on March 19, six days before the lunar eclipse and progressed New Moon. The eclipse on March 25 covered in the previous section further reflected that. The Universe hammers the same themes as frequently as required to make its point.]

24. April 8, 2024 Total Solar Eclipse

This eclipse has the cosmic components to deal a harsh blow to the USA.

Brady's description of this eclipse reflected the positive side of Uranus. The unfortunate side was noted earlier. The fact the eclipse is total, occurs in Aries, sign of the warrior, and its path slices the US east to west definitely throws several red flags, given the U.S. status quo.

Furthermore, it forms an "X" with the 2017 eclipse path of visibility. Carbondale, Illinois and various other cities are within the crosshairs. But more on that later, along with it crossing the path of the 2023 annular eclipse as well.

Sun cnj Moon cnj Chiron/9th/Aries (triple exact conjunction)

It's somewhat startling that the Sun, Moon, and Chiron, the wounded healer, are all placed in 19:24 Aries, *i.e.*, in the same EXACT degree. Like the cazimi, this is beyond unusual and another example of defying the odds, to say nothing of the cosmic strength it generates.

Consider that it occurs in the house that includes academia, courts, religious institutions and the media as well as other countries. If these matters are being "eclipsed" what lies ahead?

Mercury RX/9th/Aries cnj Eris opp Zeus/3rd/Libra

Mercury and Eris are a mere 1/20th of a degree away from an exact conjunction. They're in partile opposition with Zeus/3rd, the house of infrastructure, suggesting directed energy. Let's look a little closer in the context of Eris representing immigrants and minorities.

Bloggers such as Michael Yon, a former special forces veteran who reports from hot spots around the globe, has warned and documented the fact migrant caravans of military age men converge on the U.S. southern border on a regular basis.

Actually, he refuses to call them "migrants." He's "boots on ground" and sees these people up close and personal.

These are not all families fleeing a hostile regime.

Whether or not you're a fan of Tucker Carlson, he states that three million entered the U.S. illegally in 2023 alone and that the influx of illegals now exceeds the U.S. birthrate

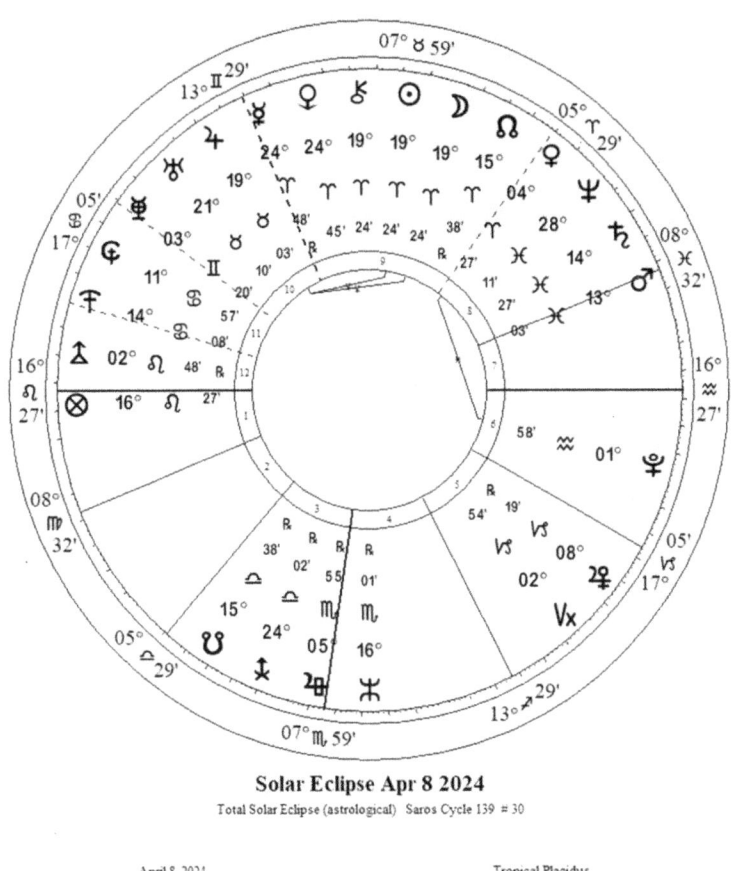

Solar Eclipse Apr 8 2024
Total Solar Eclipse (astrological) Saros Cycle 139 = 30

The website NumbersUSA.com tells us:

> *Nearly 1.4 million migrants were released into the interior in Fiscal Year 2023, with over 900,000 released by the Border Patrol alone.*

> * 850,000 visitors overstayed their visas and remained in the country illegally in 2022.
> * 600,000 aliens were estimated to have entered the country illegally without apprehension and blended into the underground workforce that employers exploit as there is no requirement to use the free E-Verify online system to verify work authorization.
> *1,018,349 individuals obtained lawful permanent residence (green cards) in FY 2022.

I'd bet dollars to donuts you haven't heard any of that on mainstream news stations.

Ask yourself, "Why not?"

On a personal note, I lived in Texas for 35 years. When I saw the 2017 and 2023 eclipse paths crossed not that far from where I lived, I decided it was time to leave. Granted, I'm a fiction author as well as an astrologer and have a good imagination. But it is not my imagination that things in this country are definitely circling the drain.

According to an October 2023 communication from the Heritage Foundation, the Chinese Communist Party has infiltrated the U.S. for decades. Chinese police stations have been installed in many major cities to spy on and intimidate Chinese Americans into toeing the Chinese Communist Party's party line. It's no secret they've worked their way into our universities and been stealing our technology. Small cells of Chinese military-aged men are among the caravans breaching our border.

Intelligence reports state that terrorist sleeper cells have been set up in dozens of cities across the country. These include Washington, D.C.; San Francisco; Santa Clara; Los Angeles; and San Diego in California alone. Also listed were Houston, Arlington and Dallas in Texas. Boston, Chicago, Cleveland, New York, Detroit, Kansas City, Denver, Oklahoma City, Tucson, Seattle, Philadelphia, Raleigh, Charlotte.

It's not a matter of if but when they activate these forces against us on our own soil.

Need I go on?

This volatile rolling stellium that comprises the Sun, Moon, Mercury, Eris, Chiron, the North Node and Venus represents a whole lot of unfriendly energy in Aries, a Cardinal Fire sign that's prone to violent action.

Venus is in Aries, too, but in the 8th house of death. She's in her debility, so not much help as ruler of the 3rd (infrastructure) and 10th (leadership) houses.

This planetary convention occurs in the 9th, which you should be familiar with by now. Note that eclipses in 2000, 2016, 2017, 2023, and 2024 also occurred in the 9th in either the eclipse or Sibly chart.

Are they conveying some sort of message?

(On a personal level the 9th includes your attitude, philosophy of life, higher learning/academia, expectations, and legal matters, but depending on where you live, the placement is likely to be in a different house which changes the implications.)

Pluto/6th/Aquarius opp Vulcanus/12th/Leo (anaretic)

Pluto opposing Vulcanus suggests a standoff between the military and hidden enemies with significant power.

Eclipse ssxtl Jupiter/10th/Taurus cnj Uranus

In the house of the president and government leadership, Jupiter is only two degrees from Uranus, suggesting a huge disturbance as it exchanges a friction-laden semi-sextile with the eclipse.

In other words, Jupiter will inflate its effects in the house where the head of state resides along with public opinion. Jupiter's mundane representation includes bankers, merchants (wholesale), judges and clergy.

Will they be behind this explosive event?

Mars/8th/Pisces cnj Saturn

Mars is accidentally dignified in the 8th house of death, which is more often than not a warning. The effect may be softened in Pisces, however, though Neptune in Pisces is ripe ground for deception and confusion. Mars' conjunction with Saturn implies he's in cahoots with bureaucrats and conservatives.

Mars like Saturn is not strong in Pisces, sign of the martyr as well as the savior. Mars is the traditional ruler of the 4th, the house that includes endings. The cusp is in Scorpio, sign that rules life, death, transformations, debt, and intense experiences. Its modern ruler is Pluto.

Saturn/8th/Pisces tri Kronos/11th/Gemini

Saturn in the house of death, which is in Pisces, the last sign of the zodiac, has a ring of finality to it. The trine from Kronos suggests whatever occurs is well-executed by a group, a coup if you will.

The lack of aspects other than conjunctions suggests each planet and trans-Neptunian is free to operate independently.

Zeus/3rd/Libra opp Mercury RX/9th/Aries

This Mercury - Zeus opposition suggests a firestorm of accountability. Remember Mercury is retrograde, a time when progress is unlikely as the past comes home to roost. He's also partile conjunct Eris.

On the positive side, if something apocalyptic does transpire, Mercury retrograde suggests it may not last. Whether the resulting change is positive is another story.

The path of this eclipse intersects the path of the 2017 eclipse over Carbondale, Illinois. Food for thought, Carbondale is an area where a significant amount of fracking has occurred in the past, if not now. The New Madrid fault and super volcano are in that region as well.

Does "X" mark the spot where all hell will break loose?

Besides, there's another "X" to consider as well.

Stay tuned. More on that later.

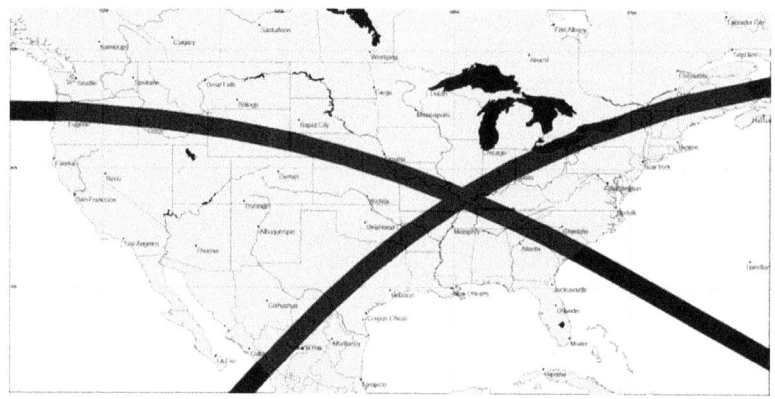

April 2024 Eclipse Interaction with Sibly Chart

This eclipse makes some interesting aspects with the Sibly chart. Will it soften or exacerbate what the eclipse chart alone has to say?

E-Kronos - Hades Midpoint /7th/Cancer cnj Sibly Sun/7th/Cancer

The Sibly Sun at the midpoint of eclipse Kronos and Hades suggests the president/government is caught between two polar opposites, *i.e.*, heaven and hell.

What does that tell us? Could this dire situation go either way, depending on his response?

E-Mars cnj Saturn/3rd/Pisces tri Sibly Sun/7th/Cancer

E-Mars cnj Saturn/3rd/Pisces qncx Sibly Saturn/10th/Libra

This could indicate communities taking authoritative action to effect change. Taking the situation into their own hands would defy the feds. Or is the 3rd referring to our

The Dark Side of Eclipses

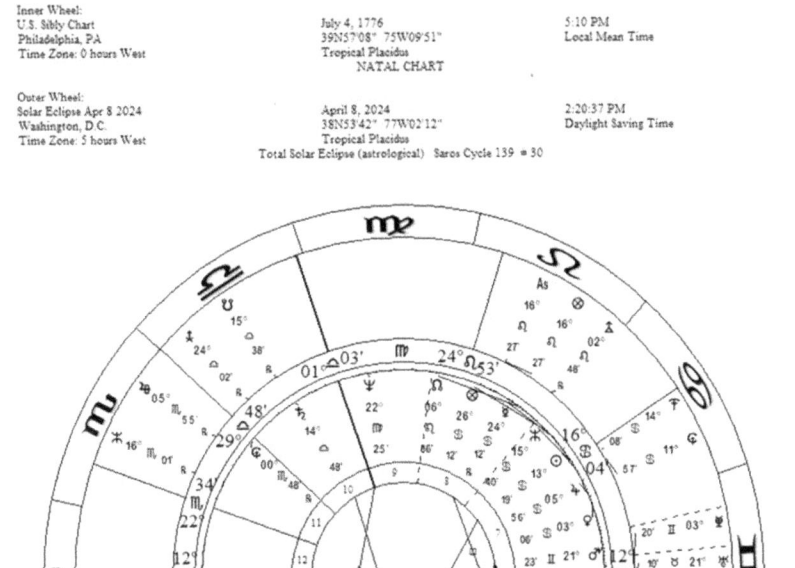

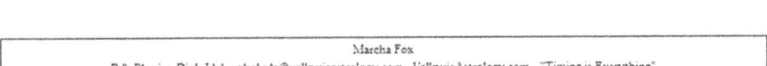

southern border under attack and needing a change of direction from the president? Or both?

Saturn itself represents conservatives, bureaucrats and the elderly. Will they be the ones who take action and force action?

Clearly far-left policies got us into this mess. The real question is exactly what were their motives facilitating a potentially destructive situation by allowing the invasion of literally millions of illegal aliens?

The American dream eroded during the Obama and Biden administrations from being based on equal opportunity to work hard for success to being taken care of at government (taxpayer) expense.

In the words of historian W. Cleon Skousen:

> *"Since the genius of the American system is maintaining the eagle in the balanced center of the spectrum, the Founders warned against a number of temptations which might lure subsequent generations to abandon their freedoms and their rights by subjecting themselves to a strong federal administration operating on the collectivist Left. They warned against the "welfare state" where the government endeavors to take care of everyone from the cradle to the grave....*
>
> *"The Founders also warned that the only way for the nation to prosper was to have equal protection of 'rights,' and not allow the government to get involved in trying to provide equal distribution of 'things.' (W. Cleon Skousen, "The Five Thousand Year Leap" 1981, pg. 29-30 as quoted in* American Crossroad of Trust *by Thomas H. Fairbanks.)*

Illegal immigrants receiving more benefits than veterans who fought to maintain freedom worldwide is not popular among millions of patriots footing the bill with their taxes.

Saturn rules the Sibly 2nd house of resources and the treasury. What impact will this situation have there?

Eclipse/4th/Aries

The eclipse lands in the Sibly 4th house, house of endings and new beginnings as well as land, families, the opposition party and history. Ending are followed by a new beginning. What will it be?

E-Eris cnj Mercury/5th/Aries sqr Sibly Cupido/2nd/Capricorn

E-Eris cnj Mercury/5th/Aries sqr Sibly Mercury/8th/Cancer

Cupido points toward financial impact to many. The pair also squares Sibly Mercury in the 8th, which is retrograde, suggestive of rethinking a lethal situation. The 8th house includes violence and death as well as debt and other life-changing situations.

E-Cupido/1st/Capricorn cnj Sibley Admetos and Eris/1st/Capricorn

The populace as a whole is aware the immigration issue has reached the boiling point even though the press ignores it.

E-Pluto/2nd/Aquarius tri Sibly Midheaven/10th/Libra

Pluto trining the Midheaven suggests transformational change of status for leadership and the country's resources/treasury as a whole.

E-Pluto/2nd/Aquarius sqr Sibly Hades/11th/Scorpio

Pluto's square to Hades looks like confrontations over resources that are likely to involve Congress or the stock market, which will not end well.

If you're not concerned about this indicator, you might want to reread the description of Hades.

And that's not all.

There are other significant cosmic events influencing the U.S. Sibly Chart.

Will they help?

Or exacerbate an already volatile situation?

25. Mars-Saturn Exact Conjunction April 10, 2024

Two days after the eclipse, malefics Mars and Saturn conjoin in Pisces, a sign where neither is particularly at home. They're not technically in debility or fall, but certainly not in a zodiacal environment that encourages their full, uninhibited expression. In other words, dysfunctional.

Saturn, as previously stated, represents conservatives and bureaucrats (but doesn't necessarily mean that all bureaucrats are conservative). Mars typically relates to the military, fires, and disputes. When these two pair up, it strikes me that conservatives may finally take action.

But in Pisces will it have any teeth? Or reek idealism?

Mars cnj Saturn/6th/Pisces tri Kronos/10th/Cancer

But maybe there's hope. Whatever action is taken is done with finesse. They're operating from the house which includes the working class, farmers, the military, labor unions, and healthcare.

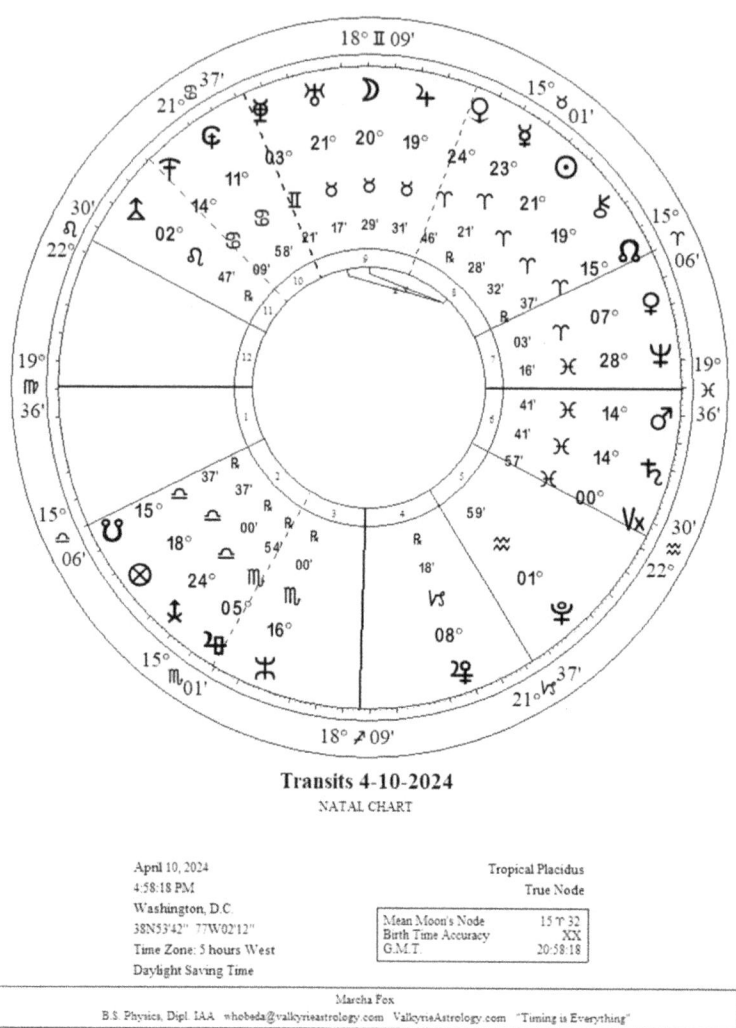

Transits 4-10-2024
NATAL CHART

They don't interact with any other planetary neighbors, but there are some other interesting configurations worth noting.

As we've seen before, considering the major planets and luminaries (and yes, to astrologers Pluto is a major planet regardless to what deluded astronomers say) plus Chiron and Eris, are all confined to only four signs of the zodiac.

Thus, the energy remains unbalanced as it has for awhile.

Both the 8th and 9th contain what are known as rolling stelliums, *i.e.* clusters of planets that are not necessarily conjunct, but in fairly close sequential degrees in the same sign.

Sun, Mercury, Chiron, and Eris/8th/Aries

These suggest information relative to something harmful that relates to immigrants and creates a dangerous situation.

Is this telling us when all those covert cells of militant immigrants are called into action?

Jupiter, Moon, and Uranus/9th/Taurus

This trio with the Moon in the middle suggests extreme emotions relative to a huge disturbance.

Sun/8th/Aries ssxt Moon and Uranus/9th/Taurus

Sun/8th/Aries cnj Chiron - Mercury Midpoint

The Moon and Uranus poke the Sun, indicating this emotional reaction pertains to harmful news provided by the Sun, which represents the president.

Zeus, Apollon, Part of Fortune, and South Node/2nd/Libra

Mercury/8th/Aries opp Zeus/2nd/Libra

Eris/8th/Aries opp Zeus/2nd/Libra

The 8th covers foreign debts, banking, and reserves. With Zeus and Apollon with the Part of Fortune and South

Lunar Node in the 2nd of finances, treasury, economy and resources, this implies many will be hit with financial issues as something is left behind.

Vulcanus/11th/Leo opp Pluto/5th/Aquarius

This looks like a rather unfriendly confrontation between the House of Representatives and the Senate, though other

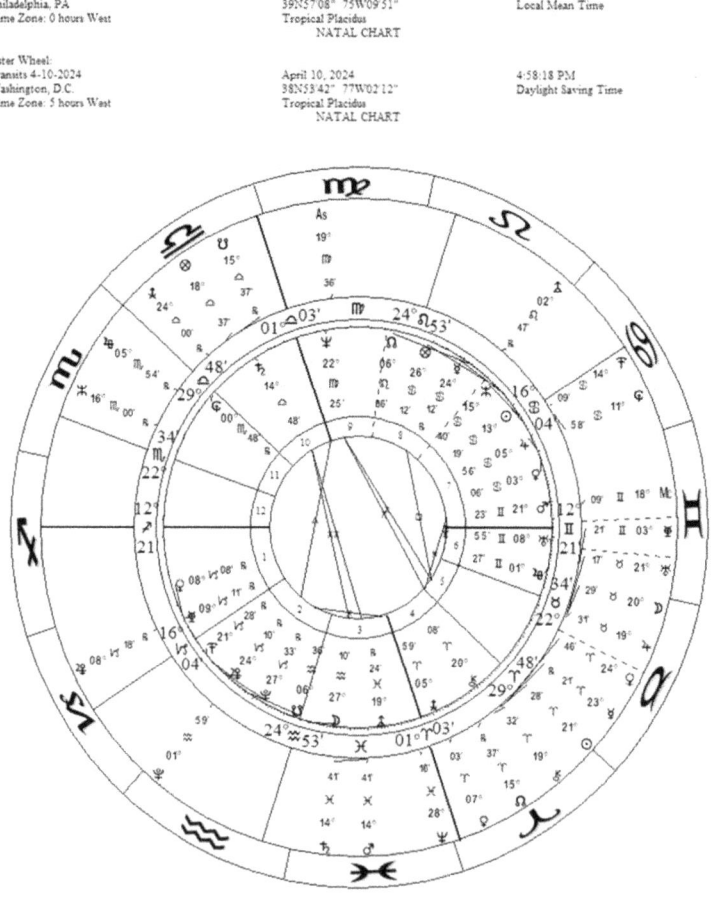

groups may be under fire as the nation's self-image is annihilated.

Mars-Saturn Conjunction Chart with Sibly Chart

Transit Mars cnj Saturn/3rd/Pisces qncx Sibly Saturn/10th/Libra (partile)

The Saturn-Mars conjunction indicates authoritative action that brings a change of direction relative to infrastructure issues based on public opinion. Will the people finally be heard?

Transit Pluto/2nd/Aquarius tri Sibly Midheaven/10th/Libra

Pluto, which can operate like the phoenix, implies major changes to the U.S. reputation that have financial implications.

Transit Sun and Mercury/4th/Aries qncx Sibly Neptune/9th/Virgo

More shifts are indicated that effect an ending or new beginning and facilitate a new direction related to other countries, courts, or media.

Transit Venus, North Node, Chiron, Sun, Mercury, and Eris/4th/Aries

A potentially violent ending is suggested by so much energy in Aries.

Transit Sun/4th/Aries sxtl Sibly Mars/7th/Gemini

The transit Sun sextile Sibly Mars in the house of alliances and known enemies implies conflict with another country that constitutes an ending and/or new beginning.

Transit Zeus/10th/Libra sqr Sibly Mercury RX/8th/Cancer

Transit Zeus/10th/Libra sqr Sibly Cupido/2nd/Capricorn

Zeus forms a T-square with Sibly Mercury and Cupido. The effect on many of what appears to be a financial situation is resulting in a power play from the government, but rethinking the situation is required.

Transit Pluto/2nd/Aquarius tri Sibly Apollon/6th Gemini

Pluto trining Sibly Apollon suggests a huge impact to the working class.

Jupiter, Moon, and Uranus rolling stellium/5th/Aries

There will be a huge emotional reaction related to the nation's self-image, children or Senate.

26. U.S. Sibly Chiron Return April 20, 2024

Less than two weeks following the April eclipse and the Saturn-Mars conjunction, the U.S. experiences a Chiron return. Chiron, the "wounded healer," indicates areas where injury or disappointments occur. It's cycle is approximately 50 years.

Chiron is in the Sibly 4th, which includes land, history and historical self-perception, family policies, and the opposition party. The 2024 Return chart also has Chiron in that house, yielding implications that disappointments or injuries will hail from those areas.

The last return was May 5, 1974. I remember the 70s. They were not easy times. Previous to that was June 8, 1923. You can check your history books, but as I recall they weren't exactly stellar times, either.

This implies trouble, though Venus conjunct Chiron may soften this effect.

Mercury stationed retrograde in Aries on April 1, 2024 so is in effect for the ~50 year duration of this return chart. This indicates the need to rethink and redo important policies that have not been effective. In a return chart it demands dealing with unfinished business or cleaning up a huge mess.

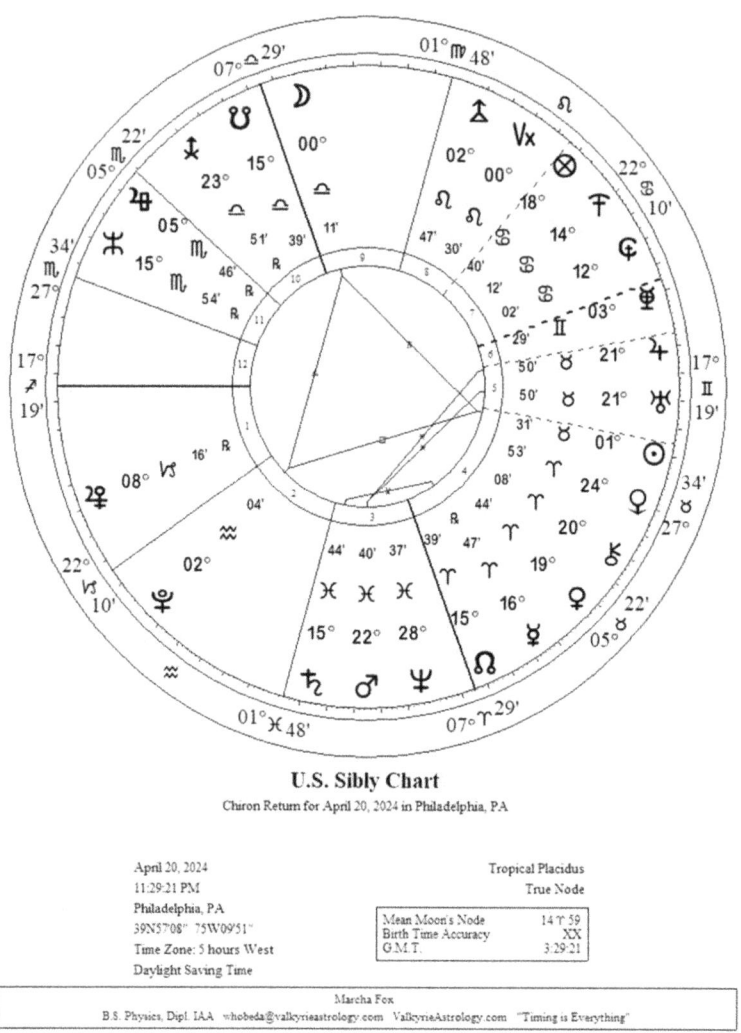

U.S. Sibly Chart
Chiron Return for April 20, 2024 in Philadelphia, PA

The Mars - Saturn conjunction has separated, but now we have another *EXACT* conjunction between Jupiter and Uranus, which is rare in itself given it only occurs every fourteen years. Coinciding with a return chart is definitely another odd coincidence, if you believe in such a thing.

The conjunction was exact at 10:47:12 PM while the Chiron Return was 11:29:21 PM, only 52 minutes 9 seconds later. Ordinarily, I would address the conjunction alone like was done for the Mars - Pluto and Mars - Saturn conjunctions, but these are so close I'll simply address it here, in the context of the Chiron return.

Jupiter cnj Uranus/5th/Taurus

This stands out as an indicator of unexpected massive change or other disturbance. This occurs in the 5th, which includes the Senate, children, sports, speculation, and the entertainment industry as well as the national self-perception, as noted earlier.

Astrologer, Richard Tarnas, states this is an excellent time to start a new endeavor. It brings innovation and confidence so we can always hope it delivers much-needed positive change.

Could this relate to the child trafficking issue that's been so carefully covered up for decades? Bring much needed cosmic help to the Senate? What about sports and the entertainment industry?

Consider what Uranus signifies in mundane astrology: Aeronautics, eccentrics, political agitators, explosions (literal and figurative), science, electrical grids, and humanitarian efforts. I would also throw in the UFO/UAP issues that have surfaced the past few years. Will it bring full disclosure on that subject at last?

Jupiter/5th/Taurus cnj Uranus sxtl Mars/3rd/Pisces

This aspect brings us back to 3rd house issues. If children are heavily involved, this could relate to Primary Education. It could likewise relate to infrastructure, which includes buildings, roads, dams, the power grid, and neighboring countries.

Mars/3rd/Pisces cnj Saturn - Neptune Midpoint

Does Mars confined between Saturn and Neptune show another situation that can go either way? Annihilation or restructuring? Neptune tends to dissolve what he touches while Saturn rebuilds. Mars completed his conjunction with Saturn and is moving toward Neptune. That conjunction occurs April 28, 2024.

Outer planet conjunctions are relatively rare and indicate major cycles. What does that tell you?

Sun/4th/Taurus sqr Pluto/2nd/Aquarius tri Moon/9th/Libra qncx Sun (anaretic) (Course adjustment loop)

Vertex/8th/Leo sxtl Moon/9th/Libra

Vertex/8th/Leo opp Pluto/2nd/Aquarius

Vertex/8th/Leo sqr Sun/4th/Taurus

The anaretic Sun, Moon and Pluto form an aspect pattern I refer to as a "course adjustment loop." It looks like a Grand Trine, but it's not.

The square between the Sun and Pluto suggests financial trouble. Will this bring the long-expected demise of the fiat dollar? The Sun - Moon quincunx indicates a change of course. The Moon represents the national mood while the 9th has been hammered lately, whether it involves academia, religious institutions, mass media, the courts, or foreign influence.

The Moon - Pluto trine indicates financial transformations. The Moon on a world point degree carries global effects. The U.S. dollar's influence worldwide has been fading for quite some time. It helped stabilize the U.S. economy when it was the world reserve currency used to trade oil, which began just after World War II.

That status is being jeopardized and threatened by other currencies. When it ends, it will have a tremendous impact on the cost of oil products and the overall U.S. economy. Of course those pushing a "green" agenda aren't concerned with the price of oil.

The Vertex opposes Pluto and squares the Sun, forming a T-square. The vertex is an energy point that tends to relate to fated events. His presence in the 8th in an anaretic degree aspecting the Sun, Moon and Pluto carries some heavy weight for a return chart with a 50 year cycle.

Vulcanus/8thLeo opp Pluto/2nd/Aquarius

Vulcanus in the house of mortality, banking, and foreign debt opposes Pluto. This shows a potential blast, perhaps one of the nation's creditors calling in overdue debt or more bank failures.

Zeus/10th/Libra opp Eris/4th/Aries

Zeus in the house that represents the head of state, ruling party, and national/civic reputation, suggests a thunderous response.

Hades in the 7th doesn't bode well for alliances or treaties.

The Lunar Nodes indicate an ending/new beginning with U.S. status left behind.

Let's see what it tells us with the Sibly Chart.

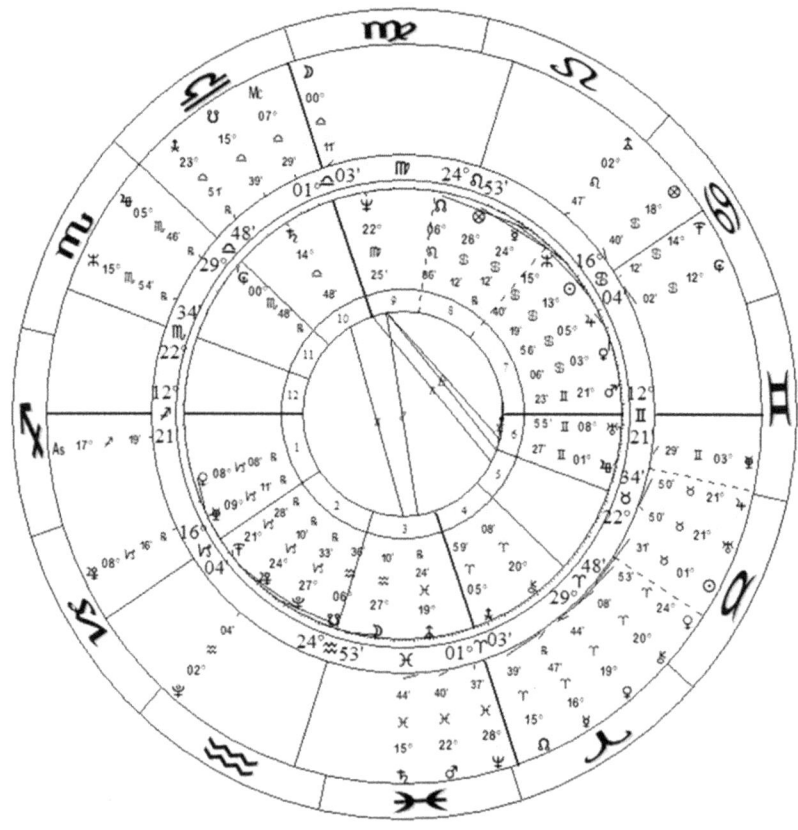

U.S. Sibly Chiron Return with Sibly Chart

The ascendants of the Sibly chart and its Chiron return are only five degrees apart, giving the return chart additional strength to impact the nation.

CR-Jupiter cnj Uranus/5th/Taurus tri Neptune/9th/Virgo

The Jupiter-Uranus conjunction in the 5th suggests a huge upset due to action by the Senate. It could relate to children as well.

Their joint trine to Neptune, the planet that represents socialism, idealism, pollution, oil, drugs, and pharmaceuticals--take your choice--indicates involvement of the courts, other countries, and the media.

If this relates to U.S. currency being ousted as the Petro-dollar, it will have severe financial impact, not only here, but worldwide. For a moment, think back to the Fentanyl crisis pouring over the southern border and how well it fits Chiron. If the dollar collapses, however, that could conceivably help end the drug trade if the financial benefits disappear.

CR Kronos - Hades Midpoint/7th/Cancer cnj Sibly Sun

The president is caught in the proverbial position between a rock and a hard place.

CR Vertex/8th/Leo sqr Sibly Hades/11th/Scorpio

Fated destruction of groups that could include Congress. For those that have been wondering when the SHTF, this is a good candidate.

CR Mars/3rd/Pisces opp Sibly Neptune/9th/Virgo (partile)

This shows a need for balance between action and ideals as well as some serious negotiations with other countries.

CR Saturn/3rd/Pisces qncx Sibly Saturn/10th/Libra

CR Sun/5th/Taurus qncx Sibly Midheaven/10th/Libra

A shift in leadership is being demanded by pundits and communities. Infrastructure, as usual, is another concern.

CR Moon/9th/Libra cnj Sibly Midheaven/10th/Libra (anaretic)

The anaretic Moon on a world point approaching the Midheaven shows the National Mood is loud, apparent, and impacts the world.

CR Moon/9th/Libra tri Sibly Apollon/6th/Gemini

The trine from the Moon to Sibly Apollon suggests a demand for peace by the working class and common people, the backbone of America trying to save what's left of their country.

CR Moon/9th/Libra ssxtl Sibly Hades/11th/Scorpio

Groups are crumbling, or being disbanded by the Courts, contributing to the National outcry.

It just keeps getting better and better...

27. A Step Back in Time

Bear with me a moment while I step back in time. I promise there's a reason, as you'll discover in a moment. Those who fail to learn from history are doomed to repeat it, right?

In May 2013 massive tornado outbreaks occurred in Oklahoma about which I wrote lengthy astroblogs. At the time I didn't check, but sure enough, an annular solar eclipse occurred May 10, 2013 at 19:31 Taurus, the chart shown on the next page.

Eclipse/7th/Taurus ssxtl Jupiter/8th/Gemini

Uranus/5th/Aries sqr Pluto/3rd/Capricorn

Mars/7th/Taurus tri Pluto/3rd/Capricorn

The planets show numerous hostile aspects. Jupiter in the house of death teasing the eclipse itself suggests all effects will be aggravated. Uranus clashing with Pluto in the 3rd is rather ominous, especially for neighborhoods and school children, as is Mars in cahoots Pluto, which offers another reminder that trines between malefics are not to be celebrated.

Saturn/12th/Scorpio tri Neptune/4th/Pisces

Saturn in Scorpio, the sign of death, which occupies the house of hidden enemies in cahoots with Neptune in the house of endings and beginnings doesn't look friendly, either.

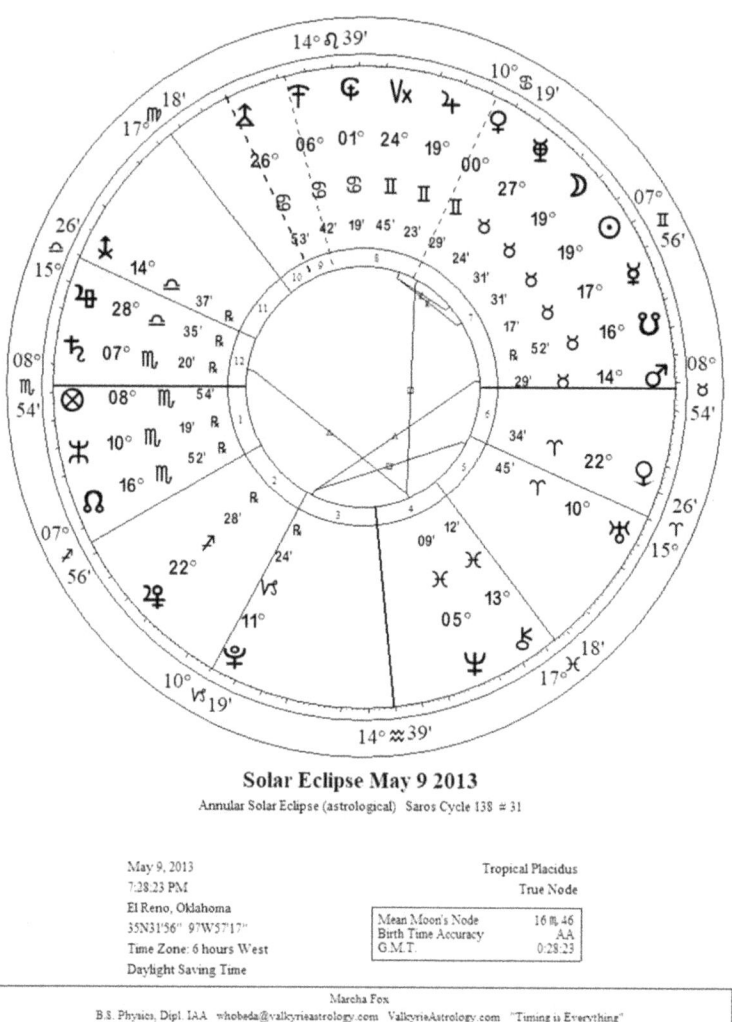

Solar Eclipse May 9 2013

Hades, which by now you've probably determined spells death and destruction, is anaretic in Gemini (an Air Sign) in the house of death.

You may remember these tornadoes. The one that hit El Reno on May 31, 2013 was an EF-5, multi-vortex tornado with 295 mph winds, was 2.6 miles wide, left a 16.2 mile track on the ground over the course of 40 minutes, induced 115 injuries, and 9 fatalities (including three professional storm chasers, which is why it made national news). It was the widest and second strongest tornado in recorded history.

Next time you're driving, pay attention to your odometer to get a sense of how far those distances really are. You can read more about it in my blog at this link:

https://www.valkyrieastrology.com/Makeover/astroblogs/Tornado2013/oktornadoesmay2013.htm.

In the blog I refer to an asteroid fly-by that occurred at the same time and occupied a significant location in the storm horoscopes, on the ascendant as I recall.

Thus, I'm inclined to believe that the presence of a comet for this upcoming 2024 eclipse is rather significant.

Comet? Holy guacamole, Batman! What comet?

Oh, yeah.

I forgot to mention that, didn't I?

Comet 12P/Pons-Brooks, nicknamed the "Devil comet" due to its "horned" appearance, will be visible during the time of this eclipse. It was discovered in 1812, seen again in 1883, with it's last pass in 1953, 71 years ago. Check it out here:

https://earthsky.org/tonight/12-p-comet-pons-brooks-outburst-millennium-falcon-bright-2024-eclipse/

Comets, like eclipses, historically represent an unfortunate omen. Seen as fireworks in the sky, the ancients believed they portended disaster on Earth (as above, so below and all that). They were also viewed as messengers of change and transformation. In modern times such beliefs are considered nothing more than superstition.

Let's dig a bit deeper to see if we agree.

The last time Pons-Brooks graced the skies back in 1953 there were several record-breaking major disasters.

North Sea floods began January 29, 1953, the result of a storm surge during which 2,142 died, most of them in The Netherlands, though Belgium and the United Kingdom were also affected. Of course I had to see if there had been a recent eclipse.

I was not disappointed.

JANUARY 1953 LUNAR ECLIPSE

A lunar eclipse occurred on January 29, 1953, the day flooding began.

Big surprise, right?

There are a few interesting aspects in the horoscope that I'll point out, but I'm not doing to go into the detail I have previously since it doesn't relate to the United States.

The Dark Side of Eclipses

Neptune/12th/Libra sxtl Pluto/10th/Leo both qncx Mars/5th/Pisces (Yod)

Note the base of the yod comprises Neptune in the house of hidden enemies with Pluto drawing public awareness pointing to Mars in Pisces at the eye. (Note Mars is in

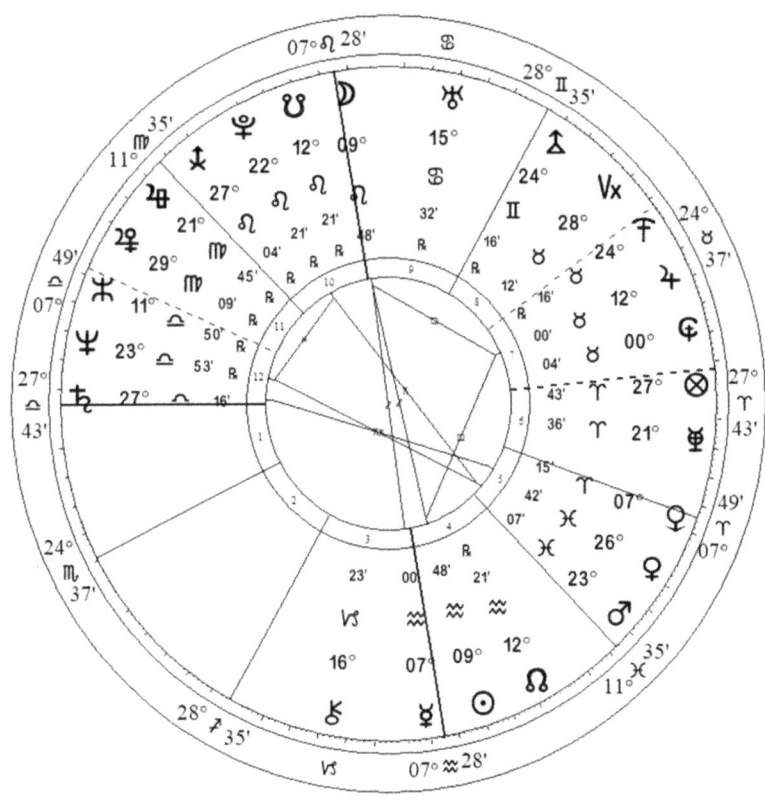

Lunar Eclipse Jan 29 1953
Lunar Eclipse (astrological)

Pisces from March 23 until April 30, 2024, the time we're examining.)

The eclipse forms a T-square with Jupiter at the apex, increasing its impact. Hades is anaretic, showing his influence in the magnitude of destruction. That T-square isn't partile (same degree) but Jupiter is partile in his

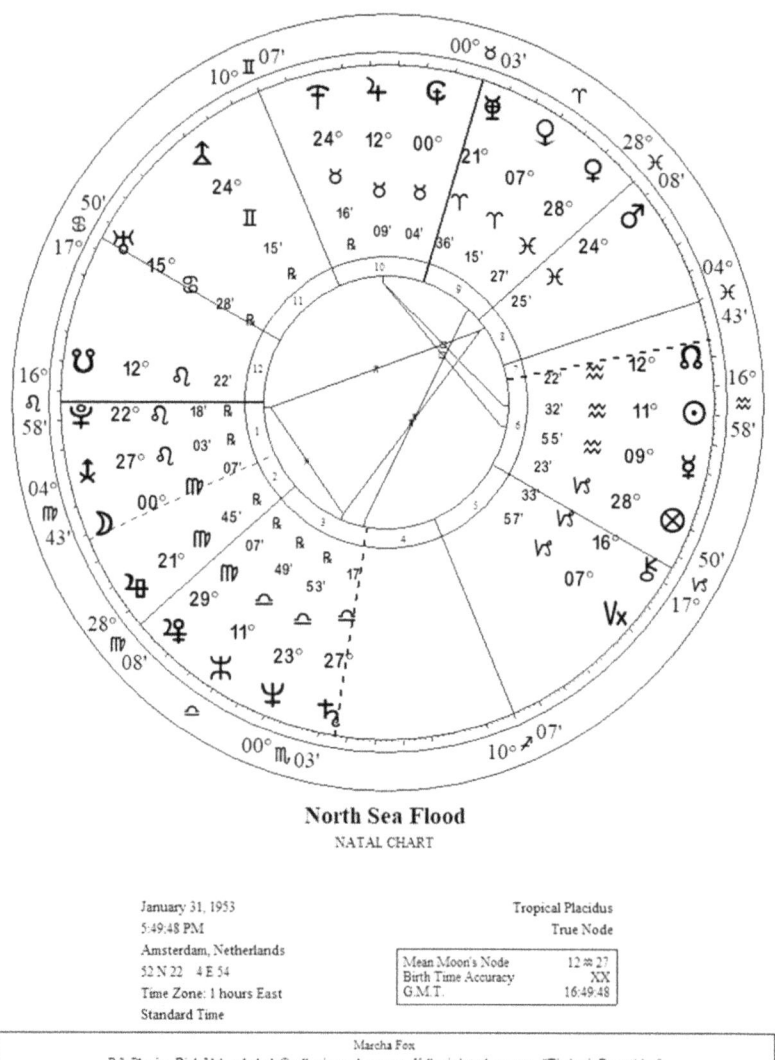

North Sea Flood
NATAL CHART

January 31, 1953
5:49:48 PM
Amsterdam, Netherlands
52 N 22 4 E 54
Time Zone: 1 hours East
Standard Time

Tropical Placidus
True Node

Mean Moon's Node   12 ♒ 27
Birth Time Accuracy   XX
G.M.T.   16:49:48

Marcha Fox
B.S. Physics, Dipl. IAA   whobeda@valkyrieastrology.com   ValkyrieAstrology.com   "Timing is Everything"

placement at "the bendings," *i.e.*, forming a T-square with the Lunar Nodes, which can function as the gates of hell. Involvement of the 7th suggests more than one country would be affected.

Pluto/1st/Leo sxtl Neptune/3rd/Libra qncx Mars/8th/Pisces

The chart for the worst of the flood in Amsterdam on January 31 carries the same yod. Pluto in the 1st shows destruction in that location, Mars in the 8th that deaths are are likely.

Jupiter/10th/Taurus sqr Sun and Mercury/6th/Aquarius

Jupiter's aspects with the lunar nodes are the same as the eclipse chart, but houses shifted to the 6th of health and 12th of hidden enemies.

Saturn/3rd/Libra qnx Venus/9th/Pisces

Neighboring unaffected countries would show compassion and concern to help.

Skipping forward a few months and "crossing the pond" to Waco, Texas, but still under the influence of this eclipse, a tornado outbreak hit on May 11, 1953 from which 600 were injured and 114 died. *(By the way, the April 8, 2024 Total eclipse is visible from Waco.)*

Looking at the chart for the Waco tornado on the next page, this outbreak shows ominous aspects, as expected.

Sun/7th/Taurus sqr Pluto/10th/Leo and qncx Neptune/12th/Libra

The Sun only squares another cosmic body for a few days, but when he does, something is likely to reflect that energy.

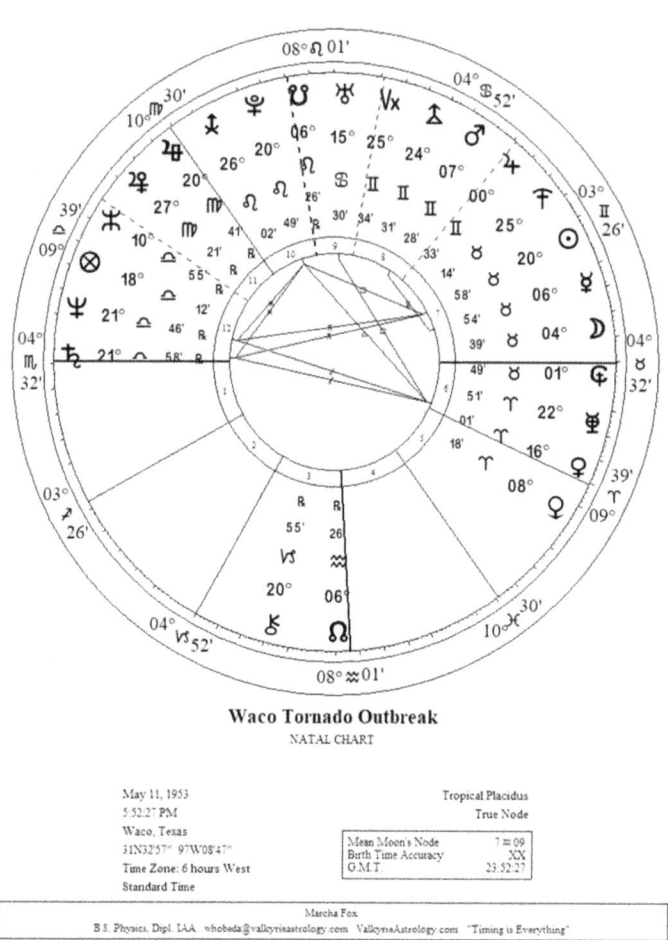

Waco Tornado Outbreak
NATAL CHART

May 11, 1953
5:52:27 PM
Waco, Texas
31N32'57" 97W08'47"
Time Zone: 6 hours West
Standard Time

Tropical Placidus
True Node

Mean Moon's Node 7♒09
Birth Time Accuracy XX
G.M.T. 23:52:27

Marcha Fox
B.S. Physics, Dipl. IAA whobeda@valkyrieastrology.com ValkyrieAstrology.com "Timing is Everything"

Pluto in the 10th shows public attention to a deadly event with Neptune in the house of hidden enemies involved, as usual.

Also note that except for Venus, who had just set, all the other visible planets as well as those that require a telescope, were above the horizon. This concentrates the vast majority of cosmic energy within half of the zodiac.

Why is this important?

The April 8, 2024 eclipse also has the majority of planets above the horizon.

That means they'll be visible during totality, which will be a spectacular sight. However, you'll need to remember to look for them during the short span of darkness. You're likely to be so mesmerized by totality that you'll forget, yours truly most likely included.

Worcester, Massachusetts, not a place you'd expect tornadoes, had a massive one about four weeks later on June 9, 1953. It stayed on the ground for a record 48 miles. Japan had major floods from June 25-29, 1953.

On July 11, 1953 there was a solar eclipse and again on August 9, less than a month later, which is unusual, plus yet another lunar eclipse in between on July 26.

There are typically two sets of eclipses each year which bring interesting events.

What's my point?

These record-breaking floods and tornadoes all took place during the 1953 transit of comet 12/P.

Eclipses can deal a pretty stiff blow. But how much did the comet exacerbate the effects?

* * *

Comets entering our solar system are often a cause for concern as well. They are frequently tied to judgment in scripture, especially in John's book of Revelation

where they are part of the seven plagues of the last days....
The periodic alignment of nearby solar systems appears to generate significant energy transfer leading to natural disasters, some of great magnitude. We know this because of their annual, patterned calendar occurrences... One alignment occurs consistently in early April. Its effects upon the earth appear to be increasing in severity.
--Val Brinkerhoff
(Seven Heavenly Witnesses of the Coming of Jesus Christ)

28. The Comet is Back!

The reappearance of this comet concurrent with the April 8, 2024 eclipse is a rare and interesting coincidence.

Or is it?

If you believe in astrology, you know there's no such thing as a coincidence.

Let's step back again to consider the discovery of this comet, which was but one significant event in 1812.

We're smart enough to learn from history, right? Too bad our leaders aren't. But I digress.

Of course the War of 1812 (June 18, 1812) comes to mind, but of particular interest is the New Madrid Earthquake series (December 1811 - February 1812) with the strongest one occurring February 7, 1812.

This is the earthquake series you may have heard of that caused the Mississippi River to reverse course. Yes, that really happened. Two earthquakes occurred on December 16, 1811 with magnitudes of 7.5 and 7.0 on the Richter scale.

Another one struck the area on January 23, 1812 with a magnitude of 7.3. The quake on February 7 was another whopper at 7.5.

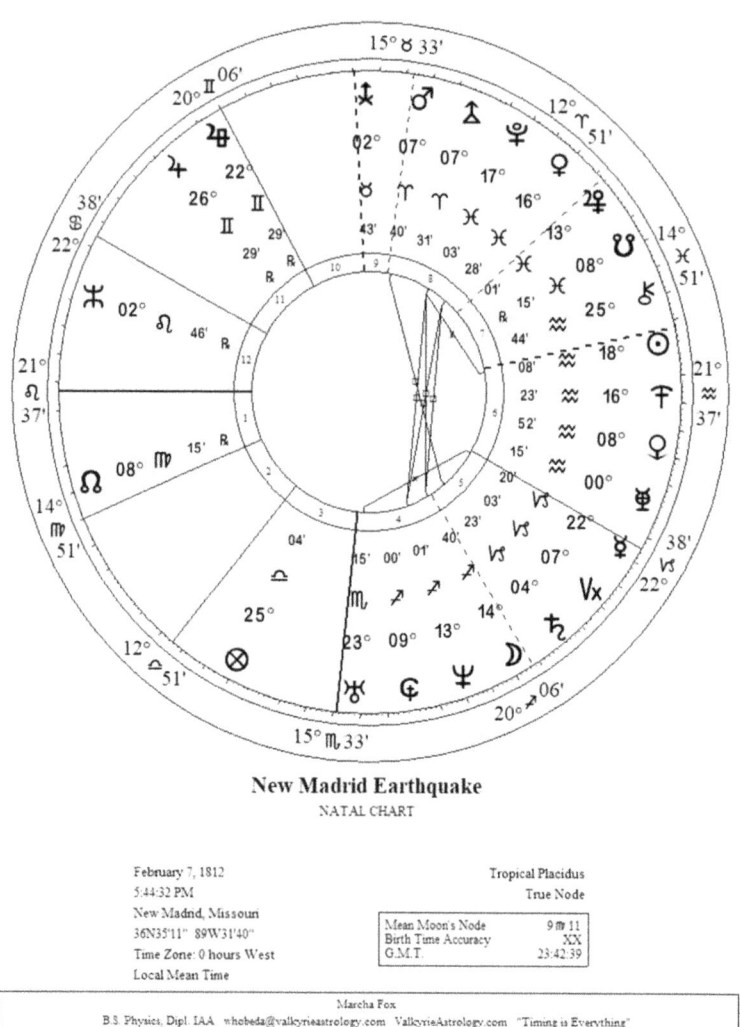

New Madrid Earthquake
NATAL CHART

February 7, 1812
5:44:32 PM
New Madrid, Missouri
36N35'11" 89W31'40"
Time Zone: 0 hours West
Local Mean Time

Tropical Placidus
True Node

Mean Moon's Node	9 ♍ 11
Birth Time Accuracy	XX
G.M.T.	23:42:39

Marcha Fox
B.S. Physics, Dipl. IAA whobeda@valkyrieastrology.com ValkyrieAstrology.com "Timing is Everything"

Their effects were felt *strongly* over on area of 50,000 square miles. The San Francisco earthquake, by comparison, was 7.9 but felt across a mere 6,000 square miles, the difference due to geological obstructions, which included the Rocky Mountains. The Midwest spreads far

The Dark Side of Eclipses

and wide, allowing vibrations to propagate across thousands of miles.

You can read more about the disaster here:

https://en.wikipedia.org/wiki/1811%E2%80%931812_New_Madrid_earthquakes#Geologic_setting

So, to summarize, 1812 brought: 1.) Discovery of the "Devil" comet; 2.) The War of 1812; 3.) The worst earthquake to occur east of the Rocky Mountains to this day.

Was there an associated eclipse?

Of course there was.

There was a partial solar eclipse on February 12, 1812. Its path of visibility was far north in the Arctic, but the interesting part is one end of its path was a few degrees west of 90 degrees West longitude. New Madrid is 89.5279 West.

Casting the chart for New Madrid, let's see what it has to say.

Eclipse/8th/Aquarius sqr Uranus/5th/Scorpio

Eclipse/8th/Aquarius sxtl Venus/9th/Pisces

Venus/9th/Pisces tri Uranus/5th/Scorpio

Neptune/;6th/Sagittarius qncx Ascendant/1st/Cancer

The eclipse occurred in the 8th house of death from which it squared Uranus, master of unexpected disturbances. The eclipse's sextile to Venus, exalted in Pisces and trining Uranus, may have softened its affects a bit.

Neptune nudging the ascendant indicates an unstable situation. As the natural ruler of water, no doubt that was a factor in the reversal of the Mississippi, though Neptune is often involved in earthquake charts.

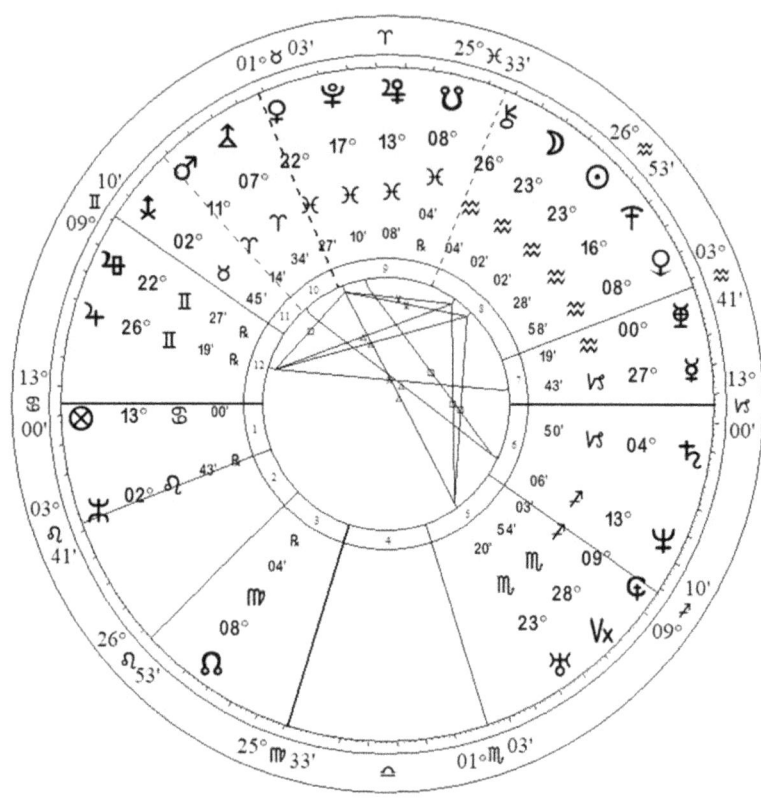

Solar Eclipse Feb 12 1812

Partial Solar Eclipse (astrological) Saros Cycle 108 = 71

February 12, 1812		Tropical Placidus
8:14:52 PM		True Node
New Madrid, Missouri		
36N35'11" 89W31'40"	Mean Moon's Node	8 ♍ 56
	Birth Time Accuracy	AA
Time Zone: 0 hours West	G.M.T.	20:14:52
Standard Time		

Marcha Fox
B.S. Physics, Dipl. IAA   whobeda@valkyrieastrology.com   ValkyrieAstrology.com   "Timing is Everything"

Jupiter/12th/Gemini sqr Chiron/8th/Aquarius

Jupiter in the 12th, which by now you should have figured out is the house of hidden enemies, is clashing with the "wounded healer," Chiron in the house of death which indicates massive injuries.

Hades/5th/Sagittarius T-sqr Lunar NN/3rd/Virgo and SN/9th/Pisces

Hades, bringer of destruction, clashes with both lunar nodes, a position known in classical astrology as "at the bendings." Placement at the apex of a T-square grants power to drive major change. Being on the cusp of the 6th house of health gives it an extra boost.

For an eclipse this is an especially sensitive placement, which clearly matched the destruction this earthquake caused.

So where am I going with this, other than the implied connection between eclipses and comets/asteroids?

Stay tuned.

It gets better.

29. Eclipse Paths that Cross

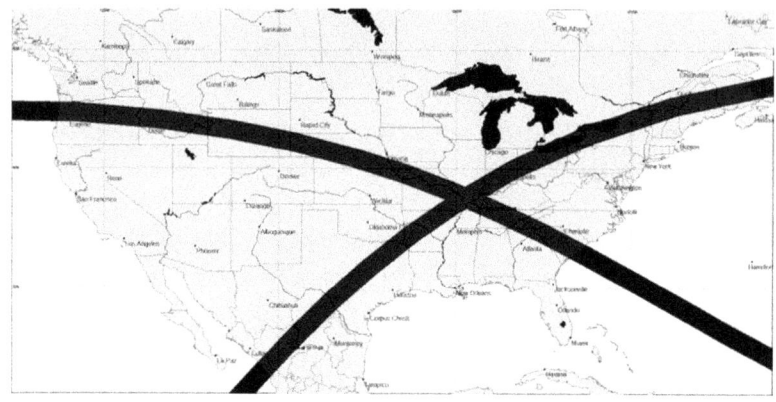

6Paths of 2017 and 2024 solar eclipses.

The following eclipse paths have crossed the U.S. in the past seven years:

August 21, 2017 (Up through South Carolina, across the Midwest through Wyoming, Idaho, and Oregon.)

October 14, 2023 (Across Texas, New Mexico, Utah, Nevada, and Oregon.)

April 8, 2024 (Maine, New Hampshire, Vermont, NY, Ohio, Indiana, Illinois, Missouri, Arkansas, Oklahoma, Texas, Mexico.)

The Dark Side of Eclipses

Paths that intersect: 2017 and 2023 (Oregon); 2017 and 2024 (Illinois); 2023 and 2024 (Texas).

If you remember the old movie, "Ghostbusters," where they were warned not to "cross the streams," I can't help but suspect that could be the case here as well.

CROSSED PATHS PART 1.0

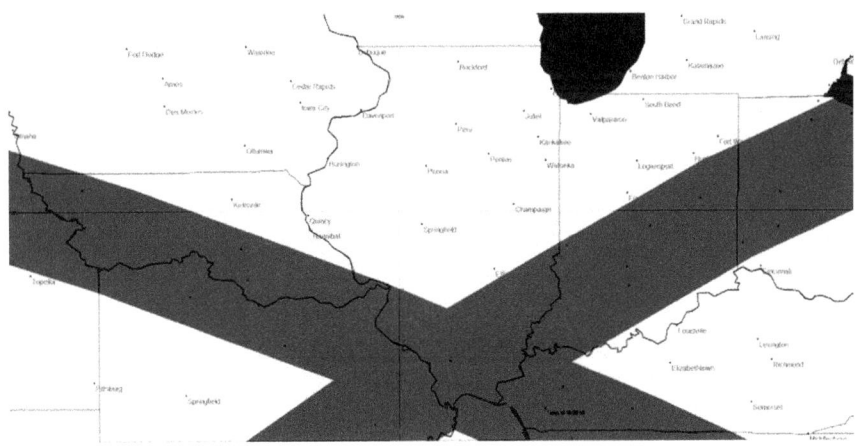

The intersection of the 2017 and 2024 eclipse paths is over Carbondale, Illinois. It's bounded by St. Louis, Poplar Bluff, Paducah, Evansville, and Alton. This area is in frightfully close proximity to the New Madrid fault and mega-volcano.

https://en.wikipedia.org/wiki/1811%E2%80%931812_New_Madrid_earthquakes

The paths of the 2017 and 2024 eclipses cross over New Madrid, where that massive earthquake occurred in 1812.

According to information from the Department of Earth and Atmospheric Science at St. Louis University, *"The* *probability for an earthquake of magnitude 6.0 or greater is significant in the near future, **with a 50% chance by the year 2000 and a 90% chance by the year 2040**.* [emphasis added]

Does "X mark the spot" and portend another literally "earth-shaking" event?

Time will tell.

I don't know about you, but personally, I'm inclined to stay away from that area on April 8, 2024. I'll be a bit too close for comfort in New York, but so be it. Those who go there to view the eclipse may get more than they bargained for.

Eclipse guru, Bill Merdian, has noted that the longitude of the beginning and end points of visibility often correspond with locations where its effect is felt.

What about a direct overhead hit?

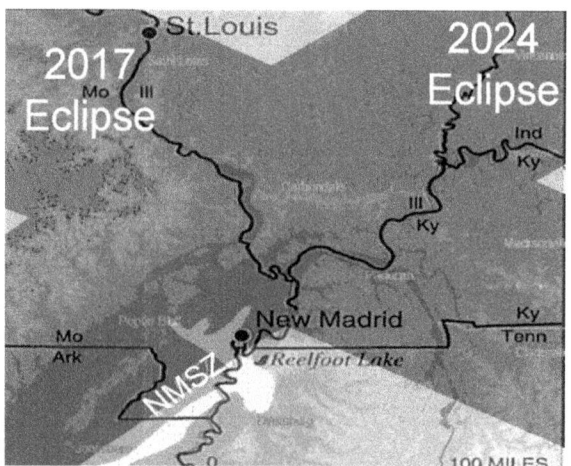

7Intersection of 2017 and 2024 eclipse paths showing New Madrid Seismic Zone (NMSZ)

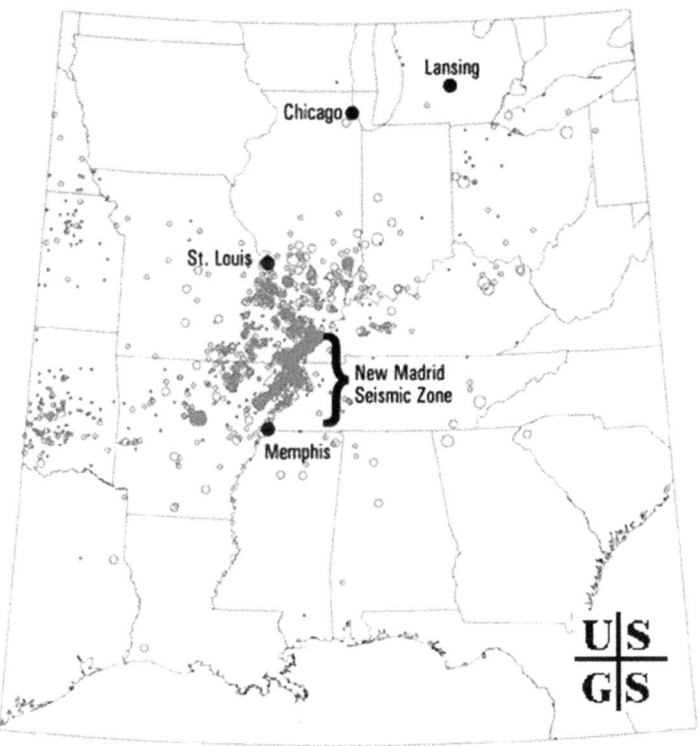

8. Attribution: By United States Geological Survey. Public Domain, https://commons.wikimedia.org/w/index.php?curid=1084834

I don't know if you're familiar with the podcaster, Clif High. Clif is really out there and wears even more bizarre tin foil hats than I do. I don't buy everything he says, but his prognostications occasionally hit the bullseye.

Could this be where the "big event" Clif referred to manifests? Clif has some weird, linguistic computer algorithm that analyzes internet activity and converges on keywords that appear to portend the future.

In an interview conducted toward the end of 2023 with individuals who are remote viewers, their predictions collaborated. Both mentioned "ejecta" as a keyword and that the news media might try to make it seem like a meteor impact. The implications are that an energy weapon might be used to trigger the volcano or fault.

If you're shaking your head at the concept of an "energy weapon" I suggest you do some research as I suggested earlier on the devastation in Lahaina, Hawaii, which witnesses report was no typical wildfire. As expected, there was a media blackout with access to the area walled off.

Or maybe such an event won't require any help, the eclipse and comet alone sufficient. There's no doubt that Mother Earth is less than enchanted with the behavior of some of her unruly occupants.

St. Louis University states, "A quake with a magnitude equal to that of the 1811 - 1812 quakes could result in great loss of life and property damage in the billions of dollars. Scientists believe we could be overdue for a large earthquake and through research and public awareness may be able to prevent such losses."

You can find the entire article here:

https://www.eas.slu.edu/eqc/eqc_quakes/NewMadridGeneral.html

Solar Eclipse September 18, 1895

The next earthquake of note in the New Madrid fault was in Charleston, Missouri on October 31, 1895, a little over 84 years later. An eclipse occurred approximately six weeks earlier on September 18, 1895. It's path was in the South

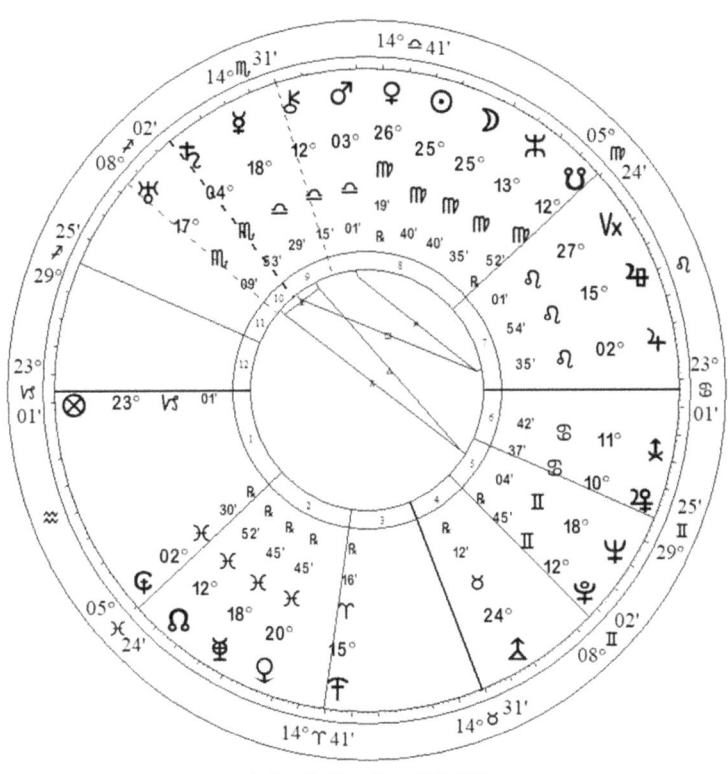

Solar Eclipse Sep 18 1895
Partial Solar Eclipse (astrological)   Saros Cycle 152 # 6

September 18, 1895
2:55:32 PM
Charleston, Missouri
36N55'15" 89W21'02"
Time Zone: 6 hours West
Standard Time

Tropical Placidus
True Node

Mean Moon's Node   12♓02
Birth Time Accuracy   AA
G.M.T.   20:55:32

Marcha Fox
B.S. Physics, Dipl. IAA   whobeda@valkyrieastrology.com   ValkyrieAstrology.com   "Timing is Everything"

Pacific, so there was no direct geographical connection as in 1812. Nonetheless, you can see a timing correlation.

The orbital cycle of cosmic troublemaker, Uranus, is roughly 84 years. Uranus hadn't quite made it back to where it was in 1812, but was in the same sign, *i.e.* Scorpio, the sign that rules death (sorry if you've already figured that out.)

Uranus/10th/Scorpio qncx Neptune/5th/Gemini

Uranus/10th/Scorpio ssxtl Mercury/9th/Libra

Mercury/9th/Libra qncx Neptune/5th/Gemini

Uranus and Neptune were vying for an adjustment that would be unexpected and create instability while Mercury, ruler of all movement, shook hands with Neptune, indicating it would come in waves. I believe for earthquakes those waves are P-waves and S-waves.

Jupiter collaborating with Mars indicates a huge blast of energy with Mars in very comfortable cosmic territory in the 8th. In other words, Malefic Mars along with the eclipse itself and Chiron were all clustered in Earth sign, Virgo, in the house that rules death.

In my experience it's common for disasters such as tornadoes, hurricanes, and earthquakes to occur when the Sun is in the 8th, regardless of the zodiacal sign. Mars in debility in Libra may have toned him down a bit, but this was still a major quake with a magnitude of 6.8 that was classified as "severe."

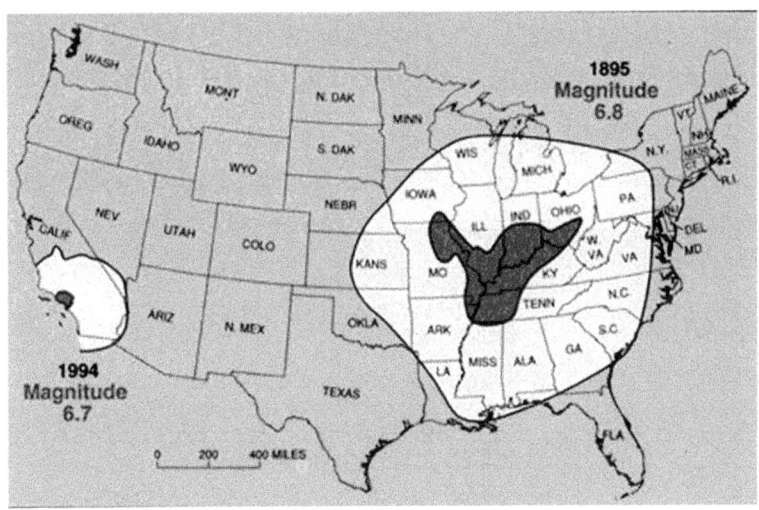

9. This illustrates the area affected compared to an earthquake of similar force in California in 1994. USA map attribution: By User Soronk on de.wikipedia - http://quake.wr.usgs.gov/prepare/factsheets/NewMadrid/, Public Domain, https://commons.wikimedia

Even if you don't believe in astrology (which is doubtful if you've made it this far), consider the physics involved. With the Sun and Moon in conjunction by longitude and declination, the combined gravitational force could be enough to trigger a quake. The Moon alone is responsible for the tides.

What might an eclipse that sweeps *directly over the same location* bring?

Does "X" mark the spot?

Were there any earthquakes on August 21, 2017, you ask? Yes, but it was in Ischia, on the island of Campania in Southern Italy.

What's interesting is it occurred at 18:57 GMT while the eclipse was in totality in Washington, D.C. at 19:30 GMT, a mere 33 minutes later.

The latitude of Ischia is 40 degrees 44 minutes North and that of Washington, D.C. is 38 degrees 91 minutes North, a difference of only one degree and 14 minutes.

Make of that what you want, and decide whether or not that was a coincidence.

Crossed Paths Part 2.0

The April 2024 Total eclipse path was crossed by the path of the Annular Eclipse on October 14, 2023. The intersection for those two is in Southwest Texas.

The paths that cross in the Lone Star State are in a sparsely populated region between San Angelo, Austin, San Antonio, Del Rio and Piedras Negras.

What's happening in that locale?

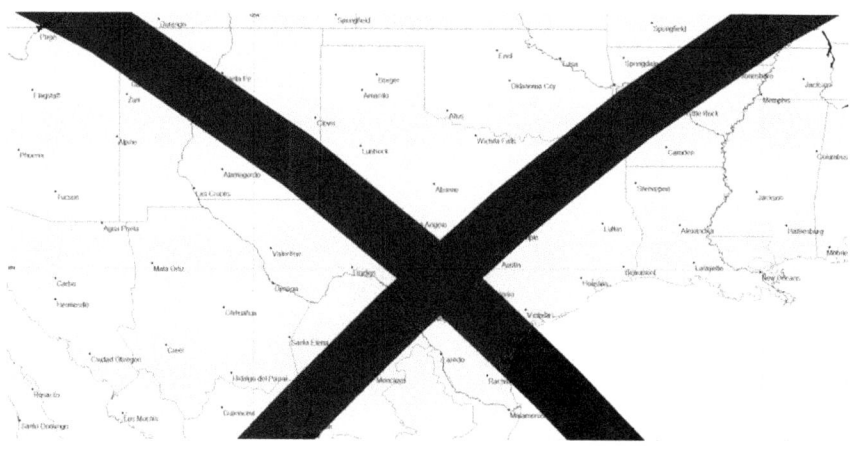

Eris suggests immigrant issues being in partile conjunction with Mercury (movement) in the 2024 eclipse and conjunct the North Node (something coming in) for the 2023 eclipse.

Is this where illegal aliens are congregated? Might they start a war? An alternative to another pandemic to interfere with the 2024 election?

The October 2023 annular eclipse paralleled Texas's southern border; The April 2024 eclipse path parallels the Canadian border with northeastern states.

Is Texas where the border crisis with illegals reaches critical mass?

10You know what it means when you "X" something out. Is this what God is telling us?

30. Enough is Enough

Astrologers never like to be wrong. It tarnishes our reputation, not only on a personal basis for our clients and followers, but for the discipline itself. There are enough naysayers and skeptics out there that say astrology is bogus and doesn't work.

Believe me when I say that in the case of these eclipses, I very much hope that I am wrong. But experience, to say nothing of my gut, say otherwise.

I would not have gone through the trauma of moving from Texas to New York if I didn't believe there were hard times coming. While I believe the entire United States is headed for trouble, I believe it will be worse in Texas. I have numerous friends and family members still living there which is an ongoing concern.

Maybe things won't be as bad as they appear. I do not mean to sensationalize, but the preponderance of cosmic evidence does not make this look like a nothing-burger. It's also in agreement with numerous bloggers, journalists. financial analysts, and other prognosticators who do not (to my knowledge) use astrology.

Those who do not see signs all round them that the U.S. is swaying on the edge of a precipice are simply not paying attention. If you are one of them, I encourage you to do some research beyond the mainstream media. If you're unaware of the pervasive censorship that has sullied the press's credibility since the COVID "plandemic" it's time to face the truth.

I realize any statements I made in support of President Trump were offensive to some. As a result, you may not have gotten this far reading, but I'll say it anyway. I did not approve of everything he did. However, I believe he was trying to save the country. I believe that he won by another landslide in 2020, but it was stolen via election fraud that has been proven, even in court. I have no doubt that the same forces will attempt it again.

If you're unaware of the World Economic Forum and their agenda for a world government controlled by the elite, that's another area you should research.

Their plans for the planet are no secret.

Have you looked up at the sky and seen it slashed with suspicious looking chemtrails that spread and erase our beautiful blue skies? No, they are not contrails from airplanes that disappear long before stretching from horizon to horizon. That is one of the most evil of all plots that tries to convince us of "climate change" while it poisons us and the planet.

Don't believe me?

Visit *https://www.geoengineeringwatch.org*.

Yes, "climate change" is manmade. But they're the cause, not cow farts. These intense storms are being generated artificially.

I'll admit that my beliefs are also based on various prophesies found in the Holy Bible as well as other religious sources. Native American prophecies say much the same. Hopi elders long ago stated when "cobwebs cover the sky" (chemtrails) and "black snakes cover the land" (highways) the end times are near.

If you're not impressed by those sources, just take a look at the disaster movies produced by Hollywood over the past few decades. The film industry is part of the 5th house so fits the multitude of cosmic influences hailing from there. Some say insider information drove their production, whether disaster films or those about UFOs, such as *Close Encounters of the Third Kind*.

As stated earlier, the WEF is not secretive about their agenda, which goes farther back in time than you can imagine. We've been moving in their direction for centuries, even millennia.

We're living in crazy times. I was born in 1947 and have seen a lot, from the 60s and 70s to the insanity of the Twenty First Century. I may not live long enough to see how this ends.

And that's fine with me.

Good luck. Don't be fooled by the lies. And most of all, be safe.

Namaste.

Appendix A

Letter from Archbishop Carlo Maria Vigano

In his famous book the 'Gulag Archipelago' author Aleksandr Solzhenitsyn makes this statement: "We didn't love freedom enough. And even more – we had no awareness of the real situation."

Archbishop Carlo Maria Viganò, a passionate and inspiring voice for freedom, shared a letter he wrote a few days ago to Medical Doctors for Covid Ethics, with The Gateway Pundit.

In his letter, Archbishop Viganò shares the challenges facing society and the worldwide coup d'état being attempted by global elites.

Read his message:

Dear Dr Frost, dear Friends, at the beginning of this new year, allow me to address my best wishes to all of you. I am grateful to have this opportunity to share with you some thoughts regarding the present situation.

For the past four years we have been witnessing the implementation of a criminal plan of world depopulation, achieved through the creation of a false pandemic and the imposition of a false vaccine, which we now know to be a biological weapon of mass destruction, designed with the aim of destroying the immune system of the entire population, causing sterility and the onset of deadly diseases. Many of our friends and acquaintances have died or been severely damaged by the adverse effects of this experimental gene serum. Many have discovered, too late, that they have been the victims of a global plan with a single script under a single direction.

What is even more serious is that this neo-Malthusian project of mass extermination, to which is added the will to control each of us through graphene oxide nanostructures, has been announced to us for some time by those in the World Health Organization and the World Economic Forum who conceived and implemented it. The rulers of all Western states, hostage to Bill Gates and Klaus Schwab, have become accomplices to this crime, demonstrating their malice and premeditation by their behavior: falsifying data on alleged infections, doctoring statistics that attribute deaths and adverse effects to Covid-19 but not to the gene serum, prohibiting effective treatments, imposing harmful protocols that have no scientific basis, banning autopsies, and preventing or thwarting accurate reports to health authorities.

In this attack, unprecedented in the history of the human race, we have witnessed the complicity of all national and international institutions, the entire medical profession, and the media. A social engineering operation has been carried out to manipulate consensus through terror, threats, blackmail, and the violation of citizens' most sacrosanct fundamental rights. The judiciary has been silent, the armed forces have looked the other way, and teachers and priests have zealously cooperated.

We are well aware of the perpetrators of this crime against God and humanity. Of course, the multinational pharmaceutical corporations have profited disproportionately from mass vaccination, and they are now preparing to accumulate still more billions of dollars from the sale of treatments against the turbocancer that their serums have caused. Those who peddle the vaccine have profited from administering these poisons to pregnant women, children, and the elderly. They have funded the self-styled experts, paying them to propagandize false efficacy and safety on the mainstream media. Multinationals have profited and, due to the lockdowns, have taken the place of small businesses, restaurants, and local shops. Energy suppliers have profited and are still profiting, and thanks to the crisis created by the system, they have made huge profits, while the costs of electricity and gas are forcing businesses to increase prices and close. Those who took advantage of the restrictions to work from home, those who sold masks that were not only useless but actually harmful, those who provided Plexiglas barriers and hand sanitizer, and those who managed the measurement of fever in public places also took their cut of profit. Many of them, who understood perfectly well what was happening, preferred to remain silent so as not to miss the opportunity to make money off of the lives and health of the rest of us.

But it's not just money that is the motive for this crime. Behind the lust for enrichment motivating many is the will to power of the subversive Davos elite, which aims to establish the New World Order. The psychopandemic has been a dress rehearsal for the attack they are now making against the economy, the social fabric, and indeed the very life of humanity.

Fifteen-minute cities, digital identity, electronic money, and the destruction of agriculture and ranching all serve the same purpose, stated in the Agenda 2030 and the Rockefeller Foundation's "Great Reset" project. The wars in Ukraine and Palestine also have the same purpose: to destabilize the international order, create permanent crises, and fuel conflicts that will impoverish individual nations and feed the globalist leviathan. Gaza's huge oil fields are tempting targets for those who want to appropriate them in order to keep Europe and the United States under blackmail, especially when the same people are imposing insane energy policies in the name of a fake climate emergency.

Today, the perpetrators of these crimes have a name and a face. Their accomplices in governments and institutions, who are guilty of high treason and very serious crimes, all come from the World Economic Forum and were students of its program called "Young Global Leaders for Tomorrow." Others, like George Soros, support them by means of philanthropic foundations that fuel social strife, civil war, and color revolutions around the world.

This global coup d'état must be denounced, and those responsible must be tried and judged by an international court. But above all, it is necessary for all of us to understand that this all-out war against humanity is not motivated only by the lust for wealth and power, but mainly by a religious motive – a theological reason. This reason is Satan's hatred: hatred of God, hatred of God's Creation, and hatred of man, who is created in the Image and Likeness of God. Bill Gates, Klaus Schwab, George Soros, and the hundreds of servants whom they blackmail in governments all hate God. They hate life, which only God can give. They hate love, which comes only from God. They hate peace, which can reign only where Christ reigns. As Tucker Carlson said a few days ago, we are facing people who serve Satan and the demons of hell, just as normal people worship and serve God.

This, then, is a battle in which body and soul, matter and spirit are made the object of a mortal attack by men and spiritual powers. But let us not forget that, if our enemy avails himself of the help of infernal spirits, we have on our side the Lord God of the armies arrayed – Dominus Deus Sabaoth – and all the hosts of Angels and Saints, infinitely more powerful. God is Almighty: let us never forget that. And He is Father: He does not abandon His children in times of trial.

I therefore exhort you, dear friends, to fight this battle with the spiritual weapons that God places at your disposal: prayer, trust in the Lord, and the awareness that this enemy will not be defeated where it is most organized and fearsome, but by striking it where it is weak. This weakness comes from its corruption, from its being subservient to evil, from the execrable sins that it has committed and still commits against God's little children.

Because I tell you that the men and women who in these four years have submitted and endured lockdowns, violations of their rights, job deprivation and social segregation are not willing to tolerate the crimes that this cursed network of perverts and pedophiles commits against children. Therefore, bring to light and courageously denounce the network of complicity and crimes of politicians, bankers, actors, journalists, prelates, and famous people who are united by their blood pact, and the whole castle of lies and deceptions that they have hatched will collapse, dragging with it the entire globalist plan, woke ideology, gender theory, the fake climate emergency, health fraud, and digital currency. Simul stabunt, simul cadent, says the Latin maxim: just as they stand together, so also they will collapse together.

Stay strong, therefore, under the banner of Christ and in the army of God, Who is Almighty, and Who on the Cross has already won the war that is now entering its final stages. Gather around the Lord, call on His Holy Name, and He will give impetus to your battle. Remember the words of Saint Paul: "I can do all things through him who strengthens me" (Phil 4:13).

Carlo Maria Viganò, Archbishop

January 2, 2024

Appendix B

Rules of Communism

This list has been circulated online in recent years and in various other sources since at least the 1940s. According to snopes.com, the origin is unknown and unlikely to be

"a list of 'Communist Rules for Revolution' discovered by Allied forces in Germany in 1919.'"

However, regardless of its origin, why are they so recognizable if they're false? No one knows who built the Georgia Guide stones, either. That doesn't negate what they say and efforts seen in modern culture that indicate their truth.

1. Corrupt the young, get them away from religion. Get them interested in sex. Make them superficial. Destroy their ruggedness.

2. Get control of all means of publicity.

3. Get people's minds off their government by focusing their attention on athletics, sexy books, and other trivialities.

4. Divide the people into hostile groups by constantly harping on controversial matters of no importance.

5. Destroy the people's faith in their natural leaders by holding the latter up to contempt, ridicule, and obloquy.

6. Always preach true democracy, but seize power as fast and as ruthlessly as possible.

7. By encouraging government extravagance, destroy its credit and produce fear of inflation with rising prices and general discontent.

8. Foment unnecessary strikes in vital industries, encourage civil disorders, and foster a lenient and soft attitude on the part of government toward such disorders.

9. By specious argument cause the breakdown of the old moral virtues, honesty, sobriety, continence, faith in the pledged word, and ruggedness.

10. Cause the registration of all firearms on some pretext, with a view to confiscating them and leaving the populace helpless.

* * *

Here are Marx's and Engel's ten commandment from the Communist Manifesto:

1. Expropriation of property in land and application of all rents of land to public purposes.

2. A heavy progressive tax.

3. Abolition of the right of inheritance.

4. Confiscation of all the property of all emigrants and rebels.

5. Centralization of credit in the hands of the State, by means of a national bank with state Capital an exclusive monopoly.

6. Centralization of transport in the hands of the State.

7. Extension of factories and instruments of production owned by the State; the bringing into cultivation of wastelands and the improvement of the soil generally in accordance with a common plan.

8. Equal liability of all to labour. Establishment of industrial armies especially for agriculture.

9. Combination of Agriculture with industry, promotion of the gradual elimination of the contradictions between town and countryside.

10. Free education of all children in public schools. Abolition of children's factory labour in its present form. Combination of education with industrial production etc. etc.

* * *

[For commentary on the following, see

https://www.theblaze.com/45-communist-goals]

* * *

On Jan. 10, 1963 Congressman Albert S. Herlong. Jr. from Florida read the list of 45 Communist goals for America into the Congressional Record. The purpose of him reading this was to gain insight into liberal elite ideas and strategies for America that sound too familiar today.

The list is attributed to Cleon Skousen, researcher and author of "The Naked Communist."

1. U.S. should accept coexistence as the only alternative to atomic war.

2. U.S. should be willing to capitulate in preference to engaging in atomic war.

3. Develop the illusion that total disarmament by the U.S. would be a demonstration of "moral strength."

4. Permit free trade between all nations regardless of Communist affiliation and regardless of whether or not items could be used for war.

5. Extend long-term loans to Russia and Soviet satellites.

6. Provide American aid to all nations regardless of Communist domination.

7. Grant recognition of Red China and admission of Red China to the U.N.

8. Set up East and West Germany as separate states in spite of Khrushchev's promise in 1955 to settle the Germany question by free elections under supervision of the U.N.

9. Prolong the conferences to ban atomic tests because the U.S. has agreed to suspend tests as long as negotiations are in progress.

10. Allow all Soviet satellites individual representation in the U.N.

11. Promote the U.N. as the only hope for mankind. If its charter is rewritten, demand that it be set up as a one-world government with its own independent armed forces.

12. Resist any attempt to outlaw the Communist Party.

13. Do away with loyalty oaths.

14. Continue giving Russia access to the U.S. Patent Office.

15. Capture one or both of the political parties in the U.S.

16. Use technical decisions of the courts to weaken basic American institutions, by claiming their activities violate civil rights.

17. Get control of the schools. Use them as transmission belts for Socialism and current Communist propaganda. Soften the curriculum. Get control of teachers associations. Put the party line in textbooks.

18. Gain control of all student newspapers.

19. Use student riots to foment public protests against programs or organizations that are under Communist attack.

20. Infiltrate the press. Get control of book review assignments, editorial writing, policy-making positions.

21. Gain control of key positions in radio, TV & motion pictures.

22. Continue discrediting American culture by degrading all form of artistic expression. An American Communist cell was told to "eliminate all good sculpture from parks and buildings," substituting shapeless, awkward and meaningless forms.

23. Control art critics and directors of art museums. " Our plan is to promote ugliness, repulsive, meaningless art."

24. Eliminate all laws governing obscenity by calling them "censorship" and a violation of free speech and free press.

25. Break down cultural standards of morality by promoting pornography and obscenity in books, magazines, motion pictures, radio and TV.

26. Present homosexuality, degeneracy and promiscuity as "normal, natural and healthy."

27. Infiltrate the churches and replace revealed religion with "social" religion. Discredit the Bible and emphasize the need for intellectual maturity, which does not need a "religious crutch."

28. Eliminate prayer or any phase of religious expression in the schools on the grounds that it violates the principle of "separation of church and state"

29. Discredit the American Constitution by calling it inadequate, old fashioned, out of step with modern needs, a hindrance to cooperation between nations on a worldwide basis.

And replace our nation of "laws, not men" with royal decree emanating from appointed judges and executive orders. Replace elected officials with bureaucrats.

30. Discredit the American founding fathers. Present them as selfish aristocrats who had no concern for the "common man."

31. Belittle all forms of American culture and discourage the teaching of American history on the ground that it was only a minor part of "the big picture." Give more emphasis to Russian history since the Communists took over.

32. Support any socialist movement to give centralized control over any part of the culture – education, social agencies, welfare programs, mental health clinics, etc.

33. Eliminate all laws or procedures which interfere with the operation of the Communist apparatus.

34. Eliminate the House Committee on Un-American Activities.

35. Discredit and eventually dismantle the FBI.

36. Infiltrate and gain control of more unions.

37. Infiltrate and gain control of big business.

38. Transfer some of the powers of arrest from the police to social agencies. Treat all behavioral problems as psychiatric disorders which no one but psychiatrists can understand or treat.

39. Dominate the psychiatric profession and use mental health laws as a means of gaining coercive control over those who oppose communist goals.

40. Discredit the family as an institution. Encourage promiscuity and easy divorce.

41. Emphasize the need to raise children away from the negative influence of parents. Attribute prejudices, mental blocks and retarding of children to suppressive influence of parents.

42. Create the impression that violence and insurrection are legitimate aspects of the American tradition; that students and special interest groups should rise up and

make a "united force" to solve economic, political or social problems.

43. Overthrow all colonial governments before native populations are ready for self-government.

44. Internationalize the Panama Canal.

45. Repeal the Connally Reservation so the U.S. cannot prevent the World Court from seizing jurisdiction over domestic problems. Give the World Court jurisdiction over domestic problems. Give the World Court jurisdiction over nations and individuals alike.

***

A slightly revised list from:

https://www.ethanallen.org/45_communist_goals_from_58_years_ago

1. Capture one or both of the political parties in the United States.

2. Get control of the schools and teachers' associations. Soften the curriculum.

3. Gain control of all student newspapers.

4. Infiltrate the press.

5. Gain control of key positions in radio, TV and pictures.

6. Eliminate all laws governing obscenity by calling them "censorship" and a violation of free speech and press.

7. Break down cultural standards of morality by promoting pornography and obscenity in the media.

8. Present homosexuality, degeneracy and promiscuity as "normal, natural, and healthy."

9. Infiltrate the churches and replace revealed religion with "social" religion.

10. Eliminate prayer or any phase of religious expression in the schools on the grounds that it violates the principal of "separation of church and state."

11. Discredit the American Constitution by calling it inadequate and old-fashioned.

12. Discredit the American founding fathers as selfish aristocrats [and racists].

13. Belittle American culture and discourage the teaching of American history.

14. Discredit and eventually dismantle the FBI.

15. Infiltrate and gain control of big business and unions.

16. Transfer some of the powers of arrest from the police to social agencies. Treat all behavioral problems as mental health or social problems.

17. Discredit the family as an institution. Encourage promiscuity and easy divorce.

18. Emphasize the need to raise children away from the negative influence of parents.

19. Repeal the Connally Reservation, allowing the World Court jurisdiction over nations and individuals alike.

Appendix C

Georgia Guide stones

The Georgia Guide stones were granite slabs in Elbert Country, Georgia, dedicated on March 22, 1980. They eventually earned the reputation as the U.S. Stonehenge.

No one knows for certain who built them or why. You can find comprehensive information about them here: https://en.wikipedia.org/wiki/Georgia_Guidestones

The following words were engraved on the granite pillars in the English, Spanish, Swahili, Hindi, Hebrew, Arabic, Traditional Chinese, and Russian languages.

Maintain humanity under 500,000,000 in perpetual balance with nature.

Guide reproduction wisely – improving fitness and diversity.

Unite humanity with a living new language.

Rule passion – faith – tradition – and all things with tempered reason.

Protect people and nations with fair laws and just courts.

Let all nations rule internally resolving external disputes in a world court.

Avoid petty laws and useless officials.

Balance personal rights with social duties.

Prize truth – beauty – love – seeking harmony with the infinite.

Be not a cancer on the Earth – Leave room for nature – Leave room for nature.

* * *

No official explanation for them was ever given, but many associated them with the goals of the New World Order. They were partially destroyed by an explosion July 6, 2022. What remained was dismantled for safety reasons.

Much of what they profess as advice was incorporated into the sustainability goals of U.N. Agendas 21 and 2030.

APPENDIX D

UN Agendas 2021 and 2030
UN Agenda 21

U.N. Agenda 21 was instituted 23 April 1992. The message of its 17 goals was sustainability. Agenda 21 is a legally non-binding statement of intent and not a treaty.

While it sounded great, in reality its tenets would ultimately dismantle the sovereignty of the United States as a nation along with all others in a series of steps toward achieving world government under the guise of sustainability.

Its four sections were:

Section I: Social and Economic Dimensions is directed toward combating poverty, especially in developing countries, changing consumption patterns, promoting health, achieving a more sustainable population, and sustainable settlement in decision making.

Section II: Conservation and Management of Resources for Development includes atmospheric protection, combating deforestation, protecting fragile environments, conservation of biological diversity (biodiversity), control of pollution and the management of biotechnology, and radioactive wastes.

Section III: Strengthening the Role of Major Groups includes the roles of children and youth, women, NGOs, local authorities, business and industry, and workers; and strengthening the role of indigenous peoples, their communities, and farmers.

Section IV: Means of Implementation includes science, technology transfer, education international institutions, and financial mechanisms.

Its Sustainability Development Goals (SDGs) emphasize the interconnected environmental, social and economic aspects of sustainable development by putting sustainability at their center.

The short titles of the 17 SDGs are: No poverty (SDG 1), Zero hunger (SDG 2), Good health and well-being (SDG 3), Quality education (SDG 4), Gender equality (SDG 5), Clean water and sanitation (SDG 6), Affordable and clean energy (SDG 7), Decent work and economic growth (SDG 8), Industry, innovation and infrastructure (SDG 9), Reduced inequalities (SDG 10), Sustainable cities and communities (SDG 11), Responsible consumption and production (SDG 12), Climate action (SDG 13), Life below water (SDG 14), Life on land (SDG 15), Peace, justice, and strong institutions (SDG 16), and Partnerships for the goals (SDG 17).

See Wikipedia for more detailed information:

https://en.wikipedia.org/wiki/Agenda_21

UN Agenda 2030

U.N. Agenda 2030 continued the goals of Agenda 21. Per Wikipedia, "The resolution is a broad intergovernmental agreement that acts as the Post-2015 Development Agenda. The SDGs build on the principles agreed upon in Resolution A/RES/66/288, entitled 'The Future We Want.'

"This was a non-binding document released as a result of Rio+20 Conference held in 2012."

The U.S. signed into it in 2015 under the Obama administration.

It has received a lot of criticism as being unrealistic and was further disrupted by the COVID Pandemic, which upset many of the goals.

Detailed information can be found on Wikipedia:

https://en.wikipedia.org/wiki/Sustainable_Development_Goals

About the Author

"Whobeda," a name which came about in an interesting way, is the pseudonym for Marcha Fox, the story of which she shares with a few select friends and clients with the world at large left to wonder.

She graduated from Utah State University with a Bachelor's Degree in Physics in 1987 and worked as a NASA contractor from 1988 to 2009, at which time she retired and came out of the closet as an astrologer and began its pursuit full-time.

She studied astrology originally to debunk it, instead becoming converted to its truth. She graduated from the International Academy of Astrology in 2012 and taught for them for two years. She now delights in seeing some of her former students doing the same.

Her website, ValkyrieAstrology.com first appeared on the internet in 2006. Her clients span the globe, testimonials available on the website.

In addition to astrology, she's an award winning fiction author. The Star Trails Tetralogy has been highly acclaimed by reviewers for its accurate science content (truth be told, she got a physics degree so she could write accurate science fiction.) She collaborated her most recent work with Pete Risingsun, an enrolled member of the Cheyenne tribe, to write The Dead Horse Canyon Saga. Two volumes of the planned trilogy are complete and with this work complete, she and coauthor, Pete, will get to work on volume three.

She's the mother of six, grandmother of 17, and great-grandmother of an ever-increasing number that at last count was eight with two "in the oven." Being a great-grandmother didn't really have an impact until she realized two of her daughters were now grandmothers.

For those who wonder, she's a Capricorn with a Virgo rising and Gemini Moon who lives in the Finger Lakes region of New York State, having fled Texas in 2023 based on information you'll find in this book to say nothing of the summer heat.

www.ingramcontent.com/pod-product-compliance
Lightning Source LLC
Chambersburg PA
CBHW061147170426
43209CB00011B/1582